D0707156

Wind, Whales and Whisky

A Cape Breton Voyage

Silver Donald Cameron

Macmillan Canada
Toronto, Ontario Canada

Copyright © Paper Tiger Enterprises 1991

All rights reserved. The use of any part of this publication reproduced, transmitted in any form or by any means, electronic, mechanical, recording or otherwise, or stored in a retrieval system, without the prior consent of the publisher is an infringement of the copyright law. In the case of photocopying or other reprographic copying of the material, a licence must be obtained from the Canadian Reprography Collective before proceeding.

Canadian Cataloguing in Publication Data

Cameron, Silver Donald, date.
  Wind, whales and whisky: a Cape Breton voyage

ISBN 0-7715-9138-1 (bound)   0-7715-9175-6 (pbk.)

1. Cape Breton Island (N.S.) – Description and travel.
2. Sailing – Nova Scotia – Cape Breton Island.   I. Title.

FC2343.4.C35 1991   917.16'9   C91-094517-9
F1039.C2C25 1991

1 2 3 4 5 GP 96 95 94 93 92

Cover design by David Montle
Front cover photograph by Silver Donald Cameron
Back cover photograph by Chris Latchem

Macmillan Canada wishes to thank the Canada Council for supporting our publishing program.

Macmillan Canada
A Division of Canada Publishing Corporation
Toronto, Ontario, Canada

Printed in Canada

Printed on paper
containing over 50%
recycled paper including
10% post-consumer fibre.

For *Silversark*'s people:

for Chris and Peter, Edwin and Jerry,
for all the others who lent a hand,
for Mark Patrick,
and, above all, for Lulu

East and by north
Send thine eyes forth
O'er waves with great whales foaming,
Where sportive seals
Dance their wild reels
Through mighty flood-tides roaming.
　　—Ancient Celtic devotional poem quoted by
　　Scott Macmillan and Jennyfer Brickenden
　　in *Celtic Mass for the Sea*

"The cruising of a boat here and there is very
much what happens to the soul of a man in a
larger way. We set out for places which we do
not reach, or reach too late; and, on the way,
there befall us all manner of things which we
could never have awaited. We are granted great
visions, we suffer intolerable tediums, we come
to no end of the business, we are lonely out of
sight of England, we make astonishing
landfalls—and the whole rigamarole leads us
along no whither, and yet is alive with
discovery, emotion, adventure, peril and repose.
"On this account I have always thought that
a man does well to take every chance day he can
at sea . . . for he will find at sea the full model of
human life."
　　—Hilaire Belloc, *The Cruise of the Nona*

"To deal with men is as fine an art as it is to
deal with ships. Both men and ships live in an
unstable element, are subject to subtle and
powerful influences, and want to have their
merits understood rather than their faults found
out."
　　—Joseph Conrad, *The Mirror of the Sea*

CONTENTS

ACKNOWLEDGEMENTS

The passage from *Celtic Mass for the Sea*, music by Scott Macmillan and script by Jennyfer Brickenden is reprinted on page iv by permission.

"Slitting the Deadman's Throat" by Bill Howell, *Antigonish Review* #77–78, Spring-summer, 1989. Excerpt on pages 20–21 reprinted by permission of the author.

Excerpts from James Organ's diary (pp. 27–30) are reprinted by permission of the author.

Excerpts from "Planting Scarecrows and Raising Tourists," by George Butters, first published in *The Cape Breton Letter*, September/October 1987, aer reprinted on page 92 by permission of the author.

"Freedom Trail" (CAPAC), (p. 125) words and music by Dennis Cox, from *The Welcome Table*, available from Dennis & Lori Cox, Capstick, N.S., B0L 1E0 or from the Canadian Society for Musical Traditions, Box 4232 Station C, Calgary, Alberta T2T 5N1.

The Cape Breton Giant, by James D. Gillis, published by Breton Books, Wreck Cove, N.S. B0C 1H0. Excerpt on pages 155–6 reprinted by permission.

"The Barbarian" by Kenzie MacNeil. Excerpt on page 176 reprinted by permission.

"Song for the Mira" by Allister MacGillivray. Excerpts on pages 188, 308 reprinted by permission.

"Working Man" words and music by Rita MacNeil. Excerpt on page 203 reprinted by permission of the author.

"The Ballad of Springhill" by Ewen MacColl and Peggy Seeger. © Copyright 1960 (renewed) by StormKing Music Inc. All Rights Reserved. Excerpt on page 203 reprinted by permission.

"Down Deep in a Coal Mine" and "The Man with the Torch in his Cap", © Waterloo Music Company Ltd., 3 Regina Street North, Waterloo, Ontario N2J 4A5. Excerpts on pages 204 and 205 reprinted by permission.

"James Bay" by Rita Joe from Song of Eskasoni. Excerpt on page 276 reprinted by permission.

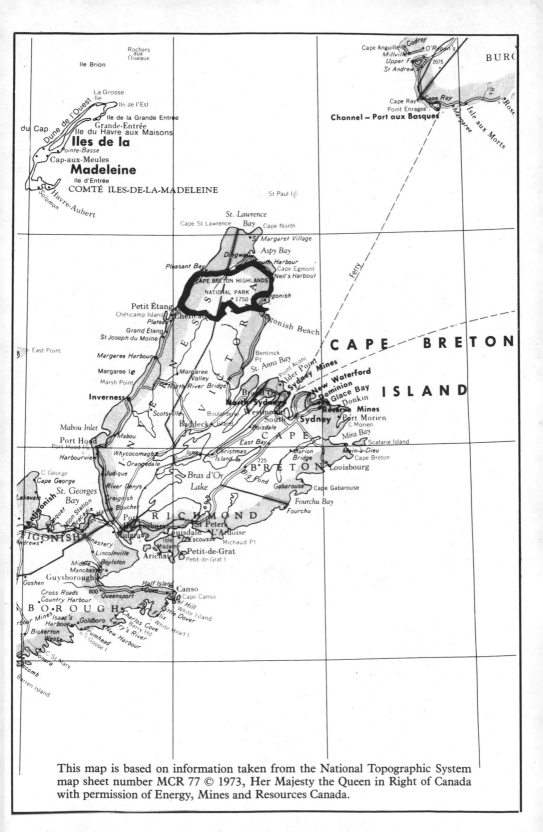

This map is based on information taken from the National Topographic System map sheet number MCR 77 © 1973, Her Majesty the Queen in Right of Canada with permission of Energy, Mines and Resources Canada.

PROLOGUE

A ship, said the master shipwright David Stevens, is more like a living thing than anything else a man can build with his hands.

On this brilliant July afternoon, *Silversark* races down the west coast of Cape Breton Island. Her varnished masthead and her tanbark sails trace scallops and swirls on the deep blue of the sky, while foam-crowned waves rolling down from Prince Edward Island slap and gurgle along her black hull.

Silversark is a handsome, muscular 27-foot cutter, but for nearly nine years she was a big project inside a small barn in D'Escousse, Cape Breton. In 1976, when I shaped her stem and laminated her frames, Lulu was single and living in Denmark, and I was divorced, and Mark Patrick was not even born. In this summer of 1990, Mark is twelve, and Lulu and I have celebrated a decade of marriage.

Today, Lulu sits at the tiller, while Mark lies along the coaming, watching the endless patterns of the wake. There is a certain wonder in this moment. This is the deck which Peter Zimmer spray-painted at Claude Poirier's body shop before we even laid it down. Those are the stanchion bases fabricated by Lulu's brother Terry. Her father and I framed the cockpit where we sit. Lulu painted and varnished almost everything on deck and below.

Small jobs, each of them. How can they add up to a little ship, shouldering her way through the seas of the Gulf of St. Lawrence as though she were indeed a living thing?

Silversark was built to cross oceans, but things have not yet worked out that way. In the meantime, yachts sail into D'Escousse every year from England, France, the United States, even Switzerland. Their crews marvel at Cape Breton's beauty, its clean water, its friendly people, its uncrowded anchorages.

Cape Breton, they say, offers some of the finest cruising on earth.

So why not explore it ourselves?

And why not explore its spirit as well as its waterways? When you enter a village under sail, you enter quickly into its life—any village, anywhere. Cruising sailors belong to the freemasonry of the sea, along with the fisherman, the merchant seaman, the ferryboat skipper. The professionals are at the wharf, and you meet them as your lines go ashore. Then the dreamers appear, asking questions and longing to be invited aboard—for cruising people personify a great fantasy: running away to sea, the ultimate dream of freedom.

Admittedly, a voyage around Cape Breton Island in a sailing vessel is hardly a passage in new and uncharted waters. The French trader Nicolas Denys published his description of a voyage around the island in 1672, and his sailing directions can still be followed. The Sieur de la Roque circled the island in 1752 to enumerate its inhabitants for Louis XV. (He found 4,122 of them.) Lieutenant Samuel Holland did a complete survey under sail fifteen years later, and Thomas Chandler Haliburton, the creator of Sam Slick, made a similar tour in the 1820s.

But new eyes see differently. I had lived in Cape Breton for nearly twenty years, and Lulu had been born there, but much of the coast itself would be new to us. Approaching from seaward, we would see a different island.

We sailed from D'Escousse in early July on a voyage of discovery and rediscovery, tacking back into the past even as we reached forward on the summer winds. For Cape Breton is a reality more resonant than it appears to the casual visitor and a voyage takes place not only on the water but also in the mind. Cape Breton has been—still is—an island of dreamers and shamans, of fallen empires and pioneering science, of impassioned music, of sunken treasure, robber barons, gallant soldiers, Communists and cannibals.

A savage, sacred landscape.

A sovereign state of the mind.

DEPARTURES

The three wine-red sails flapped lazily skyward, and then fell silent as they filled before a whisper of southerly breeze. *Silversark* slipped away from the wharf towards Bernard Island, which defines D'Escousse Harbour. We jibed into the dog-leg passage at the entrance. Close under Don MacLean's big silver-roofed barn we bore away again between red and green buoys towards the bald green knoll of Quetique Island—once crowned by a solid white lighthouse but now surmounted only by the pencil line of a skeleton tower. And I remembered The Skipper, fifteen years earlier, pointing out courses to enter the harbour.

"Put your stern towards Quetique Island and sail towards MacLean's barn till you want to scream," he said. "You can go close in, plenty of water in there by MacLean's. Then you sail due west. Brings you right in the harbour. Going out is just the opposite."

Outside, in Lennox Passage, we jibed again and steered west. D'Escousse is on the north side of Isle Madame, the largest island in a wooded archipelago in the Atlantic approaches to the Strait of Canso. Lennox Passage, 15 miles long, separates Isle Madame from Cape Breton proper. It provides a sheltered route from the Bras d'Or Lakes to the Strait of Canso, avoiding a long offshore detour around Isle Madame. Like many beautiful things, however, the Passage has a bad reputation. Nicolas Denys claimed it could be traversed only by longboats, "and even with them it is necessary to be on the lookout." The 1968 edition of the *Gulf of St. Lawrence Pilot* said the Passage is "so narrow, crooked and full of shoals, that its navigation by a vessel of moderate size requires local knowledge."

Well, maybe so, as The Skipper would say. Off to starboard, on the Cape Breton shore, Quetique, Cascarette and Indian islands are flanked by rocks—and up ahead lies the Goillon Reef, whose rocky spine dries at low tide. A long reef runs off the west end of Bernard Island, its yellow weed discolouring the water as we pass it. Tricky? Indeed: I've scraped my keel on some of these rocks and reefs myself.

Yet the channel provides 12 feet of water everywhere, and a few decades ago the Passage was speckled with the sails of ferries and freighting schooners, carrying passengers to Mulgrave, Canso, Arichat and St. Peter's, hauling coal and potatoes between Sydney and Prince Edward Island, bringing stoves and cutlery and molasses and window glass to general stores in a dozen villages. Three of those schooners belonged to Leonard Pertus, better known as The Skipper.

I learned to sail in Lennox Passage, and Leonard Pertus—pronounced PurTOOSE—was my teacher. I remember him on this very patch of water, seventeen years ago, with the tiller tucked up under his right arm, as he pointed with his left hand.

"See there, Cameron? That's what they call 'backstays on the clouds.' "

We were sailing my schooner *Hirondelle* on a passionate late-summer day of gusty winds and racing patches of cloud shadow.

To the west, over Louisdale and Burnt Island, great shafts of sunlight streamed to the ground through smoky, broken clouds.

"Backstays on the clouds?"

"That's right," Leonard nodded. "The old people say it's a sign of wind."

The old people. I chuckled. Leonard was eighty-three; who, I wondered, would "the old people" be?

"Your vessel was a lot bigger than this one, Leonard," I said.

"Oh yes," he agreed. "I never sailed a vessel this small before. She's a good little sailer, though."

For me, *Hirondelle*'s thirty-three feet represented a good big chunk of sailboat. But Leonard was accustomed to his father's ship, *Theresa*, fifteen times as bulky at a 148 registered tons, or to his own lumber-carrying schooner *Maple Leaf*, of 89 tons.

I was new to D'Escousse then, but I knew of the great days of sail, when wooden ships from the coves and harbours of Nova Scotia sailed all over the world. Before Confederation, Nova Scotia's seamen and shipwrights made the little colony one of the busiest trading nations on earth—and the richest of Canada's founding provinces. A century ago, villages like Arichat and Digby could boast more than 150 ships each, some of them schooners like Lunenburg's *Bluenose*, whose likeness you can see on any dime. Leonard's schooners were like that.

I came to Nova Scotia in part because of those ships. Growing up in British Columbia, reading Kipling and Norman Duncan and Thomas Raddall, I slowly realized that the rocky coasts of which they wrote were actually part of my own vast country. I developed an image of home: a trim little Nova Scotia village where leafy trees would tower over crisply painted wooden houses clustered around a cove. A village where people fished and farmed and cut wood, a place where men and women had skilled hands and really knew their neighbours. A rooted, solid place, with a safe harbour: a tiny port in which a person might moor a little schooner, if one were still to be found. A village, in short, like D'Escousse. But I would not have dared to hope that in 1973 my village would still boast a skipper from the days of sail.

When I found *Hirondelle* that spring, hauled up on a beach in Lunenburg, she was not yet a schooner, just a beautiful hull with an empty cabin and a primitive make-and-break engine. So I spent the summer in that most nautical of Canadian towns, shaping masts, building rudimentary berths and tables, installing toilets, compasses, hatches and handrails. At last, one August day, with a friend who knew even less about sailing than I did, I pointed *Hirondelle*'s new bowsprit out of Lunenburg Bay and headed east, bound for my village in my own little ship.

There are no secrets in D'Escousse, and my boat was well-discussed long before we beat into the harbour two weeks later. Was Leonard in the crowd on the wharf when we tied up? I never knew—but he had heard all about the first schooner to make her home in D'Escousse since he sold his own *Maple Leaf* in 1928. There are no secrets in D'Escousse, and so I had heard about The Skipper, too. Excellent, I thought: someday I will be a grizzled old salt, but right now I need a tutor.

Leonard owned an ageing motorboat called *Lutetia*, and when I saw someone pumping *Lutetia* soon after I came home, I introduced myslf. The Skipper was a sharp-eyed elf, perhaps five foot five, friendly and dignified. The hand I shook had the mottled, papery skin of old age, but his blue eyes missed nothing, and he bore himself afloat like a man half his age. I said *Lutetia* seemed a solid, comfortable boat. The Skipper gave a Gallic shrug.

"She's pretty old. Twenty years or more."

"She doesn't show it much."

"Oh, she's good for a few seasons yet. But the age is there. Are you going to pump your boat?"

"Yeah, and pick up a few things I left aboard."

"Well then I'll go wit' you. We'll take my skiff, it's right here, eh? No point hauling yours down off the beach."

We rowed out into the harbour, where *Hirondelle* danced at her anchor. Leonard cleared her bilges with a few strokes of the pump, commented that she was good and tight, looked over the rigging with a critical eye, and opined that we might tighten the mainmast shrouds.

We had no time to sail that day, but we sailed together all autumn, taking out visitors and neighbours, talking of ships and navigation. Gradually I learned how the wind shapes the ripples and how to jibe safely in a strong breeze. I watched in admiration as Leonard laid *Hirondelle* up against the lee side of the wharf under the jib alone and felt the tiller tremble as the schooner foamed down Lennox Passage under the foresail alone. As the fall grew colder, I realized with delight that Leonard and *Hirondelle* together were restoring the community's feeling for sail.

Leonard lived with his daughter Susan Murphy, who ran the post office. He wasn't a man to use three words where one would do, but as we drank tea in the kitchen of the house he bought during the Great War for $650—"a good sound house, all double partitions downstairs"—he talked a bit about his life. At seventeen he went to sea with his father, Captain Alfred Pertus. In 1912, when he was twenty-two, his father retired. Leonard became skipper of *Theresa*.

In April, when the ice went out, they would go aboard the ship, which had been frozen in the harbour all winter, bend the sails and "go to the west'ard," to Liscomb or Musquodoboit, where they could get a load of lumber for New York.

"We'd leave here," said Leonard, "snow on the ground. By the time we got to Cape Cod people would be in shirtsleeves, cutting their lawns." They'd sail past Montauk, into Long Island Sound, unload the lumber and pick up hard coal to bring back.

"Wouldn't take too long to come back," Leonard remembered. "Favourable winds, generally, that time of year—sou'west wind, westerly wind. Quite a bit of fog, though." They'd navigate by dead reckoning, calculating their position from their speed and course and their last landmark.

All summer and fall they carried lumber, lath and shingles from New Brunswick and the Gaspé to New York, coal from Cape Breton to St. Pierre and Prince Edward Island, produce from PEI to Halifax. It was a free and interesting life, but a dangerous one. Leonard's uncle drove a schooner on the reef at Cape La Ronde, five miles from home, in a December blizzard. The ship was lost with its cargo of coal, and the crew counted themselves lucky to scramble ashore in a skiff, through the freezing surf. His uncle never went back to sea.

"I lost the *Theresa* myself," Leonard said ruefully. "Well, she was ripe, she'd leak like a basket, couldn't carry much sail any more. I shouldn't have taken her out that year at all. Anyway, I

had loaded shingles in New Brunswick to go to Crapaud, Prince
Edward Island. Going in, in the evening, just about sundown, by
God I got caught. Narrow, dredged channel there, and she went
aground.

"We ran our anchor out, but the wind come nord-east that
night, a gale of wind, and we were hung up there. The next day
the wind hauled to the west. I hauled her off with the anchor,
and the keel come off her. Keel floated up on top of the water.
She filled full of water, of course. Oh, she was ripe, she was
pretty well gone with rot. She was thirty-five years old then.

"So that summer I didn't go sailing. I went to New Glasgow
and worked at the steel plant. In the spring I went to Boston and
got on a steamer there, running down south to the West Indies,
stayed there all summer and didn't come home until February.
Then I got married." He chuckled, as though he still didn't
quite believe he got married, though his two sons and three
daughters provided hard evidence that he did.

"And on my way from Boston I went down along the waterfront and spotted a schooner, a Bay of Fundyman, loaded with
fertilizer, and she was for sale. So I went aboard, and he told me
what price he wanted. I said I'll let you know in two or three days
if we'll take her—I didn't have the money, but Dad had the
money. Sure enough, Dad wired that we'd take her after she'd
gone to Wolfville—that's where she was owned, in Wolfville. It
was in April they called and said she was all discharged and
ready. So we went up. We loaded with lumber and went to the
States." His father came out of retirement and put in two
seasons on the new ship, the *Maple Leaf*.

It was a good business. They'd get a dollar per thousand board
feet for carrying shingle and lath, and the *Maple Leaf* could carry
fifteen or sixteen hundred thousand. *Theresa* carried a crew of
six, but *Maple Leaf*, much smaller, could get by with a skipper,
mate and two deckhands. A mate would earn $40 or $45 a
month, deckhands perhaps half that, and you could make a
round trip to New York in a month. *Maple Leaf* cost $3,800;
with luck, she could pay for herself in half a season, and
Leonard sailed her eleven years.

Leonard, his father and two deckhands were bound for
Halifax from PEI at the beginning of December 1917, with the

hold full of loose potatoes and a deckload of a thousand bushels of turnips "froze hard as bullets."

"We got caught in a breeze of wind—we were off of Jeddore, east of Halifax, you know where that is—and the wind hauled to the north, going to blow. We were carrying sail too much, and we tore our mains'l and blew the jib off of her. Got worse, and we had to lay to. Course we went offshore quite a ways, you know, got all iced up." He shook his head. Ice destroys a ship's stability, makes her prone to capsize. I told Leonard he had a reputation for being cool and sensible no matter what happens. He shrugged.

"What can you do, eh? When you're caught, you're caught. No point getting excited, you'd only discourage the crew. You do the best you can, it's all you can do."

They limped into Halifax December 4. On December 6, *Maple Leaf* lay alongside the old Central Wharf, under an overnight dusting of snow. Leonard went out to sweep her. The heavy wooden hatch covers were off, ready to unload potatoes.

"Beautiful morning," said Leonard, shaking his head. "Flat ca'm, not a breath o' wind." Suddenly he was knocked off his feet by a concussion accompanied by a colossal roar; the hatch covers dropped into the hold, the windows in the deckhouse blew in, the lids flew off the galley stove. Then the ship lifted and surged forward on her dock lines, crashed downward, lifted and crashed again. Just up Halifax Harbour at the Narrows, the freighter *Imo* had collided with the French munitions ship *Mont Blanc*, setting off what was then the most powerful man-made explosion in history. A square mile of Halifax had been obliterated. Almost 2,000 were killed; 9,000 were wounded and hundreds were blinded by flying glass.

Miraculously, Leonard, his crew and his ship suffered only trivial damage. Leonard walked to the wharf office, where the windows were all blown in and the secretary, cut and frightened, was crying. He sent her home and set out to find his sister-in-law, a nun, who was teaching in a South End school. The explosion spent its main force in the North End, a couple of miles away, but even behind the shelter of Citadel Hill the damage was extensive.

"It didn't look too good," Leonard said gravely. "Most of the

windows were broke in the stores and houses, doors stove in—
there was a lot of lives lost, you know. But I didn't see that.
Where I was there wasn't too many on the street. Anybody had a
home, I suppose they'd want to get home."

He found his sister-in-law unhurt and tried to send a telegram
home. But the lines were all down. He went back to the ship.
That afternoon the coals spilled from scores of stoves set the
wrecked North End ablaze.

"The wind sprung up from the north, and then it started to
snow. You could see the fire from the ship, flames high in the
sky, even though it was quite a ways from where we were."

Leonard was always suspicious about the explosion.

"No need of that collision," he said, his brow furrowed.
"Perfect weather, good visibility, there was a pilot on each boat
to keep them away from each other. Keep to your right, eh?
Same as the highway, you got to keep to your right. Lots of room
at the Narrows for two ships." *Imo* was far from her proper
course, and since both her pilot and her captain were killed her
behaviour has never been satisfactorily explained.

"How could it be an accident?" Leonard demanded. "I still
think it must have been a put-up job." In any case, with the sails
ripped and the city in ruins, it was the end of the season for
Leonard. They laid up *Maple Leaf* in Halifax's North West Arm,
and his father gave up sailing for good.

Even in his eighties, Leonard still had the bearing of an
officer. As we brought *Hirondelle* in one day, Arthur Terrio
caught our dock line. Leonard tried to tell him to pay out slack,
but Arthur didn't grasp the instructions. After a couple of futile
attempts, The Skipper barked, "Just take the end of the line,
Terrio, let the rest come aboard. Come *on*, Terrio, what kind of a
farmer *are* you?" Arthur—who became my father-in-law seven
years later—was a village elder; nobody else could have talked to
him like that.

Another time Arthur's son Pat was similarly confused, and
Leonard took the lines from him, snapping, "Look, Terrio, I
thought you were a sailor." Then Leonard messed it up himself.

"Look, Pertus," said Pat, "I thought you were a sailor."
Leonard's face broke into a huge grin—but he kept it hidden
from Pat. There are things a skipper shouldn't hear.

By 1928, even the coastal trade was done with sailing vessels. When Prince Edward Island went to wide-gauge railways, coal cars could roll right on the ferry and off into Charlottetown; there was no need of schooners to bring Cape Breton coal. As roads improved and trucking grew, sailing ships came to seem unreliable. In 1928, said Leonard, "there was no more trade for them at all. You'd go into a broker's office looking for a cargo, and he'd say, 'You got a farm at home?' That was poor encouragement, wasn't it?"

Leonard went ashore and worked as a carpenter. Talking about that, he pointed out the built-in cupboards in the kitchen. "Not bad for an old fellow, eh?" When he was eighty, he put a new keel in *Lutetia.* He took off her cabin, turned her upside down in Claude Poirier's shed, cut a tree from his woodlot on Bernard Island and had it milled to size, then carefully shaped it and fit it in.

Later on, he sailed in steamers and tugboats. He didn't leave the sea for good until he was seventy-one. I don't exactly mean that he retired; in Nova Scotia villages people don't really retire. Growing old in D'Escousse doesn't mean being shunted into a home that is really a ghetto for obsolete wage earners. Growing old in D'Escousse just means your life runs down as gradually as the grass turns brown.

Even in his eighties, Leonard Pertus was not an old man; he was Leonard, and his friends were often fifty years his juniors. He would go mackerel fishing with Jim Morrison, a masonry contractor in his thirties, or with Stanley Boudreau, who had just turned thirty. Stanley loves to tell about the summer day he and The Skipper were driving around in Stanley's Mustang.

Things were different in the 1970s; as they toured around, visiting friends, they were sharing a sociable beer. Then a car shot out from a side road right in front of them. Stanley crammed on the brakes, narrowly avoiding an accident. Leonard just sat quietly in the death seat. When the danger had passed, he said, "People are terrible, Boudreau. If we hit that fellow, you know what people would say? They wouldn't ask, 'Are they hurt? Is Stanley's car all smashed?' No, they'd say, 'There's Pertus and Boudreau, drinking again.'"

The Skipper was not really a drinking man. All the same,

when the ship was moored and the sails furled, you could pour him a finger or two of Bacardi and he wouldn't object. He drank it neat. I added water to mine, and he frowned.

"You've drowned your drink, Cameron," he said.

On November 19, 1980, Lulu and I dropped in to see him. I had sold *Hirondelle*, and *Silversark* was taking shape in the barn. Leonard had given me a hand putting an addition on the barn, but we hadn't sailed together for several years.

Around Susan's immaculate kitchen table, half a dozen people were drinking rum and playing forty-fives, a card game to which Nova Scotians are devoted. Leonard's sister Leontine was there, and his son John, and various other relatives and neighbours. When Leonard won a trick, he slapped down his cards with gusto and winked at us. Susan passed homemade fudge, and later she produced a cake. It was a special cake, for a special occasion: Leonard was ninety years old.

Treasure him, I told myself as I watched him enjoy his birthday. Try to grow old with The Skipper's grace, dignity, humour. Live with zest, if you can, at ninety.

He was under the weather after the party. A hangover, a cold, a touch of the flu. Two weeks later he was dead. I walked into the post office that day and met Claude Poirier.

"Leonard," said Claude, shaking his head. He looked at me sadly. "Who's going to teach us now?"

I nodded. Nobody would teach us how to handle our boats in a breeze, how to foretell the weather, how to moor under sail, how to "scandalize" a schooner's mainsail. Nobody else knew how.

I think of him often: his cheerfulness, his serene acceptance of calms and gales alike, the pleasure he took in his calling. In that first summer of our sailing, I asked him how he liked going back to sea in steamers and tugboats. Was steam as good as sail?

"No," he said, very firmly. "Not interesting. A motorboat, you just take the wheel and she goes. You hear that engine roaring, you're making good time. But it's not interesting. A sailboat, you have to know something.

"I'm eighty-three out, eighty-four on November 19 if I'm living, and there's still nothing I like better, on a fine day with a good breeze, than to go out in a sailboat."

Leonard, I thought, as we sailed through the waters where he taught me, I'd like your spirit with us on this voyage.

"Huh," I said out loud.

"What?" asked Lulu.

"The Skipper," I said.

"He'll be along when we need him," she said.

The wind picked up, and we sailed through the narrows by the Martinique lighthouse, steering for the bridge at Burnt Island.

STAR

OF

BETH.

We wanted to anchor that first night in one of the osprey-haunted, roadless coves in the western end of Lennox Passage. But we faced a serious obstacle: The Honourable Isadore LeBlanc Memorial Bridge. That's only my name for it; officially, the bridge is nameless. But if ever a man deserved to have his name on a bridge, that man was The Honourable Isadore LeBlanc.

LeBlanc was the Member of the Legislative Assembly for Richmond County around 1910. He had an Acadian accent as thick as a good *potage*, and he once shocked the Legislature by declaring, "I *designed* de County of Richmond, I *built* de County of Richmond, I *own* de County of Richmond h'and I *run* de County of Richmond." He was teasing his effete urban colleagues: *The County of Richmond* was the name of his ship.

His grand ambition was the construction of a bridge onto Isle Madame, about which he hectored the Legislature incessantly.

"Mr. Speaker," he cried, "h'in de h'old days, h'it was all sea transport—and down in de Ile Madame, we done fine. We built de ships, we sailed de ships, we made a good living.

"But today, dat's all goin'. Now h'it's road transport, and we got to have a bridge onto de Ile Madame. Wit'out dat bridge we're going to go down and down and down, and dere's nothing more h'important before dis 'Ouse dan a bridge onto de Ile Madame."

Eventually, it is said, the Premier of the day grew weary of LeBlanc's jeremiads. He rose in the House to say the government would build no such bridge. The project would be prohibitively expensive, because the bridge would have to cross Lennox Passage, which was a large body of water. There weren't enough people on Isle Madame to justify it.

"So," said the Premier, "we aren't going to build that bridge, and I hope the Honourable Member for Richmond will find another subject for his stirring addresses to this House."

Up popped Isadore LeBlanc, aflame with righteous fury.

"Mister Speaker!" he cried scornfully. "I got a t'ing or two to say to de Premier! In de first place, 'e says dere's not dat many people in de Ile Madame—Mr. Speaker, dere's six t'ousand people, and dat's no small number where I come from.

"In de second place, 'e says de bridge would be h'expensive, because Lennox Passage is a big body of water! H'it's not a big body of water—hell, I could *piss* halfways across!"

"Shame! Shame!" cried some Honourable Members. "Order! Order! You're out of order!"

Above the tumult rose the stentorian voice of LeBlanc.

"H'I know goddam well I'm h'out of h'order!" he bellowed. "If I was in order, I could piss *all* de ways across!"

He carried the day. The House voted for the bridge.

As it turned out, two bridges were required, leapfrogging across Burnt Island from Isle Madame to Cape Breton. When The Skipper and I sailed together, those spidery, antiquated steel bridges still gave the world its only road access to Isle Madame. At the centre of the longer bridge was a swing span, turned by Stanley Forgeron's horse; walking in circles around an auger in the middle of the span, the horse slowly cranked the bridge open—for Farley Mowat, for instance, when he sailed through Lennox Passage in *Happy Adventure* on his way to Expo 67.

But in December 1970, when the tanker *Arrow* broke up off Arichat, on Isle Madame's south coast, the authorities hastily built an impromptu causeway just west of the old bridges in order to keep wandering slicks of Bunker C out of Lennox Passage. By the mid-1970s, when the oil slicks were gone, the swing bridge was too badly rusted to repair. Eventually it was replaced by a permanent causeway pierced at just one point by a lift bridge—which *should* have commemorated the Honourable Isadore LeBlanc.

All the water which once flowed between the islands now pours through that narrow gap—and, oddly enough, it almost always flows eastward. The prevailing winds blow in the same direction. Together, the two constitute an irresistible force.

When *Silversark* approached the bridge, the wind and tide were both against us. The bridge tender opened the span. We tacked into the opening—and the current thrust us back out, carrying *Silversark* bodily sideways. We tried and failed again. We waved the bridge tender to close the bridge while we dropped the anchor nearby.

Sitting in the cockpit, we considered the options. Hope that the tide would change? Not likely. Pray for a favourable wind? We might spend a long time on our knees. Ask a passing motor vessel for a tow? Probably the best bet. And then—

BAM! BAM! BAM!

It sounded like a cannon firing, half a mile behind us. I snatched up the binoculars and saw puffs of smoke rising along the shore, right beside a boxy, dorylike grey sloop.

"A make-and-break, by God!" I said.

The make-and-break is an antique form of two-cycle gasoline engine, a device of unparalleled simplicity and viciousness. *Hirondelle* came equipped with one. I called it Stinky Sam, and it made every effort to burn me, drown me, blow me up and maim me.

To start a make-and-break, you squirt raw gasoline from an oil can directly into the combustion chamber, creating explosive vapours all around you. Seizing the massive cast-iron flywheel, you manually roll the engine over. Then you scramble clear.

With luck, the gasoline fumes explode *inside* the combustion chamber, and the engine starts. With more luck, the flywheel may not seize you by a finger or a sleeve and break your arm. If you are triply lucky, the engine will turn over in the direction you had in mind. But there are no guarantees; the engine is just as happy rotating backward, propelling the boat stern-first.

A make-and-break has no transmission and no clutch, so the boat moves forward (or backward) the moment the engine starts. Mind you, the engine frequently will not start at all, in which case you blow helplessly around the harbour, bouncing off ships, wharves and buoys. To prevent such mishaps, beginners are well-advised to keep the boat firmly tied to a wharf or a mooring until the engine has declared its intentions.

I said "firmly tied." I once asked a charming woman to take a rope around a bollard on a high, splintery wooden wharf in Lunenburg and bring two ends back aboard. When the engine started, she was to cast off one end and haul the line aboard as the boat moved off. Alas, I neglected to insist that she fasten both ends of the rope *firmly*.

To my great surprise, the engine actually started—and forward, too. *Hirondelle* moved off smartly, pulling my unsuspecting friend straight up the face of the wharf. She let go just in time to land heavily on the stern of the schooner, which was fast moving out from under her. Showering the vessel and its master with splinters and curses, she very nearly ended a promising relationship right there.

BAM! BAM! BAM!

A make-and-break. I'd know that sound anywhere.

And the boxy grey sloop was moving.

Stinky Sam (and his diesel-powered successor, Sweet Sue) ultimately persuaded me that engines in sailboats are an abomination—dirty, smelly, unreliable, explosive, expensive. Engines require holes in the boat for propeller shafts and cooling water. They lull you into trusting them in tight situations—and then they fail. So *Silversark* has 10-foot oars clipped to the rigging—the simplest form of auxiliary power, quite sufficient to move her short distances in calm weather.

But in making the drastic decision to rely on oars, I had not considered the problem of Isadore LeBlanc's bridge.

The grey sloop continued BAM-BAMing its way up towards us, standing tall in the water. Her nameboard bore the words *Jesus Loves III*. She was towing a workmanlike dory called *St. Mary Magdalen*. Her helmsman sported a bushy beard and a baseball cap. He was tall and ruddy, dressed in olive-drab work clothes. We knew him by repute: a solitary homesteader who lived on an isolated waterfront property a mile beyond the bridge.

He waved gravely to us as he passed, BAM-BAMing his way towards the bridge. We gravely waved back.

The bridge did not open.

The sloop circled in front of the bridge, her skipper calling to the bridge tender. Nothing happened. The sloop went around again and again, her tiller hard over, her skipper standing in the cockpit with his hands cupped around his mouth.

"Hey! Come on! Open the bridge! Open the bridge!"

Nothing.

The make-and-break fell silent. The bearded fellow lowered his anchor over the stern.

Bells rang. Traffic gates closed. The bridge slowly opened.

The bearded one tried to start his engine. BAM! Then silence. Another BAM! And more silence.

Cars were stopped on either side of the bridge. People got out and looked down. They saw two sailboats—*Silversark* and *Jesus Loves III*—lying at anchor, not moving.

"I don't want to be here," said Lulu. "I don't know what game they're playing, but I don't want anyone thinking we're part of it."

Finally, the lift span began to drop. It fell into place, the gates went up, and traffic began to flow.

BAM! BAM! BAM!

Jesus Loves III had her engine running. Her master tried to haul his anchor while the little sloop made tight circles around her anchor line. Finally the hook came up in a solid two-foot ball of glistening chocolate-coloured kelp. *Jesus Loves III* began circling in front of the bridge again while her skipper stripped kelp off his anchor and called to the bridge tender.

"Hey! Open the bridge! Come on! Open the damn bridge!"

Nothing happened.

He stopped his engine again. Once more he lowered his anchor over the stern.

Bells rang. Traffic gates closed. The bridge slowly opened.

Once again, motorists lined the guard rail, staring down at the two anchored vessels. Once again, we cringed.

Eventually, the bridge closed again.

But this time, the master of *Jesus Loves III* was not starting his engine. He was busy at the base of his mast.

Lulu looked through the binoculars.

"He's taking his mast down!" she said. "He's going to go *under* the bridge!"

Sure enough, he was slackening his rigging. The afternoon was fading, the sun slanting downward. The foul tide still poured out below the bridge. We were thinking about supper.

"He's getting in his dory!" cried Mark.

The bearded sailor was clambering—rather awkwardly—into *St. Mary Magdalen.* He shipped his oars and began rowing.

"He's coming here!"

Indeed he was. In a few moments he had pulled up beside *Silversark*, hot and sweaty but smiling.

"Hi," he said. "I was wondering if you might happen to have a little short piece of three-quarter hose, just maybe five or six inches? And also a drink of water."

"I think I've got some hose," I said. "I'll take a look."

"I'll get you a drink," Lulu said. "Come on aboard."

He climbed over the lifelines—"It's kind of difficult, that leg is wooden"—and introduced himself.

Richard Mayes.

His problem, he explained, was a leaky hose in the cooling system which made his engine overheat. He could motor only for a few minutes without shutting it off—and once it was hot, the engine was balky. The bridge tender knew that, said Richard, so he opened the bridge only after Richard shut his engine off. The bridge tender had covered himself: he couldn't be accused of anything: he had opened the bridge. It wasn't *his* fault if *Jesus Loves III* couldn't get moving again.

"I gather he doesn't like you," I said.

"I had a lot of trouble with that family," Richard said. "I'm a Christian, I guess they find that hard to take. Look, if the current's not too bad when I get goin', I could probably tow you through if you want."

I had a sudden vision of the two boats circling around in front of the bridge, blowing horns and shouting vainly.

"Sure," I said, "but don't worry about it. We'll get through somehow or other."

"You could be here a long time waiting for an easterly."

He rowed back. We watched as his mast came down level with his deck, protruding over the stern. BAM BAM BAM! Lifting his anchor, he motored towards us.

"Too much current!" he shouted. "But come by when you get through!"

"All right!"

BAM BAM BAM! The old engine echoed in the square-sided cavern under the bridge, then faded slowly as Richard motored down the passage to his home.

Next morning *Silversark* slipped through the bridge, towed by Ron Boudreau, an eel fisherman from nearby Louisdale. The night's fog had burned off, yielding a pearly-grey morning. We sailed into a light southwesterly breeze, tacking down the Passage to Richard's homestead. As we came closer, we saw the gaunt grey skeleton of a massive wooden ship standing on the beach, partially concealed by a long low shed. In letters six feet high, the side of the shed bore the motto: STAR OF BETH.

We anchored. Richard rowed out and took us ashore.

Richard's land gradually rises inland to the top of a long wooded ridge. He bought it from an ad in the back pages of a sporting magazine. *Cheap Canadian properties! Nothing down!* There is always a catch. In this case, it was the isolation of the property—a mile by water from the nearest road. Richard didn't care. Born in Texas, he was then living in Saint John, New Brunswick. He moved to Cape Breton in a 23-foot sloop he had built himself.

Richard builds boats in much the same style that Caterpillar builds front-end loaders. Massive timbers, husky bolts, heavy planks, muscular ironwork. All his boats are flat-bottomed and square-sided. The larger ones have beefy solid-wood keels projecting downward from the centre-line, with auxiliary keels out on each side, a system which ensures that if the boat settles on the bottom, she sits more or less upright. Over the years, his boatbuilding projects have grown bigger and bigger. His dory *St. Peter* is only 10 feet long. *St. Mary Magdalen* may be 14 feet. *Jesus Loves III* is 25 feet. The new vessel, *Star of Bethlehem*, is a 52-foot trading ketch. She will not be his last. God only knows— I say this reverently—how big his ultimate ship may be.

"I had to shorten *Bethlehem* on the sign there because the shed's too short," he remarked.

The shed contains a small sawmill, powered by a portable generator. To build a ship, Richard cuts his own logs up on the ridge, skids them down the hill behind a little four-wheeled all-terrain vehicle, muscles them onto the saw table and slices them into timbers. He shapes the timbers, bolts them into place and soaks them with used motor oil to prevent them from cracking and warping when they dry out—which is why *Star of Bethlehem* already looks weathered and grey.

Star of Bethlehem is perhaps 16 feet wide, with 10 feet of headroom in the hold. She is more like a car ferry than a yacht. Her masts would do for telephone poles. Using a complicated set of guys, props and tackles, Richard raised both masts himself. Her bottom consists of close-fitted four-inch timbers covered by two layers of diagonal planking, with tar and plastic sandwiched between them. She will crush rocks and shatter icebergs.

The grandeur of Richard's project overwhelms his actual home, which looks like a smokehouse: tall and narrow. The whole building is no more than 10 feet square. Like the bottom of *Star of Bethlehem*, the walls are made of small logs laid on top of one another within a framework. A red crucifix is nailed above the door. Just outside is his well, three feet deep, two feet across, lined with short wooden posts, and full of water.

The house had a half-built addition, slightly taller than the original building, twice as long, sheathed in waferboard.

"I'm expecting guests this summer," Richard explained. "I needed someplace to put 'em."

"How did you get the waferboard down here?"

"Just balanced it across the dory and rowed it home."

Inside the original house, the walls are lined with shelves of bulk food. A plank counter holds wash basins and pails. The main living space is dominated by a cast-iron wood stove. A steep ladder leads up to a low sleeping loft.

"Richard," said Lulu, looking first at the ladder and then at Richard's wooden leg, "how do you—oh, yes!"

"Right." Richard smiled. "The leg stays downstairs."

We wanted to dig some clams. Richard lent us a small plastic pail and a clam-digging tool—a broken steel spring leaf—and gave us directions. We set out along the shore.

Richard's cabin stands by a notch on the shore inside a rocky spruce-capped islet. Just to the west are two or three tiny coves, separated by grass-covered micro-peninsulas and jagged sandstone outcrops. The layers of sandstone were loose; grabbing and tugging, we pulled out brittle inch-thick sheets of perfectly flat stone, like thin slabs of concrete. All around us, the birds were soaring and wheeling, crying and wading—blue jays and sandpipers, finches and terns.

The shore was strewn with small shards of sandstone, perfect for skipping. Our crew included an expert. Mark picked up a handful of stones and casually whipped each one across the little cove, *skip-skip-skip*, clean into the trees on the other bank. Lulu and I joined in, freckling the water with overlapping circles, exulting in the stone that flies fast and flat, just touching the surface before lifting again as though it had drawn energy from the water itself—and groaning at the perfect skipping stone which fails, making one high hop and then splashing lifelessly into the water.

Mark switched to "cutting the devil's throat," firing his stones edgewise into the water so that they plunged without a splash, piercing the surface with a single low, wet *thrk!*

A couple of summers ago, Mark threw stones with Bill Howell, who later wrote about the blameless joys of stones and water:

a broken window costs at least five allowances;
a broken ocean or lake is free.

Meanwhile, consider the great curve of Canada
on the globe of the world in your mind.

This is the exact opposite of
skipping anything.
            This has nothing to do
with holding grudges.
            This has everything
to do with instant revenge.
            This is the gloat
that no one else will ever know.
            This is always
the sure kill without a wave goodbye . . . .

The black mud of the shoreline was speckled with clam vents. But when we began digging with the spring leaf, we turned up broken clams: they were clustered so thick in the mud that we could hardly drive the spring steel down without striking one. We put the spring leaf aside and dug with our hands, clawing down into the mud and picking clams out of the walls of shallow holes. It was like picking apples.

The pail was soon full. We heard the popping sound of a light engine. Looking up, we saw Richard's four-wheeler weaving its way along the shore.

"I figured we were all hungry, so I got a pot of mackerel and rice ready to go," he called. "How you doin'?"

"Great! Look at the clams!"

Richard grinned and wheeled around.

Richard's one-pot supper—cooked on a wood stove, in July— consists of a pot of rice steamed almost completely and then covered with a layer of spiced whole mackerel. As the mackerel steam, their juices and spices seep down through the rice. Richard served the meal with hot pickled peppers on the side— *really* hot peppers, the way Mexicans and Texans like them.

Later, back aboard *Silversark*, we quenched the fires in our mouths with cold beer. Richard was pleased: he drinks no hard liquor, and his last beer had been in March.

"I'm gonna make me some home brew," he said. "I've done it before, I don't know why I'm not doin' it now."

As the rosy light of sunset painted the surface of the water, he talked about other projects—a survival handbook he wanted to write, and a survival knife he had designed. The knife would serve as an axe, a saw and a hammer; its waterproof compartment would contain fish-hooks and line, snare wire, matches, a compass and much else.

"There's survival knives on the market," he said, "but they're really toys. You want a knife that gives you a real chance of survivin' if you find yourself in a bad spot."

How would that happen?

"Well, I think we're in for some pretty bad times," he said cheerfully. "The Bible tells us that nation will rise against nation, and I believe that. The Persian Empire will be re-established, and I believe we'll see a nuclear war. I don't want to get too deep into philosophy here, but the prophecies are *there*, and I'm a Christian, I believe 'em."

He tilted his bottle upward, drained the last of his beer, and heaved himself out of his seat, his six-foot frame bent to fit under *Silversark*'s five-foot-three overhead.

"I get up early, and you're going to sail tomorrow."

We went on deck. The wooded shores were black, but the moon made a rippling pathway on the water as Richard rowed ashore.

I went below. Mark was in his quarter berth, his slender twelve-year-old body stretching back under the starboard cockpit seat. Lulu was curled up in the big delta berth up forward. I blew out the oil lamp and joined her. *Silversark* moved gently. One sleeps well in a boat, rocked to sleep by the ceaseless movements and lulled by the wavelets chuckling against the bow . . . .

"Ahoy! You've got a fair breeze!"

I swam up from my sleep. Who was calling? Where . . . ?

"*Silversark*! You've got a fair breeze!"

I stumbled through the cabin and threw back the hatch into a pastel dawn, all gold and palest blue in crisp, cool morning air.

To the east, a burning spot on the horizon marked the place where the sun would soon rise. The treetops were alight, but darkness lingered in the shadows. Dew lay in pools on the deck. Lennox Passage was ruffled by a gentle easterly.

Richard stood on the shore in his work clothes and cap. "Beautiful breeze for where you're headin'!" he called. "Can't waste a fair wind!"

"Thank you!" I replied.

Richard waved and turned away. Back down below, my watch told me it was five A.M. I burrowed under the warm covers in the delta berth.

"What was all that?" Lulu asked.

"Fair breeze for the Strait," I murmured. "Fine morning."

"What time is it?"

"Five."

"Good grief," said Lulu.

We lay there for a few moments, each aware that the other had not gone back to sleep.

"Well," said Lulu, finally.

"Right," I said.

"If that breeze goes around to the west later on — or if it dies — we'll look pretty silly."

"Mmm," I said.

At six, *Silversark* spun on her heel and slipped away westward. We sat in the cockpit with our morning coffee, waving to Richard. Standing on the deck of *Star of Bethlehem*, Richard waved back — a modern Noah with a proper ark, awaiting a divine catastrophe.

Lulu's instincts were right: the easterly wind eased steadily as we ran down Lennox Passage into Inhabitants Bay. Haddock Harbour opened to port, another maze of neglected islands and sheltered inlets. One island belongs to hospitable Germans who come for a month or so in the summer: waterfrontage in Europe is so scarce and pricey that it makes sense to buy cheap Nova Scotian land and fly the family out to it.

We sailed slowly past the long slender bulk of Rabbit Island, with the ragged shore of Janvrin's Island, the last fragment of the Isle Madame archipelago, to port. Close in by the shore of Rabbit Island, a lobsterman hauled traps, his outboard skiff heaving in the onshore swell. Mark was still sleeping; Lulu yawned and went below. *Silversark* and I sailed on together.

Seeing this landscape for the first time, one might find it pristine and unspoiled, the very picture of coastal serenity. In fact, it is redolent of ruined dreams of wealth and industrial development. Twenty years ago, Inhabitants Bay was the outer anchorage for supertankers waiting to unload at the Strait of Canso Superport. The far shore of Inhabitants Bay—Port Malcolm, Port Richmond—is uninhabited only because its people were removed to make way for a steel mill, never built, on Bear Head, towards which we were steering. Off the port bow, on the mainland of Nova Scotia, a gigantic scar marks the site of the oil refinery John Shaheen proposed to build after his apparent success at Come-by-Chance, Newfoundland. In the fall of 1974, Shaheen brought a shipload of dignitaries here on the *Queen Elizabeth II*, which he had chartered for the purpose. But Shaheen went bankrupt and died, and that refinery, too, was never built.

Halfway across Inhabitants Bay, the breeze died completely, leaving *Silversark* rolling quietly in the slick water for fifteen minutes. Lulu and Mark woke up, put on the kettle and ate some granola. The wind came in again from the northeast, gently at first, then more seriously. *Silversark* forged onward, aiming for the red buoy off Bear Head. Another lobsterman was hauling traps there, waving as we passed. We turned at the buoy, and *Silversark* heeled before what had become a fresh breeze, carving her way directly up the Strait.

"Look!" cried Mark. "A dog swimming!" Sure enough, the dark head of an animal was moving steadily through the water from the industrial lands at Bear Head towards the mainland.

"That's not a dog," said Lulu, squinting through the binoculars. "It's—it's a deer!"

We sailed within fifty yards of it. As we passed, the deer turned around and swam back to Bear Head.

"Another Cape Bretoner who couldn't bring himself to leave," said Lulu.

We found ourselves abreast of the oil dock at what was once

the Gulf Oil refinery and is now just a collection of storage tanks on the hillside. For years, former Liberal cabinet minister Alastair Gillespie has been trying to put together a deal called Scotia Syncrude, which would use the defunct refinery to make petroleum out of coal; news about the project has become a staple of the two weekly newspapers in Port Hawkesbury, pop. 3,850, the chief community of the Strait area.

Port Hawkesbury is best visualized as a suburb with no urb to which it is sub. But because of this stretch of water, it is—or was—that rare anomaly, a Maritime boom town.

The Port Hawkesbury boom took place twenty years ago, after the construction of the Canso Causeway blocked the Strait and unexpectedly created the finest ice-free deepwater harbour on the east coast of North America. Gulf Canada built a refinery to process Middle Eastern crude from supertankers. Canadian General Electric built a heavy-water plant to supply the CANDU reactors Canada intended to export to the world. The Nova Scotia Power Corporation erected an oil-fired generating station, Georgia Pacific established a gypsum-shipping operation, and Sweden's Stora Kopparberg, through a subsidiary now named Stora Forest Industries, built a pulp and paper mill.

Then, during the 1970s, the boom stalled. CGE sold its heavy-water plant to Atomic Energy of Canada Ltd., and in 1986, when Michael Wilson noticed the world's indifference to CANDU reactors, he closed it. When the Suez Canal reopened, super-tankers faded away, and the Gulf refinery closed. The generating plant was converted to run on coal, and it still operates—but Nova Scotia's new generating plants stand right atop the coal mines of Lingan, a hundred miles away. The chief remaining industry is Stora, with a workforce of 1,300—and Stora itself faces sluggish markets and stiff competition.

But that magnificent harbour is still there, and Port Hawkesbury has faith. The town is on the Trans-Canada Highway and the Canadian National main line, though Michael Wilson has taken away its passenger trains. A new gypsum quarry is operating nearby, and several small industries have sprung up, lured by a rich stew of government development funding. Louisiana Pacific is producing a revolutionary new wall covering made of gypsum and wood fibre, and the German conglomerate Thyssen is proposing to build military vehicles—armoured cars and the like—at Bear Head.

In the mid-1980s, Port Hawkesbury was doing tolerably well. A local shipyard called Breton Industrial and Marine, now bankrupt, was building draggers, pilot boats, small freighters. Offshore oil exploration brought Petro Canada supply ships to Mulgrave, across the Strait, where Mulgrave Machine Works built up an offshore-supply business that employed thirty to fifty people. At that point, Port Hawkesbury stumbled on a brilliant promotional idea, executed it just once, and misguidedly allowed it to die.

The Great Paper Boat Race of the World sprang full-bodied from the head of Bill Martin at 12:41 P.M. on March 7, 1984, in the Industrial Commission Board Room. Martin was thirty-seven, a bearded extrovert given to quixotic ventures. His 1981 campaign for the provincial legislature was typical of NDP campaigns in rural Nova Scotia: he was drowned by hereditary Grits and Tories. When he left his job as manager of radio station CIGO, however, he successfully established a weekly newspaper despite the existence of an award-winning weekly, *The Scotia Sun*. By 1984, the paid circulation of *The Reporter* was 6,700. The *Sun*'s was 6,300.

Martin made his suggestion at a luncheon meeting of the Port Hawkesbury Chamber of Commerce, which was considering what to do about the Festival of the Strait, held annually on the Canada Day weekend. Founded by the Chamber of Commerce, the festival evolved into an independent organization which was regularly pelted with editorial tomatoes by Bill Martin. Its directors all resigned and told the Chamber to take it back. The Chamber called a luncheon meeting. Martin attended. Martin, you big-mouth, said the members, now what do we do?

Bill Martin got up and said: "Hold a paper boat race."

He was as astonished as anyone else. The idea had never occurred to him until that moment.

The Great Paper Boat Race of the World was set for Canada Day. Entries were to be constructed "principally of paper," though screws and other fasteners were allowed. They had to be propelled by muscle or wind, not by engines. Sails, if any, had to be paper. Paddles and oars could be of any material. There were no restrictions on size, design or type of paper. *But each boat had to carry a crew of three.*

Jim Organ was a pipefitter at Stora Forest Industries. He got the assignment of building Stora's entry.

Jim Organ's diary, May 15, 1984: *"Paper boat approved. Seems like it's all in my lap. Decided to sit down and draw some working prints . . . Long time drafting, as I had to build in my head and then transfer to paper. Have to design a craft which takes into account my limited abilities as a shipwright."*

Breton Marine was building a vessel. So were Mulgrave Machine and the local Knights of Columbus. Several other entries were rumoured, and at the heavy-water plant the entire engineering department had gone daffy, producing *fifteen* designs.

Jim Organ's diary, May 24: *"Solved the curvature problem of yesterday. So simple I couldn't see it . . . We have a 3-man crew so far, all union, need a rep from the company. Try for Ralph Keef. He got me in this mess anyway. If I go down so does he . . ."*

Across the Strait, the owner of Mulgrave Machine, Bob Reid, had "come into the office in a jolly mood one morning," said his colleague Jack Hoben, and declared that the company would build a boat out of SonaTubes, the heavy paper cylinders used to form concrete pilings. The design evolved from the materials: a multihulled sailboat. Michael Breen and John Bunyan worked two solid weeks on *Mean Machine,* as the 21-foot trimaran was christened. They reshaped the tubes using industrial paper towels soaked in fibreglass resin. For a sail, they sandwiched a smelt net between two layers of towel; for a mast, they used cardboard cores from Stora newsprint rolls. Breton Marine and Stora made similar masts and sails.

Jim Organ's diary, May 25: *"Went over town to see Bill Martin. Any kind of ballast allowed. Shipyard has model of Bluenose, will be hard to beat. Went to Mulgrave . . ."*

Paul Osborne was the shipyard's mechanical engineer. At twenty-six, he was underwhelmed by Port Hawkesbury's throbbing night life. But he stayed because he had an interesting and useful job; besides, his father owned the shipyard.

Paul and his buddy, Billy Butts, began building partly because "it gave us something to do in the evenings." Nova Scotia was hosting the Tall Ships that year, a moment of glory which led the race committee to hint that tall *paper* ships might not come amiss. So Paul and Billy built a tiny schooner out of corrugated cardboard soaked in resin.

"It was like building three boats, layer upon layer," Paul remembered and grinned. "We put in over four hundred hours each. We worked from seven-thirty to ten every evening, and all day every weekend. Just for fun, I kept track of the screws: we used over twelve hundred."

Jim Organ's diary, June 7: *"Couldn't sleep last night so I came in @ 4:00 A.M. . . . didn't get double crew . . . worked till 8:00 P.M. . . ."*

The Knights of Columbus were bent on fun. Bill MacInnis wondered about a couple of SonaTubes hinged horizontally, so that three fellows could each put a foot in both tubes and *walk* the vessel across the water like a set of cross-country waterskis. Or should the Knights of Christopher Columbus present themselves as a Rowing Catholic organization?

Jim Organ's diary, June 9: *"Jimmie Joe and I both got sick. Probably from the heat. Wicked hot, 85 degrees. This is my 26th day without a break . . ."*

June 15: *"Finished 3 oar ports. Mike Heighton made a dragon's head and tail. Looks great . . ."*

Bill MacInnis decided that the tubes were too big to allow the team to walk on the water. And the enthusiasts at the heavy-water plant got the word from Ottawa: making paper boats was not a proper use of taxpayers' money. Not as useful, presumably, as heavy water.

Jim Organ's diary, June 27: *"Launched this afternoon. Behaves beautifully in water. Very pleased . . ."*

On June 28, Paul Osborne and Billy Butts launched *Breton Too*. The black schooner revealed a severe list, and a pinhole leak. They beached her to add ballast and repair the leak. In racing trim, she weighed over a ton, including 425 pounds of hull, 1,350 pounds of ballast and "800 pounds of people."

The next afternoon, the Mulgravers launched *Mean Machine*. She was tight as a bottle, and she handled beautifully. Eight machine-shop mariners piled aboard and boldly sailed her across the Strait to Port Hawkesbury in twenty-eight minutes. They had a beer at the Yacht Club before paddling back in thirty-seven minutes against the wind. *Mean Machine* remains the first and only paper boat ever to cross between mainland North America and Cape Breton Island.

The afternoon of July 1 was humid and stifling. The Port Hawkesbury waterfront bristled with spectators. Bill MacInnis, Bud McIntyre and Bob Delaney launched *The Papal Boat* at 1:28. The race was called for 1:30, and *Breton Too* would brook no delay: the repair was failing, Osborne was bailing, time to be sailing. *The Papal Boat* was christened with a paper bag full of Canada Dry, "the champagne of ginger ales."

The Papal Boat consisted of two SonaTubes held together with one bolt and two smaller tubes piercing the larger ones at right angles. The tubes were not waterproofed, and they were sealed with cardboard and a single layer of paper towels soaked in resin. She had taken eight hours to build, and "she never leaked a drop," MacInnis declared proudly. Delaney and McIntyre sat forward and paddled; MacInnis exhorted them from the stern, wearing blue shorts, a white shirt and an orange tie "so I could be seen on the bottom if I fell overboard." At intervals he blew a blast on a conch shell once used by his great-grandmother to summon the men from the fields at meal times. Beside him was a small barbecue fastened to the afterdeck. At the starting line, he doused the charcoal with lighter fluid. Black smoke and orange flame shot into the sky. The other paper boats paddled quickly away from him. Unperturbed, MacInnis began to broil hamburgers.

Among them, the entries recapitulated the entire history of Western sail. The first boat must have been a couple of logs lashed together, like *The Papal Boat*. Longships like *Stora Viking* carried Europeans to America before the Magna Carta, and fishing schooners like *Breton Too* marked the end of commercial sail. *Mean Machine*, of course, echoed contemporary high-tech ocean-racing multihulls.

So *Mean Machine* should have won. But, like *Breton Too*, she was counting on the wind. *Breton Too* "sailed across great to the starting line," said Paul Osborne. "And then as the starting flag went, the wind died. Partway through, we thought it was coming again, and then we looked at the smoke from the pulp mill. It was going straight up. So there we were, rowing one long ton."

No wind, no contest. *Mean Machine* could be paddled effectively, true. But *Stora Viking's* six men rowed like Norsemen intent on pillage. *Mean Machine* came second, *Breton Too* third. Sometime that afternoon, *The Papal Boat* arrived. This was "a deliberate strategic decision," MacInnis claimed in a subsequent letter to *The Reporter*. "It was not our intention to come ashore until the hamburgers were cooked."

Jim Organ's diary, July 1: *"Won race. Unbelievable. Fastest vessel. Won overall. All worth it. Large crowd. Damn it feels good!"*

Stora Viking was prepared to defend the next year. *Mean Machine* waited in a loft. But *Breton Too's* leak turned her cardboard hull to mush, and Paul Osborne regretfully set her afire. She burned very well.

Meanwhile, Bill Martin had mail from as far away as California. Paper shipwrights contemplated canoes, kayaks, even a submarine. Bill MacInnis said *The Papal Boat* would tow a waterskier in 1985, enabling her to finish both first *and* second.

Alas, the race was never held again, although it had the potential to become what the 500 is to Indianapolis, what the America's Cup once was to Newport, what bathtubs are to Nanaimo. Martin turned Tory and went to work for the Mayor of Port Hawkesbury, who was running for the provincial legislature. The mayor was Billy Joe MacLean, who won the election and became a cabinet minister, but ultimately proved too aromatic even for the spectacularly tolerant atmosphere of Nova Scotia politics. Convicted of padding his expense accounts, he was expelled from the Legislature in a special sitting called specifically for that purpose. Martin vanished into some promoter's Valhalla in Halifax, and the Great Paper Boat Race of the World disappeared.

Still, Port Hawkesbury's paper ships and polyester men were true inheritors of a great Nova Scotia tradition. As *Silversark* sailed past the Port Hawkesbury Yacht Club, I remembered the verses of John Masefield, the master of the kraft:

I must go down to the sea again, to the lonely sea and
the sky;
And all I ask is a sulphite ship, and a kleenex to wipe
my eye,
And a newsprint sheet, and a windward beat with the
J-cloths all a-shakin'
And a cardboard spar pointin' at a star, and a dawn like
waxed paper breakin'.

We passed Port Hawkesbury without stopping, holding our
course on a long reach up to the Canso Canal.

I was nervous about the canal. Since the opening of the Canso
Causeway in 1955, only the Canso Canal makes Cape Breton an
island. The causeway is the deepest in the world; in its construction half the face of nearby Cape Porcupine was blasted away
and dumped in the Strait between Auld Cove, on the Nova
Scotia side, and Port Hastings, on the Cape Breton side.

As with the Isadore LeBlanc Memorial Bridge, the Canso
Canal is the only remaining opening in the causeway. It has
high concrete walls on either side. A swing bridge lies across it.

The wind was blowing straight into the canal. Lulu would
have to steer right alongside the canal face, and I would have to
jump for a ladder, carrying a dock line. While Mark fended off, I
would scamper up the canal wall and stop the boat by taking a
turn of the rope around a bollard. Then, once the bridge
opened, two of us would tow the boat through by walking along
the bank with long tow lines, while the third steered and fended
off.

If this plan failed, of course, *Silversark* would sail on straight
into the canal until the mast hit the bridge.

Just outside the canal, we dropped the mainsail.

"All right," said Lulu. "Here we go."

I stationed myself beside the rigging, ready to jump. Lulu
closed the gap between *Silversark* and the round concrete
"islands" of the canal face.

There were no ladders. Or, rather, the ladders were on the
inside of the curves. By the time I saw one, we had passed it.

I looked up. A middle-aged man in vivid green slacks was looking back down at me. A canal tender, come to help out.

"Catch a line?"

He nodded, and I slung him the coil of line.

"Take a turn around a bollard and stop her gradually," I called. He had gone out of sight behind the top of the wall.

The boat stopped abruptly. I found a hanging rubber tire and scrambled ashore with another line. We made fast.

"Thanks," I said. "What's the procedure now? Do I go to the canal office and get them to swing the bridge?"

"Damned if I know," he said. "I'm a tourist."

COAST

OF

GHOSTS

The officials at the Canso Canal didn't want us to sign in. They didn't want to see our ship's papers. They hustled us through the lock and showed us a berth well outside the canal entrance, clear of any *real* ships which might appear.

The Gulf of St. Lawrence is not the Atlantic. The tides rise and fall at different times; before the causeway existed, the tidal currents sweeping through the Strait of Canso were legendary. Gulf water is shallower and less saline than ocean water. It warms up quickly in the summer, often reaching temperatures in the sixties and seventies. Tourist guides call it "the warmest ocean water north of Florida," which it may be.

The Gulf waters also freeze solid in the winter. On a bitterly-cold midwinter day, the air on the Gulf side of the causeway will be utterly clear above a seamless white sheet of ice. But on the other side, where the salty Atlantic water still heaves, "sea smoke" rises a hundred feet above the surface, rolling and tumbling over itself in thick, heavy banks.

The Atlantic rollers are immense, majestic; the Gulf breeds a short, sharp chop. Cape Breton's low, ragged Atlantic coast offers plenty of coves and harbours; the Gulf shore is high, bold, straight and forbidding. Port Hood and Chéticamp excepted, the Gulf harbours of Cape Breton are narrow river mouths with strong currents running in and out, their approaches guarded by offshore sandbars.

From the canal, the nearest accessible Cape Breton port was Port Hood, 24 nautical miles away. Our steady northeasterly might bring us to Port Hood in six hours, just before nightfall. But if the breeze fell light, we would find ourselves entering a strange harbour in the dark...

We sailed instead for Havre Boucher, five miles down the opposite shore, our little ship hurrying out through the widening funnel of the Strait's northern entrance. Sure enough, the breeze died away right at the harbour mouth. We shipped the oars, and Mark rowed.

Mark likes rowing: it builds muscle, and he wants to be bigger, stronger, older. Meanwhile he likes to test and monitor the growing strength of his body. During our cruise he reached his mother's height: a notable landmark, even though his mother is but a wee slip of a girl. Whenever I saw him swimming, I blinked. He used to look like a bundle of broomsticks, but now he was filling out through the chest, shoulders and thighs, building a man's body day by day, even hour by hour.

Silversark moved slowly into Havre Boucher, a pretty little basin circled by the Canadian National line from Sydney to Truro and, further up the hills, by the Trans-Canada Highway. For decades, the railway was a major employer in the village, which otherwise sustains itself as a fishing port and a bedroom community for the industries of Port Hawkesbury.

The harbour marks the dividing line between the Strait of Canso and St. Georges Bay, the largest bay in Nova Scotia. The bay was named, according to one tradition, by an English captain whose ship was attacked and set on fire by pirates.

"St. George and Merry England!" cried the captain, inspiring a vigorous defence — but the burning ship sank all the same, and the crew spent months in Havre Boucher before finding passage back to England.

That is not the only fiery ship in the village's collection of stories; another local legend — shared by the villages on the Cape Breton side — maintains that a blazing full-rigged ship occasionally appears in St. Georges Bay. People claim to have observed it through binoculars and found it in perfect trim but in flames above the deck. Cartier is said to have landed here in 1535, and fishermen say they have encountered that ship, too, sailing towards them and then fading away.

We talked with the fishermen and ate supper. As the sunset faded into darkness, we walked along a dirt road to the harbour mouth to look at the wind and sea.

"What are those sparkling things in the hayfield there?"

Fireflies. The whole meadow was twinkling with little lights flitting from one stem of grass to another. Delighted, Mark plunged into the hay.

"Look!"

He had a firefly trapped in his fist, winking on and off regularly, like a minuscule lighthouse.

"Look!"

Lulu held out her hand. A firefly had landed on it. It sat there, switching on and off, oblivious to its hostess and perfectly content with its condition.

We walked back to the boat. The firefly rested on Lulu's knuckle, glowing, fading, then glowing cheerily again.

Inside the boat it still flashed. Then it flew off.

"Where did it go?"

"There!"

The firefly perched, glowing intermittently, on the rim of a rubber boot below the companionway. We picked it up and set it outside. It flew off into the night, flashing its farewell.

A good omen.

We slipped quietly away from the wharf at seven in the morning. The west wind lay waiting for us, crisp and boisterous under a hard blue sky — not a fair wind, but a decisive one, a wind which would carry us to Port Hood on one long tack. *Silversark* heels easily at first, but in a steady breeze she soon finds her groove. She heeled ten or twelve degrees and stayed there, crashing forward into the white-capped seas, butting her way slowly towards Port Hood.

Sailing to windward is a noisy, tumultuous affair. The boat smacks into the seas, pitching and tossing and throwing spray. The wind whistles in the rigging, the sails tremble and flutter, any loose equipment creaks and thumps and rattles down below.

Despite the tumult, though, we weren't actually going very fast.

"Would she stand the jib?" I said tentatively.

"I'm sure she would," said Lulu.

The jib is *Silversark*'s second-largest sail, the sail that really pulls her to windward. In a sea, too, she needs the extra power to drive her against the waves. Heaving on the halyard, I sent the jib fluttering skyward, and Lulu sheeted it in. *Silversark* heeled a little further and took off, charging through the waves like a horse released from the corral. With Lulu steering, I had very little to do. It would be five or six hours till we closed with the land again.

Among the pleasures of sailing is the torpid, passive ease of many passages. You can read, make music, sunbathe, eat. Or you can just *be*. Even fretful people find it possible to sit back and muse aimlessly, staring at the wake or watching the slow transformation of shapes in the clouds. No doubt that meditative, rhythmic, wave-paced pulsation of time was one of the charms of transatlantic crossings before the age of air travel.

That day, I found myself looking at the plunging deck as though it were slightly out of focus, hanging between past and present. I remembered Peter Zimmer standing amidst the deck framing, methodically shaping the beams so that the plywood would land fair, and then calling for epoxy glue mixed to the consistency of "a nice-a pasta dough" before we hammered the decking down with tiny bronze ring-nails. I remembered creeping across that deck on my hands and knees, trying not to bump my back on the rafters of the barn. All that work, that thought, that care—how did it connect with the reality of this little ship forging through the seas, with the grey-painted deck rising and falling against the wide, blank ocean horizon?

In the shop, *Silversark* was a big, inert sculpture in mahogany, bronze and oak. But now, like all ships, she had developed a life of her own, a distinctive personality. It had taken a while to get comfortable with her. What sane person, after all, would go to sea in a ship built by a novelist? But we were coming to know her, to respect what she could do. She was indeed more like a living thing than anything else a man—and a woman—could build with their own hands.

I looked around. Behind us lay Havre Boucher and the mainland of Nova Scotia, already shrinking and fading, becoming hazy and indistinct. Ahead of us lay the islands of Port Hood, still too far off for any features to show. Far to the westward, the smoky bulk of Cape George marked the other side of St. Georges Bay.

And what was that white object thrusting above the horizon in the general direction of the invisible Prince Edward Island? Too big to be a ship, surely. An oil rig, moving from one drill site to another?

"What is it?"

"Dunno." I reached for the big yellow Minoltas, our workhorse binoculars. A big trapezoidal block of white, textured, slowly tapering . . . I focussed the binoculars again.

"It's a ship!" I said. "A square-rigger!"

"Go on!"

"It is! It's a full-rigged ship, hull-down."

"What's hull-down?" asked Mark.

"You can't see the ship itself because the curve of the earth is in the way. You can only see the masts and sails. It must be huge, it's ten or twelve miles away."

The square-rigger was moving fast, sailing up into the bay and along the far shore. In an hour or two she would be at the causeway. As we later discovered, she was the Colombian sail-training bark *Gloria*, out of Cartagena, on a North American tour. She spent the weekend in Mulgrave, opposite Port Hawkesbury. But for us, she was a brief glimpse of history and poetry, unexpectedly moving across our own wake like the ghost ship of St. Georges Bay.

Silversark sailed on, shouldering her way down the Cape Breton shore. The coastline here is an imposing rampart of flat-topped mountains set back from the sea, with homes and farms dotting the shelf below. But for someone who knows its history, this is a melancholy district. That high plateau, now given over to woodland which feeds the Stora mill, was once cleared and cultivated. There were whole communities back there: Creignish Rear, Rhodena, Essex, Lexington, Lake Horton, McIntyre's Mountain, Rear Long Point, MacDougal's Mountain. Farms filled the countryside from Port Hawkesbury to Mabou, and thence across Cape Breton to Whycocomagh and West Bay.

But those farms are gone, replaced by a strange, eerie forest, all spruce and balsam fir—a forest seamed by roads and pathways, and peopled with ghosts.

In Creignish Rear, the evidence was still fresh when I prowled its winding dirt roads in the early 1980s. Shingled walls lay flat on the grass. Clearings resisted the advance of the spruce trees. Occasional houses still stood with trees reaching through their staircases or their ruined parlours. Heaps of rock dotted the abandoned fields.

The first generation of settlers took the lands along the coast. One of them was a man whose name appears on the old grant map as "John MacMaster." In Creignish they still call him Iain MacEwen ic Iain, or Iain Ruadh—Red John.

In 1801, Iain Ruadh left Moidart, Scotland. He probably landed in Pictou, already a well-established Presbyterian town. Like many Highlanders, like the Stuart kings—like most of the Cape Breton Scots today—Iain Ruadh was Catholic. He moved east, first to the Scottish Catholic town of Antigonish, where he married Maggie MacIsaac, and then to Creignish with his first cousin, Donald MacMaster the Weaver. Maggie's brother John followed, settling at Long Point.

Back in the Highlands, corrupt chieftains and their Lowland overseers were burning the houses above tenants' heads and herding families aboard ships so cramped and foul that they could not even have served legally for the slave trade. Creignish was wild, with its cliffs towering behind its strip of seaside land, but its hills were blanketed with beech, maple and birch as well as spruce and fir; the waters of St. Georges Bay were full of fish; and Iain Ruadh's view was bounded only by the distant blue hills and smoky headlands of Nova Scotia.

Iain Ruadh and Donald the Weaver cleared land and built log cabins. But later, as his family grew, Red John was stirred to think about a more permanent house—a whitewashed stone cottage with a pitched roof on all four sides and a nice ridge-pole along its length. Set on a knoll high above the bay, the house said: Here I stand. From now on, my people belong to Creignish.

Iain Ruadh's stone house is a landmark, seven miles from the Canso Causeway; I picked it out with the binoculars as we sailed by. Iain Ruadh and his Maggie had five sons and seven daughters. Their son Duncan married Cecilia MacEachern, of Long Point, and in 1922, at the age of ninety-eight, Cecilia was still living in Iain Ruadh's stone house with her son, Dan Duncan MacMaster.

Meanwhile, another of Iain Ruadh's sons, Hugh, married Maggie MacIsaac of Rear Port Hastings and took up his own grant in a part of Creignish Rear known as South Rhodena. That farm passed to Hugh's son Archie, and to Archie's son Dan, who lived there until 1950, when he was eighty-two.

Dan's daughter Cassie married Angus MacInnis and moved to Port Hawkesbury. Her son Frank delighted in weekends and vacations with his grandfather in Rhodena, and nobody grieved more when the farm was abandoned. By 1980, Dan MacMaster's farm was only a tangle of rotting timbers and curling shingles in a clearing marked by neglected fruit trees.

When young Frank MacInnis started a family, he built his house in Creignish—not back in Rhodena but down on the shore, a mile or two from Iain Ruadh's stone house. But because he loved the old Rhodena farm, his uncle Donald signed it over to him. It was Frank MacInnis who first took me back into the Rear, showing me the traces of vanished communities.

Frank works in Port Hawkesbury as principal of the Community College—but, as they say, he "belongs to Creignish."

He is Iain Ruadh's great-great-great-grandson.

The Rear was cleared and settled in the 1830s and 1840s, after the first generation of Highland pioneers had taken the shore land. The Scots were pouring into Cape Breton—something like 20,000 by 1843. Between 1832 and 1838, the Crown sold 34,000 acres to homesteaders.

Some of the settlers in the Rear—like Iain Ruadh's son Hugh—were children of the shore families; others were later immigrants from the rapidly depopulating Highlands. The Rear was less convenient, particularly for men who might have supplemented their farming with a little fishing, but it satisfied what Joseph Howe described in 1830 as "the extravagant desire the Highlanders cherish to purchase large quantities of land."

The settlers suffered terrible privations—six or eight people living for five weeks on the milk of a single cow—but within a generation they had given Cape Breton the appearance of a settled community; within two generations, they were relatively prosperous. These were good years in the Maritimes, when shipbuilding and lumbering prospered, mining developed, agricultural production rose steadily from year to year, fishing and trading carried Maritimers around the world. A legislative report of 1852 remarked that half the masters of New England fishing vessels were Nova Scotians and that "there were upward of 200 men on board of them this season from the Straits of Canso alone." A Scottish editor who visited Inverness County in 1880 found living conditions much better than in Scotland itself:

> The farmers as a class are not wealthy, but they have as much bread, potatoes, meat, butter, cheese and such substantial fare as any one needs to have, while they not only grow their own wool, but in nearly all cases keep their own looms and weave it in their respective homes into excellent cloth. Add to all these home comforts a beautiful climate, and the independence enjoyed by a fine race of men living unmolested by laird or factor, on their freehold possessions, and what more can be wished for?

Nova Scotia's greatest Gaelic poet, the Bard MacLean of Barney's River, though at first depressed by the ceaseless toil of clearing and planting land, eventually concluded that:

> Canada is our country,
> The New Land of freedom and food,

A good land in which over-lords
Do not expel us in the glens.

To which the sons and grandsons of Iain Ruadh might have
added a heartfelt "Amen."

The main road of Creignish Rear was the General Line, which
runs roughly parallel with the escarpment of cliffs. Its southern
section, near its intersection with the Trans-Canada Highway,
is well maintained. Its people, remarks one wry old man, "finally got a good road after they were all dead."

The northern part of the General Line and the web of lesser
roads which push further inland are falling into ruin. Some can
be travelled in a truck or a Jeep, others only by snowmobile. A
few are so far neglected that it takes an experienced woodsman
even to discern where they once ran.

Four of the backwoods roads converge at the Forks to meet
the Mountain Road, which switchbacks down the cliff to the
imposing white church at Creignish. Jim Sandy MacDonald
lived near the Forks and remembered sixteen teams of horses
coming down the Rhodena road, heading for church. The
people would tether their horses at the top of the mountain,
where the trees shielded them from the wind, and walk down to
church.

"They were saving their horses," explained John Alex Mac-
Donald, the one-time mail driver who lived at the bottom of the
mountain. "They didn't think about saving the people."

Like most Scots, the people of the Rear gave out information
in bits and pieces, around the edges of a leisurely conversation
in Gaelic. A man near the church was surprised to find John
Sandy MacDonald from the Rear at his door at five o'clock one
morning. He came in and had breakfast, and the two talked of
the weather, the crops and the price of feed until eight, when
John Sandy rose to leave.

"By the way," said John Sandy, "the old man is dead." His
father had died that night, and he was filling in time until a
decent hour to fetch the priest.

They lived, said Jim Sandy MacDonald, "from the ground

up," cutting their own wood, growing their own vegetables, raising their own animals. "About all we had to buy was tea and tobacco." They built their own buildings and furniture, made their own clothing from their own wool. The men picked up some cash by cutting pit props for the coal mines, ties for the railway, pulpwood and firewood. Rather than carry it down the mountain in wagons, they built a chute. It must have been something to see: logs racing 400 feet down the cliff, piling up like pick-up sticks by the railway tracks.

The mountain farms had their tradesmen, too: masons, carriage-makers, wheelwrights. The coopers of Creignish Rear built quintals for the fish trade, barrels for the quarries, little firkins for salted butter. Lizzie MacQuarrie was married in the Blue Mountains, well behind the General Line, and she remembered convoys of horse-drawn sleighs piled high with new barrels, going through the frozen fields to be sold at West Bay Road and Marble Mountain.

It could be a hard, grinding life, with death nearby in a thousand guises. Dan MacMaster noticed one day that John MacLean's house had been still and silent for three winter days. He broke down the door and found MacLean frozen stiff. In the barn, the horse was so hungry he was chewing the boards of his stall. Another time, when Dan's wife, Katie, was due to have a baby, the Rear was hit by a heavy snowfall. The MacQuarries went with Dan to break the road open again for the doctor to get in, and Dan Hughie MacDonald started to do the same thing from the Forks. Katie never forgot her anxious wait, going out to the porch every few minutes listening for the returning sound of sleighbells. When she heard them, she put out a huge meal of ham, potatoes, fresh bread with homemade butter, pickles and the like; years later, she still talked about her feeling of relief.

Diphtheria struck the family of James P. MacDonald, and he had to bring a child down the mountain to the church for burial. Next day he was back with another. "In those days TB was an awful killer," says John Alex MacDonald. "They had no cure for it then. They'd just leave you in a back room and wait for you to die. It wiped out whole families, all but one or two."

For amusement, they visited, played cards, made music, danced and told the long Gaelic stories called *sqeulachd*. "Ah, there were some wonderful stories," recalled D.A. MacInnes, "but you can't tell them in English. In English they lose everything. But after an evening with those stories going around, you'd be half frightened to go home alone." Gaelic voices soft under the lamplight, mournful tunes from the fiddles: *Cailleach liath Ratharsair*, The Grey Old Lady of Raasay; *Null Thar nan Eileanum*, Over the Isles to America; *Cha Till mi Tuille*, Nevermore Shall I Return.

"*A chaora chrom, c'aite bheil thu?*" they sang. *O sheep with the crooked horn, where are you? All sheep have milk, but this has a gallon.* The crooked horn is the copper coil of a still, and parties survived all night long on this sheep's milk.

A surprising number of men married either very late or not at all. "Some of them had to stay home and take care of the old people and the farm," explained D.A. MacInnes. "They had some tough times up there, and I suppose a lot of them felt they couldn't support a wife." Duncan MacDonald, the son of the third pioneer settler in Creignish proper, married at seventy-four—and enjoyed twenty years of married life all the same. John Alex MacDonald was in his fifties when he married. James G. MacDonald had three sons, and none of them married. Little Rory the Mason had five sons, and none of them married, either. In 1980, Malcolm MacDonnell was sixty. He had only recently married, and he had a thirty-year-old wife and a young family.

In a small community like Criegnish Rear, everyone is famous for something. Lauchie MacKinnon was a Gaelic singer, the leader of the music at milling frolics, traditional Highland affairs at which neighbours gathered to shrink and shape newly woven homespun cloth. Donald MacNeil was a famous Gaelic bard—and a satirist. None of his songs survives, but people still remember his scathing verses about the family which failed to invite him to a milling frolic. Hughie D. MacInnis, Dougald MacDonald and Hughie Archie MacDougal were fiddlers. Shimon Angus MacDonald was famous for fatherhood: he sired twenty-four children by three wives, and applied for the old age pension on a trip down to the church for the baptism of his last child.

Neil MacQuarrie was famous for his caustic humour. He was a short, swarthy man who farmed a couple of miles beyond the

General Line, in South Rhodena. He was never lost for an answer.

Someone met him one day, labouring back up the mountain from the railway station down at the shore. It was a filthy day, full of sleet and snow driven by a miserable east wind.

"Where have you been, Neil?"

"To the railway station."

"And what would you be doing there, on such a terrible day?"

"I suppose," sighed Neil, "that if a man went to Hell for a wife, she'd still be wanting to go home on visits."

Another time, Neil bought a barrel of flour from a merchant in Port Hastings. A few days later he brought it back.

"Was it not good?" inquired the merchant, R.J. MacDonald.

"No," said Neil. "It was not good."

"Well, what was wrong with it?"

"I took it home," said Neil, "and my wife made some bannock. I tried a piece. It had a poor taste. I put some butter on it. It tasted no better. I put some molasses on it. Still it tasted foul. The cat was passing by, so I threw her a piece. She took two nibbles, and then retired behind the stove and licked her rear end to get the bad taste out of her mouth."

Farm after farm after farm: abandoned, disappeared. One of the schools was skidded down the mountain and converted to a house. Another remained in the woods, its walls splayed apart, a shelter only to sheep. Dan Hughie MacDonald's house, which once harboured a general store and a post office, was still standing at the Forks when I went there—but its windows and doors were gone, its shingles were blowing off, and its walls had gaping holes. Someday soon, a cold, angry wind would howl through the pulpwoods of Creignish Rear, and in the morning Dan Hughie's house would be flattened on the ground.

"The young people moved away, and the old folks died." Electricity, the telephone, paved highways and the railroad spread along the shore, but not into the backlands. The farms produced more children than they could support, and the ones who moved away came home with cash in the pockets of their

store clothes. More than one Gaelic poem damns the Eaton's
catalogue for destroying a way of life.

> It wasn't Eaton's we depended on
> 　　to keep us supplied with clothing,
> But industrious mothers with their
> 　　knitting needles in the winter.

Thus the bard Kenneth Ferguson. Another Cape Bretoner,
Murdock Morrison, echoes him:

> I'll tell you the truth
> 　　(believe it, and don't contradict it)
> It's Eaton's big catalogue
> 　　that left thousands so conceited.

A farmer lived well, in one sense, but he had no cash and no
luxuries. Even today, the houses where the old bachelors and
widows live are spartan—and there were good-paying jobs in
the new steel mill at Sydney, in the mansions of Boston and New
York, in the coal mines of Glace Bay and the mill towns of New
England.

So the young people left, and the farms fell vacant, and every
vacant farm made the community that much less vital. Schools
shrank, and then closed. Roads grew even worse. When the
supermarkets appeared, local markets for foodstuffs vanished.
Government regulations meant that it didn't pay to produce
only a few gallons of milk for sale. People began to need cash
incomes. Malcolm MacDonnell hung on in Essex until the
1960s, and when I asked him whether he regretted leaving, he
roared, "No! I should have left twenty years before." A man
couldn't make a living back there. To get work shovelling snow,
Malcolm walked five miles out to the railway and five miles
home at night—for $2.25 a day.

In 1931, Mrs. Hector Hughie MacDonald took the census in
Creignish Rear. She didn't recall the exact number, but she
reckoned there were twenty-five to thirty farms along the Gen-
eral Line alone. By 1980 there were two: and John Angus
MacDonald, the son of Little Rory the Mason—Angus Little
Rory, as he was known—was the last of the original families.

Angus's plain white house rested on a south-facing hillside by the General Line. The farm was trim, well kept, but curiously lifeless. No fields of oats or hay tossed in the breeze, no implements or machinery were strewn about the yard. The only sign of a garden was a large potato patch just below the barn. No vehicles stood waiting by the house. When Frank MacInnis unlatched the gate, he didn't close it again: Angus Little Rory had no animals to escape.

He came out to greet us, a little wiry man in his late seventies, accompanied by a boisterous young dog named Spot. He wore a peaked cap, a red checked workshirt over olive drab shirt and trousers. He spoke with that soft, liquid Gaelic accent which seems to linger over the words and caress them.

He had lived there alone since the death of his brother four years earlier. He had never held a driver's licence; he brought his groceries in by cab from Port Hawkesbury, at $7.50 a trip. His brother had a pickup truck, but Angus preferred a horse. His last horse had died a year and a half before. It died of old age.

And where was I from? Oh, down near Arichat, 50 miles away. "I was in Arichat once," Angus said. "I went down with a sleigh-load of rabbits to sell."

He missed his neighbours, yes. It was good when people could get together of a winter evening for companionship. I tried to imagine his kitchen full of people telling stories and making music. It was a plain room, with few domestic comforts. The ceiling was rough-cut boards over hand-hewn beams, the walls planked and painted. A chrome set, linoleum, a big wood-fired cook stove, a well-used couch, a small plaster Christ crucified to the wall, a big old alarm clock. The people would bring the warmth to such a room, and take it when they left.

"Oh, I was going to leave, too," said Angus with a nod. "Yes, I was going to leave, too." But he and his brother never got around to it, and after a while there didn't seem to be much point.

Just before we said goodbye, Angus looked up at me sharply.

"Are there many horses around Arichat?" he asked. "Working horses? I'd like to get another horse. It's hard to do anything without a horse."

The settlers of the Rear believed that man was made for labour, that the world's riches are not infinite. They took from the land and gave back to the land, and for all its severity their life had a certain shapeliness and flavour.

Creignish Rear was the smell of woodsmoke and new-mown hay, of the ripe cow barn and the hot kitchen where the blueberries were being boiled for jam. It was the sound of sleighbells and the crisp hiss of the runners in the hard deep snow of a silent midwinter road. It was lanterns in the darkness moving slowly up the mountain Sunday evening, each one a family returning from Mass. It was the ripple and lilt of Gaelic, the language which Scots claim was spoken in the Garden of Eden.

Creignish Rear was the ring of the axe in hard maple, the puffs of steam from the horse's nostrils, the weary muscles in back and arms at the end of the day. It was working several days on the roads to meet your property taxes. It was the steady congealing routine which finally petrified around a bachelor, imprisoning him. It was the look of serious concentration lit by flashes of mischief on the faces of the children in a one-room schoolhouse with ten grades all learning together. It was the sharp sweet burst of juice when you bit into an apple from Hugh Cameron's orchard on a keen October day.

It was nights of fiddling and stepdancing and moonshine, when you danced till your shirt was soaked in sweat. You went outside and saw the stars whirling in the coal-black sky; and though you had intended to go home that night, you opened your eyes in the morning and found you were still in Sandy John Peter's kitchen. And it was the shyness of her smile, the sparkle in her eye, that said without words that when the farm passed to you she would be there to bake the bannock, paper the walls and gather the eggs. She would give you children, and later, when you had both grown old, those sons and daughters would see that you lived out your days in the peace and dignity you had earned through a lifetime of labour and laughter.

It is hard to catch the reality of the people who are gone. But they worked and fought and loved and suffered as people have done since the beginning; they helped their neighbours, scolded their children, butchered their pigs, stoked their fires, argued politics, prayed and trusted and confessed and died. Farm after farm, they built a community, a place for their children and the children of their children. A place of their own, where no corrupt chieftain or Lowland factor could ever evict them again.

In all of Britain, says John Prebble in *The Highland Clearances*, one can find real solitude only in the Scottish Highlands, "and if their history is known there is no satisfaction to be got from the experience."

From the sea, the hills of Creignish look serene and untouched — and there is real solitude there, too. But if the history of those highlands is known, there is no satisfaction to be got from that experience, either.

"Don," said Lulu, "shouldn't we be seeing that Judique buoy?"

I jumped up and looked around. The coast of Nova Scotia had become a blue blur behind us, and the buildings of Havre Boucher had disappeared. The two islands off Port Hood were becoming hard and distinct. I snatched a couple of compass bearings, then went below, plotted them on the chart and came back on deck.

"Should be a little ahead, and well in towards the shore," I said. Lulu scanned the waves with the big binoculars. I got out the compacts. Designed for birdwatching, they fit inside a jacket pocket, and I like to have them handy as we make a new harbour.

"Got it," said Lulu. Sure enough, the buoy was bobbing in the waves between us and the shore. Sailing fast, *Silversark* was putting the buoy rapidly behind her.

"We're really moving," I said.

"Aren't we."

Henry Island, the outermost of the Port Hood islands, grew larger, came abeam, fell behind. As we entered its lee, the wind eased, the seas diminished. We looked for a green buoy between Port Hood Island and the Cape Breton shore.

"Is that it, away inshore?"

It was. A long sandbar runs out from Port Hood Island, almost closing the entrance. We sailed in, then tacked out to the island. Rust-coloured beaches lay under its steep bluffs, and a ruff of spruce trees cut the skyline. To the north, the hills declined into a shell-shaped valley of fields and farmhouses above a wide sandy beach. We had heard there was a fine little harbour along this shore, but we saw no sign of it.

Should we go to the village, on the mainland? A wharf lay along the shore directly opposite the island, and farther up the harbour we could see what looked like a set of breakwaters.

"Let's sail up to the beach near the houses and anchor. We can row ashore and look around after lunch."

Lulu tacked up to the beach and headed *Silversark* into the wind. The little ship glided to a stop. I lowered the plow anchor over the bow and paid out chain. The wind caught the sails again and blew her sideways. The chain came taut, and the boat swung back into the wind. The anchor was set. We lowered the sails.

The island's first settler was Captain David Smith, a Loyalist who landed here in 1786. The community he founded, with its traditional Nova Scotia houses, seemed settled and cared for; even the church looked occupied. But that was all an illusion.

"The young people moved away, and the old folks died."

The man we wanted to see was Bertie Smith. Bertie Smith is a direct descendant of Captain David Smith. He and his wife, Shirley, are the *last* year-round residents of Port Hood Island.

BERTIE'S

ISLAND

During lunch a Coast Guard helicopter
landed beside a light tower on a nearby spit called Smith Point.
Mark gobbled down his sandwich, hurriedly pumped up his
little Canadian Tire inflatable and rowed over.

We watched him anxiously—a diminishing figure in a little
blue-and-white boat, with a red lifejacket and a white hat. We
knew he could manoeuvre that coracle with panache and precision, and he could swim like an eel. Yes, he had rowed straight
downwind, and he might have a struggle getting back. But even
if he broke an oar or fell overboard, the wind would only carry
him across the harbour to the beach in Port Hood.

Why is it so difficult to let children make their own voyages of discovery? Each voyage is a little longer, a little more hazardous, than the one before, and if anything happened to them you would want to die yourself. But they have to go, and in the end you can only prepare them, and watch them, and pray.

Mark made his way back while Lulu and I inflated the Sea Eagle canoe. We all paddled ashore and walked up the reddish dirt road along the beach and uphill by a ruined cannery. From the hilltop, we saw a square, almost landlocked boat basin tucked behind Smith Point, occupied only by one fishing boat and a couple of runabouts. A husky, brush-cut man was working on a balky old Johnson outboard mounted on a Boston Whaler. Bertie Smith.

"I saw you out there," he said. "You should come into the harbour."

Without an engine?

"Lots of room to tack," said Bertie. "Just stay close to this side of the channel."

"Do I have to go?" asked Mark. He had his line in the water already, dangling his bait amidst the schools of small perch.

Lulu and I paddled back and raised the main and jumbo. We tacked into the channel below the old cannery. Right in the entrance, we tacked again — and immediately ran aground.

I dropped the jumbo, to keep her from driving further on the ledge, and scrambled for an oar to push her off. Lulu spotted a fishing vessel just coming up astern and flagged it down.

"We're aground — can you tow us off?"

The fisherman nodded, circled around and caught a rope. He gunned the engine, and *Silversark* floated free. The fisherman cast off the line. We were just 50 feet from the entrance — but we had a rock pile on one side and shoal water on the other.

"Could you tow us in?"

"Tow you in?" said the fisherman.

"Just inside the breakwater. We don't have an engine."

He took our bow line and roared into the tiny harbour, heading for the shallowest part of the basin. *Silversark* felt like a car being yanked into a small parking lot at 50 miles per hour. At this rate, we were going to smash into the seawall —

I whipped out my belt knife and slashed the rope. It let go like a rubber band. Lulu put the tiller hard to port, and *Silversark* coasted to the quay. The fellow in the fishing boat circled beside us and threw our rope aboard.

"Thanks."

"No problem, buddy!"

We spent three placid days on Port Hood Island, and never even visited Port Hood itself.

"You don't want to go over there," said Bertie. "The south side of the wharf dries right out at low tide; you don't get any shelter on the west side, and the north side is crowded." Once a coal-mining town, Port Hood is the "shiretown" of Inverness County, which includes the entire west coast of Cape Breton. But we were more interested in the island.

About half of the island's eighteen houses are owned by Americans, chiefly New Englanders, and about half are occupied at any given moment during the summer. Bertie Smith plants a garden, raises pigs and cattle, and cares for the other seventeen houses. His fishing boat is the ferry to Port Hood. Everyone and everything from Girl Guides to groceries come in with Bertie, at $10 a trip. One evening his boat pulled into the basin with a white wicker sofa on the cabin roof. Its owners were sitting in it.

Bertie has an oblique way of expressing his wishes. When I suggested we might move to the east side of the basin, he pointed out the merits of the north side and the ease of pulling the boat across with long ropes—by which he meant he would really prefer that we not disturb the runabouts tied to the east side.

I asked about using a phone.

"Help yourself," said Bertie. "There's one in the shed." There it was, tucked in with the tractor, pulleys, chain, old harness and bits and pieces of ancient farm machinery. Bertie had installed it for the convenience of summer residents.

I had some calls to make: to D'Escousse, to see if Chris Latchem and Sonja Susjnar had arrived; to Port Hood, to invite Richard and Ann Sherrington to visit us; to Halifax, where my half-hour TV drama *Peggy* was being filmed the following month.

Nova Scotia is an intimate little world. *Peggy* was being produced by Peter Zimmer's brother Chris, who was a potter in Judique when I first met him. *Peggy* is based on a children's game which used to be played on Isle Madame. It involves batting a six-inch wooden peg, pointed at both ends, out past a fielder. I thought it was an indigenous Acadian game, and I wrote a radio play in which the plot turned on the outcome of a peggy game.

Then I learned it had also been played in Toronto, New Hampshire, Saskatchewan and Scotland. It had a variety of other names—peacock, tiddley, one-eyed Sally, piggy, one-a-cat. When Chris Zimmer described it to Sami Ahmed, head of the National Film Board's Halifax office, Sami smiled. We played that game in Pakistan, he said. It's played all over Asia.

Both Chris and Peter Zimmer are friends of Richard Sherrington, our computer guru, colleague, supplier, client and friend. Richard and Ann live in St. Ninian's, a nearly abandoned farming community up behind Port Hood. They have been there for nearly twenty years—but they had never been to Port Hood Island. And Peter Zimmer was vacationing nearby with his family; they would come too.

Ten years ago, Peter was an industrial designer and furniture manufacturer, producing an innovative "clam chair" in Port Hood. He has a bachelor's degree in physics, and he was a sculptor, a cabinetmaker, a freelance broadcaster and a professor of fine arts before he became a furniture manufacturer. In the 1982 recession his company was torpedoed when the interest rate broke 20 per cent. While the company was being wound up, Peter hung his coveralls in our barn.

"All I need is room and board and Scotch," he said. Thus fuelled, he worked with us all summer and fall, building lustrous cabinetry in ash, mahogany and afrormosia. He laminated deck beams, built drawers and designed a chart table with a removable panel to allow a typewriter carriage to move back and forth.

Peter was with us on Labour Day, 1985, when we finally

launched the boat, and he was aboard when *Silversark* first
glided away from the wharf in the faintest of zephyrs, making a
minuscule wake in the almost unruffled water. The old master
shipwright David Stevens lived for that moment: When a newly
launched vessel first feels the wind and starts to move, he said,
she gives a little lurch — and that's the birth of a ship, the thrill of
a lifetime. I can still see Peter Zimmer's face at that moment,
split wide open by his vast, boyish grin.

Before Peter arrived in the boatshop, Chris Latchem had
come and gone. But *Silversark* actually began at Chris's kitchen
table in a crooked little house in Newfoundland. Chris was then
a marine biologist with the federal government, dreaming —
like me — about building the perfect cruising sailboat.

"I think I'd build out of cold-moulded plywood," Chris said.
Moulded plywood? As he explained the technique, I thought: I
could do that, if I took my time. A year later, Chris visited
D'Escousse. I had the boat framed, and Chris stayed for a week
to work on it. He came back later and stayed for months —
working, essentially, for the joy of it.

Chris had never sailed aboard *Silversark*, never even seen her
in the water. Just before we left, he had called to say that he and
Sonja were coming down this summer. They were several days
behind schedule, but Chris's sense of time is elastic: when he
said once that he "thought he'd dart up to Montreal for a week
or two," he was gone for two years.

I phoned Lulu's mother in D'Escousse. No sign of Chris and
Sonja. So Chris and Peter wouldn't meet this time, either.

Bertie Smith's ferry arrived, trailing fiddle music on the summer breeze. The fiddler was Patsy Palmer, a friend of the
Zimmers and Sherringtons, coming with her family for a day
hike on the island. Peter came ashore with his wife, Val Bach-
ynsky, and their baby daughter, Allison. Richard and Ann
Sherrington had their teenage daughter Sarah and her friend
Rita.

The older kids instantly took off for the island's best swimming beach, a mile down the shore. The adults sat in the cockpit
with wine and cheese and then rambled around the dirt roads,

observing the settled grace and dignity of the houses, the rioting wildflowers of July—and the junk. Smith Point is strewn with shattered plastic and rusted metal, and the island landscape is dotted with ruined cars: Cherokees with flapping fenders, Subarus fleeing from intensive care, a comically shortened Volkswagen pickup.

"Those aren't junk!" Peter objected. "Those cars are in use!"

"They are?"

Port Hood Island is where old cars come to die. Vehicles that can't even sneak through the provincial safety inspection are ferried out on 40-foot fishing boats with impromptu plank decks, or cross on the harbour ice during the winter.

"When I lived in Port Hood," Peter said, "the boys used to put an old junker out on the ice and make book on the date it would disappear in the spring."

In 1963, fulfilling an election promise, the government built a sandstone causeway to the island; Bertie Smith drove a pickup across during the four days it lasted before a savage storm took it out. In retrospect, the abortive causeway looks like a last attempt to save the island community. The island is isolated twice a year—in the fall, when the ice is thick enough to stop a boat but too thin to carry any weight, and in the spring, when it rots and breaks up into drifting fields of "clampers." During those periods, island people simply wait.

But the school system would not wait.

The island once had its own small elementary school; one of its teachers was the author Alistair MacLeod, whose powerful, incisive stories are rooted in the life of this coast. He now teaches at the University of Windsor, but he still summers with his family in his native Dunvegan, just down the shore.

After Grade 6, island children boarded in Port Hood during the school term. When the one-room school was closed in 1983, however, even the six-year-olds were separated from their parents. What family could endure that? One after another, they sold their homes to summer people and moved to the mainland. Port Hood Island had fifty-five voters in 1963, twenty in 1981. Now there are two.

Is this not bizarre? The schools shape all our lives, as though society had been created to serve the school system and not the other way around. Family vacations are fitted to the school calendar. The schools turn kids out at three o'clock, even though both parents work until after five o'clock. Whole communities wither and die because administrators declare their schools "uneconomic."

But schools are a long-term investment—and village schools don't necessarily do a poor job. Sidney Smith did all right: President of the University of Toronto, Minister of External Affairs. And he came from a small school in Port Hood.

Lulu suffers from recurrent back problems, and the next day she was immobilized in her berth. Mark found a new friend named Amos Boretto. Eventually Amos's mother, Lorna, came looking for him. Her husband was once the local United Church minister, and though they are now in Woodstock, Ontario, the Borettos still spend their summers on Port Hood Island.

"You should come to church tonight," she said. "Everyone goes, whether they're United Church or not. And then Shirley Smith opens the canteen afterwards. It's the big social occasion of the week."

Mark and I decided to go. At six that evening Bertie came down to the wharf, in jacket and tie, ready to ferry the minister from the mainland. I quickly shaved and dressed. This year, for the first time, I actually had respectable clothes aboard: Alex Tilley's "adventure clothing," which is intended to be crumpled, rolled up and generally abused, and still look decent when you pull it out of a locker. Mark was waiting on the wharf.

"My, my, don't we look smart tonight?" he said.

Smart-ass kid.

Jubilee United Church was charming and simple—white shingles and black trim outside, cream V-joint and plum-coloured mouldings inside. The service, too—conducted by a student minister, Harold King—had the simple, hand-hewn directness I remember from my United Church childhood. Simple prayers, and a gathering of children with the minister to discuss the day's lesson. ("He speaks to the children as if they were people," whispered Mark.) A prayer for illumination.

Plenty of hymns, with everyone singing. A simple benediction, and people chatting around the church door.

This is one of four churches served by Allan and Betty Darby, Harold King's summer mentors. Both Darbys are ordained ministers, whose charge covers fifty miles of sparse Protestants; more than 85 per cent of the people are Catholic. The congregations are ageing and declining, but the members cling fiercely to their local churches, even though maintenance has become a heavy burden.

The island's former Methodist church is now the community hall, in which Shirley Smith dishes out ice-cream cones and pop three times a week. The place doubles as a local museum. I wandered through it, looking at photos of the island in its prosperity—vanished fish plants, and the little cove rimmed with lap-strake fishing boats, their sails frapped against their masts, fishing gear spread out on the beach.

Bertie came in, having landed the clerics and their guests in Port Hood. Shirley locked the canteen. We lingered a moment, looking out over the water.

"Southerly wind tomorrow," I said. "Good to get out of here, but I'm not sure how it'll be to enter Mabou."

"Oh, that's a good wind for Mabou," said Bertie. "You'll slip right in with a southerly wind."

"If we go early we'll have a fair tide," I said. "You really think we can sail right over the old causeway?"

"Sure you can," Bertie said. "Just stay in the notch by the red buoy, like I told you. There's three or four feet of water there even at low tide. Must be ten or eleven feet at high tide."

I walked down to the basin. At the bottom of the hill I turned and looked back. Bertie and Shirley were walking up the hill together, silhouetted against the strong blue and gold of the evening sky.

THERE WAS
AN
OLD WOMAN
FROM MABOU

Between Port Hood Island and Mabou we managed to go aground twice in a single perfect morning.

We sailed at 6:45, clearing the basin on one long port tack, then squaring away for the red buoy at the ruined causeway. I stood in the bow, peering down into the water. Mark was below at the echo sounder, calling out the depths:

"Thirty-two feet . . . twenty-eight . . . nineteen . . . sixteen . . . twelve! FOUR!"

A huge flat rock, four feet under the surface—

WHUMP!

Silversark came down on a wave, struck the flat bottom of her keel on the flat rock, lifted up and sailed onward. The bottom fell away into obscurity again.

"Twenty feet!" cried Mark. "Twenty-four!"

Our hearts had skipped a beat or two, but the bottom of *Silversark*'s keel is an eight-inch square block of lead about five feet long, through-bolted and epoxy-bonded to 18 solid inches of laminated mahogany plank. We might have squashed a few barnacles, possibly even dented the lead, but nothing more.

The warm, steady southeasterly breeze carried us swiftly past the bluffs of Cape Linzee and Colindale. From Cape Linzee the land falls gradually towards the Mabou River; north of the river, the Mabou Highlands rise like a wall. It is only 10 miles from Port Hood to Mabou, and within an hour we were scanning the shoreline, looking for the river mouth.

I had navigator's nerves. I knew where the harbour must be — but we were approaching it obliquely, with nothing to confirm the position. Could one make a serious error in a 10-mile run down a well-defined coast on a bright, sunny morning? Yes, absolutely. When the navigation is easy, the navigator grows sloppy. *There's Sight Point, right over there.* But is it really?

We jogged on into the bight where Mabou Harbour had to be. We were right up against the land when the harbour finally opened, a narrow mouth with a high bluff to port and a low sandy point to starboard. The current was running with us, as we had planned, but the wind was blowing straight out of the river. I went forward to watch the bottom and handle the jib. Mark went to the depth sounder. We tacked under the bluff in eight feet of water and swung back across the channel.

"Eighteen . . . nineteen . . . fourteen . . . twelve!" cried Mark.

Lulu tacked.

Silversark spun on her heel — and went hard aground.

A sandbar rises abruptly from deep water on that side of the channel. As we tacked, the current carried *Silversark* sideways onto the bar. Our bow was in deep water, but our stern was pinned against the bar by a racing current which whirled little tornadoes of sand around the back of the keel. I poked down into the sand with the oar, and leaned on it. But the moment I lifted her keel off the bottom, the current pushed her higher up the bar, lodging her even harder.

"Can you give us a tow?"

I looked up. Lulu was talking to three men in a long, low fishing boat.

"Oh, maybe," said a young fisherman with a smile.

"Maybe?"

"We'll leave you there a couple of hours and maybe pull you off after that," said the young fellow. "Heading into Mabou?"

"If we can get there."

"Here, toss us your line."

It took a hard yank to pull *Silversark* free. The fishermen kept right on going, hugging the right bank of the river and then swinging into a boat basin behind a bulky lighthouse. Fishing boats lay moored all around. At the head of the basin was a low bait shed. We made fast and went to thank our deliverers. The skipper was a wiry little man named John Beaton—John C. Beaton, to distinguish him from eight other John Beatons among Mabou's 600 people. What could I give him? He shook his head.

"No, no, I'm in the Search and Rescue auxiliary, they'll give me something for it."

"Don't feel bad," said another fisherman. "We go aground in here all the time ourselves."

The harbour is a lush green fjord which runs inland another three miles to Mabou itself—which is not to be confused with West Mabou, Southwest Mabou, Northeast Mabou, Mabou Coal Mines or Mabou Harbour Mouth, where we were. Years ago, when coastal freighters and gypsum carriers came to Mabou, there was 32 feet of water over the outer bar, and the harbour was dredged right up to the village. Now there is only six feet over the bar, and the fjord is heavily silted up. The channel is tortuous and the village wharf has been demolished. We decided to stay put.

"We stayed at the Harbour one time in a bed and breakfast," I said. "With Donald Rankin. Where's his house from here?"

"Right there," said John C., pointing up the hill.

A few minutes later, a dark blue pickup pulled up beside the lighthouse. A husky man in late middle age sat behind the wheel.

"How's she goin'?"

"All right," I said. I looked at him closely.

"We've met," he said.

"Donald Rankin," I said.

Donald Rankin laughed.

"Welcome back."

Donald and Mary Rankin run their bed and breakfast mainly because they like to meet people. Because we had stayed with them seven or eight years earlier, we were practically family. Could we take a shower? Of course—and while we showered, Mary made tea and sandwiches. We called home on their phone: the missing Chris and Sonja were still missing. During the next couple of days we filled our tanks with water from their well, did our laundry in their washer and dried it on their line.

Payment? For anything? Not a word of it.

"But it's your business."

"We don't do it for the money," said Donald. "We're three miles off the highway down here; if we didn't do bed and breakfast, we'd never meet anybody new."

After our showers, we proposed to walk or hitchhike to Mabou. Donald would hear none of that: he would run us into town himself, wait while we bought our groceries and bring us back. But we wanted to walk around Mabou and look up people we knew.

"All right," said Donald, "I'll bring your groceries home and put them in the fridge. If you need a drive later, you just call."

We stopped to cash a cheque at Mabou Credit Union, which has been managed for thirty years by the gruff, forthright Francis Xavier Rankin. F.X., as they call him, has built it into a busy, efficient $5.5-million institution. I am active in the credit union movement, and F.X. recognized me.

"Come in the office a minute," he said.

"I'll go to the store," said Lulu.

I sat down in the office.

"How'd you get down here?" F.X. demanded.

By boat. We're moored at the Harbour.

"How'd you get into town?"

Donald Rankin drove us.

"Donald A."

Presumably.

"He's dead."

Well, no, I protested, he seems to be alive, he runs a bed and breakfast—

"Donald Roddie."

Maybe so.

"He's outside."

Yes, um . . . he just drove us here. Your credit union's still doing well?

"Fine. Having a good year."

No chartered banks in town?

F.X. jerked a thumb in each direction.

"Port Hood ten miles, Inverness thirteen."

And the nearest credit unions?

"Port Hood ten miles, Inverness thirteen."

Ah.

F.X. pushed back his chair.

"Nice to see you. Any time you're down this way, come and visit."

I walked up the main street towards the Co-op store. In Nova Scotia, Mabou is famous for two things: its intensely Scottish character, and its music. The Gaelic language is still a living presence in Mabou, visible even on the main street. The sign on the post office says Tigh Litrichean, House of Letters. The museum is An Drochaid, The Bridge. A box on the side of the road is labelled "Droinach"—Garbage.

Mabou is arguably the fountainhead of Cape Breton music—Scottish music, moulded and reshaped during two Canadian centuries by the Irish, the Acadians and the Micmacs as well. You can hear it on any album by my soul brother, Mabou's own "J'nALL'n"—John Allan Cameron. J'nALL'n's fans particularly admire his instrumental music: fiddle and bagpipe tunes brilliantly played on the twelve-string guitar. But he is also a robust comic singer, and his first album begins with the tale of marital infidelity which is forever identified with Mabou:

> There was an old woman from Mabou,
> In Mabou she did dwell;
> She loved her husband dearly, but

Another man twice as well.
To me right fa-liddle a-ladle
And me right fa-lora-lee.
La, la, la, la!

Ah, yes, the song was purloined from the Irish, who think the old woman lived in Wexford, but never mind. Every pretty little nook near Mabou has a fiddle tune to celebrate it: there's the West Mabou Reel, the Mabou Jig, the Hills of Cape Mabou Jig, the Trip to Mabou Ridge March, the Joys of Mabou Mines Reel, the Glenville Jig. There are tunes about Mull River, Glenora Falls, Glencoe—and that's not to begin on the tunes written for and about local people.

John Allan's mother, Katie Ann Cameron, was a fiddler, and his brother, John Donald, leads a splendid fiddle quartet called The Cape Breton Symphony. Katie Ann's brother, the late Dan R. MacDonald, was a legend: a pot-bellied, cranky, wandering bachelor who composed more than 3,000 fiddle tunes, many so sweet and piercing that they seem to come straight from the Other World.

Mabou's musical dynasties also include the Beatons, notably Kinnon Beaton, a leading fiddler, and his brother Joey, a fine Scottish pianist. Their parents, Donald Angus and Elizabeth Beaton, were outstanding Scottish musicians, and Donald Angus himself came from a family of violinists and pipers who traced their musical lineage back 200 years to Lochaber, Scotland.

Near the Beaton house, a few feet from the Cameron home, is the home of The Rankin Family, five accomplished brothers and sisters who tour the region as a band and recently released an album. The three girls—Raylene, Cookie and Heather—have also been mainstays of a popular annual medley of skits and music, The Cape Breton Summertime Revue. Cookie's hilarious portrayal of a deaf, doddering and pungent old woman is a highlight of the evening.

One day she went to the doctor
Some medicine for to find,
Sayin', Doctor, give me somethin'
For to make me old man blind,

> To me right fa-liddle a-ladle
> And me right fa-lora-lee . . .
> La, la, la, la!

Humming Mabou music, I found Lulu and Mark loading groceries into Donald Rankin's truck outside the sparkling new Co-op store. The Co-op sells everything: groceries, fishing gear, clothing, appliances and tools. The modern equivalent of the old village general store, it struck Lulu as "the nicest, cleanest store I've ever seen. You could eat off the floors in there."

This end of Nova Scotia is the heartland of English Canada's co-operative movement, established half a century ago by two dynamic, plain-spoken, charismatic priests, Father Moses Coady and Father Jimmy Tompkins. The two were cousins, from the small Irish community in the Margaree Valley, 35 miles north of Mabou. Tompkins taught at St. Francis Xavier, the Catholic university in Antigonish, and served in several parishes in the Antigonish diocese. Coady became head of the university's Extension Department, and in the 1920s and 1930s he criss-crossed eastern Nova Scotia and Prince Edward Island, preaching the gospel of co-operation, self-help and adult education. He left a trail of producer co-ops, co-op stores and credit unions behind him, most of which still have his portrait hanging on their walls. Tompkins started the co-operative housing movement; the community of Tompkinsville, near Sydney, was the first co-operative housing development in Canada.

The co-operative movement has lost most of its evangelical zeal since the days of Coady and Tompkins, and many of those tiny first-growth co-ops and credit unions have folded or merged. But the surviving ones often dominate the economic life of their villages, as they do in Mabou, and the notions of co-operation and self-help are now deeply ingrained in the culture.

While we were in Mabou, I went to nearby Glenora Falls to see two of the Co-op's most distinguished members. Dr. Phyllida Kent was head of the English department at the University College of Cape Breton. Her husband, Tom, is a tall, lean, pipe-smoking native of the English Midlands who came to Cape

Breton in 1971 to lead "Devco," the Cape Breton Development Corporation. He had been assistant editor of the London *Economist*, vice-president of a multinational chemical corporation, editor of the Winnipeg *Free Press*, policy secretary to Prime Minister Lester Pearson, and deputy minister in two federal departments. Suave, brilliant, articulate, cool, he was the classic unflappable Ottawa mandarin.

As president of Devco, Tom Kent became, in effect, the Governor of Cape Breton Island. Devco was Ottawa's response to economic catastrophe in Cape Breton's coal mines, which had been owned by a Hawker Siddeley subsidary, the Dominion Steel and Coal Company, or DOSCO. Coal once supplied nearly 60 per cent of Canadian energy needs, but by the mid-1960s it had slipped to 11.5 per cent. DOSCO's mines had shrunk accordingly—but the four remaining Cape Breton mines still employed 6,500 people and produced 4.3 million tons a year. In 1965 DOSCO announced it would close them.

Ottawa hired a consultant who concluded that Cape Breton coal could never again be economic and recommended that a federally owned Sydney Coal Corporation take over the mines and phase them out by 1981. Meanwhile, a Cape Breton Development Corporation would "strengthen and stimulate the Cape Breton economy," filling the gap left by coal.

The government put both functions in one corporation. Meanwhile, the provincial government was preoccupied with DOSCO's abandoned steel plant; it happily left Cape Breton's other problems to Devco. With its domination of the island's economy and its wide discretionary powers, Devco became the closest thing to an island-wide government that Cape Breton had ever experienced.

Devco's Industrial Development Division began abominably, offering large grants and incentives to itinerant manufacturers of cassette tapes, shipping containers, eccentric recreational vehicles, electronic instruments and Toyotas. They stayed as long as the grants lasted. After five years, Devco's portfolio represented $30-million worth of failure. Tom Kent was then Deputy Minister of Regional Economic Expansion.

"Devco was in mortal peril," Kent recalls. "But if it was done right, it was one of the most important regional development plans there was. And I was rather out of sympathy with the government, in any event."

The classic Ottawa man rapidly became a devout Cape Bretoner. Kent had a map of the island in his office, with red pins marking the places he and Phyllida had visited. "I couldn't make jokes about Rear Barra Glen any more," recalls David Newton, whom Kent hired away from the local newspaper. "He knew where it was—and he had been there last weekend."

"Kent came from Ottawa in a period when twenty senior mandarins could meet for lunch and make crucial decisions about the future of the country," remarks another former Devco colleague. "They tended to regard Cape Breton as the end of the world, but when Kent came down here and loved it, they began to feel it was okay to funnel money in here—after all, good old Tom thought it was worth doing, and things seemed to be improving."

Fired by Kent's sweeping imagination, Devco boiled with initiatives. Marinas and charter yachts appeared on the Bras d'Or Lakes. A subsidiary company began marketing the island's crafts. Restaurants and hotels sprang up. Devco was involved in modular homes, wool milling, sash and door manufacture, maple syrup, boatbuilding, lumber milling. The corporation began experimenting with aquaculture, growing oysters and trout in captivity, and it imported sheep from Scotland.

"Look, Tom Kent could make the city dump sound like a rose garden," says Steve MacNeil, another of Kent's Devco colleagues. "And he could sell it in Ottawa, too. When he talked, you could see the sheep on the Cape Breton hillside, you could practically taste the sweetness of the morning dew in the meat of the lamb."

Devco's success depended on "stimulating local entrepreneurship," Kent explains. "It therefore had to try to be a *Cape Breton* institution." To "localize" it, he hired gifted Cape Bretoners, revealing an unexpected faith in the island's own people. Ann Terry MacLellan had been Cape Breton's most popular TV personality, for instance. As Devco's Director of Corporate Affairs, she gave a trusted human face to what might otherwise have seemed an impersonal colonial administration.

Kent also took a new look at coal.

"In 1972," Kent explains, "I persuaded myself that the long decline in coal prices was over, and that a smaller coal industry was as good an industry as you were going to get in Cape Breton in the foreseeable future. It certainly made more sense than chasing footloose factories." He convinced the federal cabinet, and Devco stepped up the development of a new mine at Lingan.

The decision was prescient, as OPEC soon demonstrated. The provincially owned Nova Scotia Power Corporation subsequently built a coal-fired generating plant at the Lingan pithead. NSPC became—and still is—Devco's main customer.

By 1977, Kent felt Devco's house was in order, but provincially owned Sydney Steel was floundering. Kent became president of Sydney Steel, where he worked out an imaginative plan to ship Cape Breton steel to rolling mills in Vancouver. Then the provincial government changed, and the deal fell apart. Kent became chairman of the Royal Commission on Newspapers, and Dean of Administrative Studies at Dalhousie University.

The Kents commissioned an airy contemporary house from Sydney architect Bob Ojolick and built it in an eerily beautiful glen near Mabou. Lacking the usual web of family relationships and shared upbringing, they remain slightly exotic—but Mabou does not consider them outsiders. The Kents are particularly proud of the Co-op. When the store takes inventory, the Kents are down there with their neighbours, counting tins.

"This is a remarkably happy society in many, many ways," Kent reflects. "And a remarkably friendly and supportive one. When someone's house burns down, for example, people rally around with money and work, and they often raise quite a lot of money to help them get started again. It's a very stable society. There's virtually no policing. This house is a bit out of the way, and we're away a lot, but we've only had one act of vandalism in fifteen years." He laughs. "That was pretty minor. Someone peeled the NO off my NO HUNTING sign.

"It's never been an isolated island, you know. People travel all over the place to work—a lot of them are drillers or sailors, things like that—and they travel when they retire. If you pick up this week's Inverness *Oran*, you'll see a front-page story about a couple of local farmers who are selling the hay off thirty acres of land and donating the proceeds to development projects in Swaziland. One of them visited Swaziland somehow or other and saw that a little money could do a lot of good there.

"But that's not unique. When the Co-op reached its fiftieth anniversary, the members celebrated by establishing an endowment to support self-help projects in Third World countries."

Self-help projects within Inverness County are the mandate of Incor Investments, a publicly funded agency headquartered in a little red building in Mabou. Incor's executive director, Frazer Hunter, is a tow-headed Scottish farmer, lured to Cape Breton by Tom Kent to raise imported Scottish sheep. He offers a gloomy analysis of Canada's economic personality. Our country, he says cheerfully, is cursed with excessive resources. We sell fish, wheat, trees, minerals. Our munificent endowment makes us peevish and self-indulgent, like a tycoon's brat.

Not so in Japan, Taiwan, Singapore, Britain, Switzerland. Societies with minimal resources learn to live by their wits. People become inventive and competitive when the chips are down—"but in Canada, our chips are never down. We don't take risks, we don't develop our human resources. We're more comfortable with failure than success. That's why economic development is such an uphill battle in this country."

Frazer Hunter says these depressing things with a cherubic grin. He is suffused with joy, his veins are coursing with adrenaline. After ten years in Cape Breton, he and his wife, Angela, anted up their own chips: borrowing something like a quarter of a million dollars, they have bought a dairy farm a few miles back in the hills behind Mabou. Frazer is terrified and ecstatic.

"It's been our dream for years," says Angela later. "We couldn't ever have done it in Scotland. The land there is all in the hands of the landed gentry. The Duke of Buccleuch, you know, owns most of the land between Edinburgh and Glasgow. He owns whole villages—shops, houses, everything. Everyone's a tenant. We could never have owned a farm there."

The Hunters have just moved to their comfortable farmhouse on a small river, backed by a steep wooded hill with pastures above it. The Hunters have three boys, all around Mark's age, and so we lose him for a day and entertain the Hunters aboard *Silversark* in the evening.

But that's to come later. Right now I am interested in another local project: the only distillery in North America designed to brew premium single-malt Scotch whisky. The president of Glenora Distillers is Bruce Jardine, whom I know. If I call him from Frazer's office, he might arrange a tour.

"Well, no doubt," says Frazer. "But why don't you just take my car and run out there? It's only a few miles up the road."

From Highway 19, Cape Breton's oldest legal distillery—not yet open for business—looks like a tiny whitewashed village straddling MacLellan's Brook. A nine-room inn faces a low warehouse. The third side of the courtyard is the inn's reception, bar and dining room. The fourth side is MacLellan's Brook, and beyond it stands the long two-storey building of the distillery, with the distinctive kiln building at the end. The whole complex is tucked right under a ridge of small, steep, spruce-clad mountains at the edge of a meadow.

The place is aswarm with tradesmen—carpenters, plumbers, electricians. Bulldozers and dump trucks snarl around the buildings. The first batch of malt is due from Montreal tomorrow. Jardine will arrive soon. Meanwhile, a bearded, jean-clad Glaswegian named Harry Cockburn takes us though the distillery.

Cockburn is Group Engineer with Morrison Bowmore of Glasgow, who own three of Scotland's eighty distilleries. Morrison Bowmore have a technology transfer contract with Glenora and actually own a piece of the company. Scottish law requires that whisky be aged for at least three years, and for Glenora's whisky to be called Scotch, it has to follow the dictates of the Scotch Whisky Association, right down to the label on the bottle. Glenora's whisky will be aged for five years; while it is maturing, the company will market a single-malt whisky made in Scotland to its specifications by Morrison Bowmore. Sales of blended Scotch have been dropping, but single-malt sales have been rising.

Why would Morrison Bowmore want to encourage competition in the whisky business? Cockburn laughs.

"We're considered a renegade outfit in Scotland," he says. "We've already helped set up distilleries in Paraguay and Korea, which was quite a radical step. But if our Korean partners can wean the Koreans from rice wine and persuade them to drink Scotch, they'll open up a market bigger than they can serve themselves. And once people have learned to drink one Scotch, you know, they want to try others."

The equipment seems at once new and Olde Worlde. Huge oaken tanks hold a mash of malt, yeast and water; in forty-eight hours it ferments into a "beer," which is 7 per cent alcohol. Two tapering copper stills run up the height of a two-storey building. The "wash still" takes the alcohol level up to 21 per cent, and the "spirit still" takes it to 63 per cent.

Will Glenora's really be a superior whisky? Cockburn nods.

"The climate here is very like Scotland's—the same humidity, temperature range and so on," he says. "The water is excellent—it comes from MacLellan's Brook, and it's fed by mountain springs. Well, now, if the water is good, and the ambiance is good, the whisky should be good."

Good enough to compete with the Scottish distilleries?

"It'll be very good whisky." Cockburn smiles. "For *great* whisky, of course, you need a hundred years of experience or so."

Bruce Jardine is tall, florid, harried and exhilarated. This is a $4.2-million project, and with no product to sell, its funds are flowing out as fast as the waters of the brook. But there will be products soon. Glenora will market a vodka from Jamaica and four varieties of rum under the name "Smuggler's Cove," as well as the Morrison Bowmore Scotch, which will be called "Kenloch."

The Scotch Whisky Association would not approve any name with the word *glen* in it. No confusion, please, with Glenfiddich and Glenlivet and similar patrician whiskies—even though Jardine comes from Glencoe, and the distillery was planned for Glenora Falls and actually built in Glenville. The association eventually approved "Kenloch." But Kenloch is the Inverness County garbage dump, right? Jardine smiles inscrutably.

The rum will do well. In Atlantic Canada, rum sells. Rum constitutes more than half of all liquor sales in the region—a direct result of the old seaborne trade with the West Indies. For generations, Canadian schooners carried lumber and salt fish south and returned with cargoes of salt, molasses and rum.

"I don't know whether it's true or not," says Jardine, "but I've heard that there's more rum sold in Atlantic Canada than in all of the United States."

The whisky trade has an interesting system for financing its maturing inventory. For about $600, you can buy a barrel of Glenora's whisky right now—200 litres, 63 per cent alcohol. Glenora will purchase it back after five years, and it guarantees a set rate of return. Better yet, the distillery will repay your original investment even if the world price of whisky has fallen. If the price has risen—and it has been rising steadily for many years—Glenora will pay the higher price. A barrel of Scotch may bring a return as high as 50 per cent per annum.

And, *in extremis*, it's your Scotch. If you don't like the deal, tote your barrel home and drink the whisky.

To reach Mabou's new restaurant, The Mull, from Frazer Hunter's office, you have to pass the Mabou Village Gallery. The gallery window is full of Cape Breton pottery, weaving, glass, wood and leatherwork. Inside, the walls are hung with photographs and paintings, chiefly by Suzanne Chrysler Mac-Donald. A cheerful woman greets you. She is happy to talk about the works and the people responsible for them. She is Suzanne Chrysler MacDonald.

Mark has been taking photographs, and Suzanne has fine photographs of beaches and shorelines. The two of them are soon enmeshed in a discussion of composition, colour, f-stops and shutter speeds. Suzanne's husband, Alex, arrives. What began as a browse turns into a visit. Suzanne was raised in Quebec, Alex in Mabou. We find ourselves talking about nicknames.

Like most other Cape Breton villages, Mabou was settled by a few families. The district is still dominated by Beatons, Mac-Donalds and Rankins, and the Scottish sensibility truly approves only a few first names: Alexander, Angus, Donald, Hugh, Kenneth, John, Malcolm, Roderick, Ronald and a handful of others. The Mabou phone directory lists seven Angus Beatons, six Donald MacDonalds, four John Rankins, three Alexander MacNeils.

I know these frustrations intimately. There's a Donald Cameron in Mabou, and there are two in Port Hood, eight or more in Halifax, a dozen in Vancouver, more than twenty in Toronto. Donald Cameron is or was the registrar of Mount Allison University, the founder of the Banff Centre (later a senator) and the operator of the Port Hawkesbury A&W. Donald Cameron is Nova Scotia's Premier. Several Donald Camerons work in the media, and at least two of us are published writers.

How's a boy to make a name for himself when everyone else is making the same name? Fifteen years ago, folksinger Tom Gallant heard my woes, looked at my hair—then *prematurely* white—and said, "*Silver* Donald Cameron!" Brilliant! Much later, I recalled that the format was traditional even in my own family: I had an Ottawa Valley ancestor named Black Sandy.

Like Creignish, Mabou has produced a good crop of nicknames, double names and patronymics: The Gobha Ban (The White-Haired Blacksmith), Diddle Iddle (who liked to hum along with the fiddles—"diddle-iddle-iddle"), Tangle Eyes (whose eyes were crossed), Blue John, Dave Colorado (who had worked in Colorado), Dan the Dyer, John the Bard, Dougald the Miller. In 1816, a twenty-two-year-old immigrant named Allan MacDonald settled on a nearby ridge. He became Allan the Ridge, and his descendants are still "the Ridge MacDonalds." A family of MacMillans are "the Dancers."

"Do you know what they call me?" demands Alex MacDonald.

"Silver Alex MacDonald? Alex Suzanne?"

"I am Alexander Angus Johnny Ban. Alexander, the son of Angus, the son of White Johnny."

"Alex," says Suzanne, "these people are hungry. They're just going to The Mull—and where are you going after that?"

"To visit Maureen and Ronald MacKenzie."

"Well, come back after supper and I'll drive you."

"But—"

"No buts. I'll drive you. Enjoy your supper."

There must be a civic ordinance in Mabou against allowing visitors to walk.

The Mull belongs to Charles and Eleanor Mullendore. Mull River is a nearby village, and "mull" is a Scottish term for a headland. "The mull" is also the snuff box passed around after a Scottish banquet, and traditionally made from the head of a ram—mouth, wool, glass eyes and all. It's a curious blend of elegance and barbarism: little silver trays, with tiny spoons chained to them, sunk into the skull right between the horns. The celebrants spill a wee spoonful on the back of a hand and snort it. The banquet hall erupts in sneezes. If these were not mature Caledonian gentlemen—decked out in kilts, sporrans, dirks and lace—you'd swear they were doing cocaine.

Shouldn't Charles add a proper Scottish mull to his restaurant? He rolls his eyes. Like many other businesses on this coast, The Mull relies on tourists, and tourists want a little authenticity—but not too much. They expect bacon and eggs, steaks and seafood. They do not expect sheep's-head snuff boxes.

"We've revived some Scottish dishes, though. We sell a lot of marag—make it ourselves. People love it. We can't keep it in stock. Want to try some?"

Absolutely. Scottish cuisine is solid, workmanlike and sustaining, the gastronomical equivalent of a stone cottage with an open fire. Oatcakes, bannock, cock-a-leekie soup. Marag is a white sausage of oatmeal, onion, spices and suet, packed into an intestine. It sounds repellent, and it looks dead. Fried and eaten with hot mustard, though, it is wonderful—bright, spicy, subtle and substantial.

Suzanne drove us down the harbour and then up into the foothills of the Mabou Highlands. Off a dirt road, all by itself, a fawn-coloured new house of traditional design stood at the top of a long, sloping lawn. Three young boys came boiling out of the door. Maureen and Ronald stood smiling behind them.

When Lulu knew her at university, Maureen Rankin was already passionately interested in Celtic culture. Maureen later went to the Hebrides to study Gaelic and came home with a soft-spoken, red-headed souvenir from South Uist.

"Will you take a wee dram?" asked Ronald once we had

settled around the fireplace in the pine-panelled living room. In the other room, thumps and bangs and shrieks of laughter told us that Mark and the three boys were getting along fine.

Ronald is a carpenter and a cabinetmaker, Maureen a teacher, and the two of them built their house themselves. It is a comfortable, happy house, tight and snug and easily maintained; a Celtic house, in which Gaelic is the language of family life.

"I really liked your article on the Gathering of the Clans," said Maureen. "That whole thing is so completely false. It turns history upside down."

It does. For essentially commercial reasons, Nova Scotia— *mainland* Nova Scotia, primarily—has taken to hosting the International Gathering of the Clans, welcoming the chieftains from Scotland and staging tartan extravaganzas for tourists. There *is* a worldwide Scottish culture, centred on the music, the language, the stories, the humour, the romanticism, the shared emotional circuitry around such values as loyalty, courage and learning. But it has little to do with clans and tartans.

The Gathering of the Clans is filled with bitter ironies. The Highlanders came to Canada because the clan system was shattered, betrayed by the chieftains themselves. Claiming as personal property the lands they held in trust for their people, the chieftains enriched themselves by evicting their clansmen and replacing them with sheep. Today there are plenty of Chisholms in Mabou, Inverness and Port Hood. Half the people of Antigonish seem to be Chisholms. But in Scotland, by 1878, there was only one Chisholm left on the clan lands in Strathglass. In 1854, when the Duke of Sutherland tried to raise a regiment for Crimea, he could not enlist even one man in all of Sutherlandshire.

"We have no country to fight for," said the duke's broken tenants. "You robbed us of our country and gave it to the sheep. Since you have preferred sheep to men, let sheep defend you."

What is a Highland chieftainship? A bauble drained of honour, a heritage of shame.

But Maureen has a sunny nature, and her indignation is a fast-moving cloud in a summer sky. We stayed late, and ended the evening with tea, oatcakes and homemade cheese. The boys joined us, and Maureen prevailed on Kenneth to get his violin and play *Mrs. MacLeod of Raasay*. Angus had left his bagpipes elsewhere, but he had his chanter, the recorder-like part of the instrument which the piper fingers. He brought it out and played the sad, melodic *Lord Lovat's Lament*.

Full circle: for the lament commemorates Simon Fraser, 11th Baron Lovat and Chief of Clan Fraser, who was beheaded in London in April 1747, for his part in the last and greatest of the Jacobite risings. Though he was a fat, shifty old rascal, I might go to see Lord Lovat if he came to Nova Scotia.

But not his successors, in any of the clans.

Chris and Sonja arrived next day. Their geriatric Volvo station wagon was jammed with camping gear. Two racing bicycles stood on the roof. Chris was in training for a four-day road race from Montreal to Boston and back. From Montreal to Cape Breton they had taken turns: one rode for 100 or 200 miles while the other drove, and then they switched.

After Chris dropped his bicycle off in Margaree Harbour, our next port, we all went for tea with Donald and Mary Rankin.

"You going to Meat Cove, Bay St. Lawrence?" asked Donald. "Funny people down there, you know. In Meat Cove they don't know how far they are from Chéticamp." He laughs. "That's true. I was down there once, I asked a fellow how far it was. He said, 'I don't know, I've never been there'. They're nice enough people, but they're different. They don't talk much."

We did want to go to Bay St. Lawrence, if we could.

"Mmm," said Donald. "If I were you, I wouldn't bother with Margaree. That's another narrow entrance, and the bar runs out a long ways. If you've got the wind, I'd go straight down to Chéticamp. Then you've got fifty miles off your trip. Chéticamp's a good harbour.

"This can be a dangerous coast, all the same. I remember coming home from Chéticamp in 1952. It was October, Hallowe'en eve. A gale came up, and we were caught. The whole coast was just a froth of white all down along. Inverness was closed, there was no entrance there at all. Out in front of Margaree it was all white breakers. We were jogging along at quarter-throttle, trying to hold her up to it. The seas were coming right over the bow.

"We went in behind Margaree Island, trying to find some shelter, but there was no shelter to be had. I didn't think we were going to make it. We finally got into Mabou—there was plenty of water over the bar then. It was the only harbour we could get into. By the time we got in I was seeing things in strange colours, and the next day my blood pressure was 220. I thought we were gone for sure."

John C. Beaton towed us out of Mabou at 6:15 in the morning. Inside the harbour, we could hardly feel the wind, but beyond the sheltering headland a strong westerly was heaping up the seas over the bar. John C. took it slowly. The two boats reared skyward and plunged into the troughs. John C. gestured: did we want to go back? Standing on the foredeck, I shook my head. Once past the bar, *Silversark* would find this a good sailing breeze.

We plugged onward, rolling and pitching, slowly moving towards the outer buoy. At seven we rounded the buoy, cast off the tow line and made sail.

On a bluff high above us, a man sat in a dark blue pickup truck, watching the little ship scudding down the coast. It was Donald Rankin.

FOUR-
AND-
TWENTY
VIRGINS

Despite its name, Mabou Coal Mines is one of Cape Breton's most haunting scenes—and I still have never been there. On our way to Mabou, Donald Rankin drove up a back road and stopped at the peak of a hill. Through a gap in the trees, we saw the country falling away to reveal sweeping hills, sloping fields and crescent beaches. Mabou Mines.

The coal mines are long since gone, like those of Inverness and Port Hood and the gypsum quarries at Mabou Harbour. Only one coal mine is operating in Inverness County, at St. Rose, a few miles north. Mabou Mines today is a summer colony of artists like film-maker Robert Frank and composer Philip Glass. As we passed by from seaward, it looked calm, surreal, frozen in its own loveliness like an impeccable painting.

"I wonder if we couldn't pole that jib out?" asked Chris.

Thus began the basic pattern of the next 80 miles. I navigated; Lulu steered; Chris and Sonja experimented with the sails. Chris knows sails far better than I do. He has built a racing catamaran, taught sailing and sailed across the Atlantic. During the building of *Silversark* Chris also worked with Steve Callahan in Maine, using the same wood-epoxy system to build the 21-foot *Napoleon Solo*. When *Solo* was completed, Steve and Chris sailed her to England.

"What's the sea like, out in mid-Atlantic?" I asked him. "Just like this."

Chris flew home from England, but Callahan's return trip was epic. Six days from the Canary Islands, something massive struck *Napoleon Solo*—possibly a whale, conceivably a submarine. Callahan just had time to scramble into an inflatable emergency raft. There he lived for the next seventy-six days, drifting clean across the Atlantic to be picked up by fishermen near Guadeloupe. His book *Adrift* is a detailed account of the ordeal.

"We should have a preventer on that main," Chris observed. "And some vanging tension on the jib."

A little tighter here, a little more slack there. An extra tug on the halyard. More weight forward. Each little change made the boat roll less, steer better, go faster.

"How would this boat do for an Atlantic crossing, Chris?" "Perfect."

"Chris, pass me the suntan lotion," said Sonja. "Lulu, do you want some, too?"

The sun, once our friend, is now a danger. Mark, Lulu and I used #12 sunscreen lotion. Chris and Sonja used #40—"axle grease," said Chris. A few years ago none of us would have used lotion at all, but at least two Cape Breton friends—Ann Sherrington is one of them—have suffered malignant melanomas. Why? Will we soon hear about a newly discovered hole in the ozone layer over the North Atlantic, too? Smear on the grease. And this blue water flows from the St. Lawrence, which drains the Great Lakes. What chemicals are swishing past our stern, flushed down the river from the sewers of Chicago, Hamilton,

Detroit, Montreal? In these waters, the world's sickness is invisible. The sea and the sky *look* beautiful.

The breeze held steady, and the coast slipped past.

"Inverness," I said, pointing the binoculars at a village on a bluff. "The harbour's to the right, in that notch."

"Dad," said Mark, "how does that song go?"

"What song?"

"The one about Inverness. About the virgins."

"I only know two lines," I lied.

> Four-and-twenty virgins,
> They went down to Inverness;
> And when the night was over,
> There were four-and-twenty less.

"That's not all of it."

"No, but it's all I can give you."

The lusty breeze kept blowing, driving big seas onto the shore. From seaward, breakers are hard to judge. You see their smooth backs, not their foaming faces. But along the shoreline we could see blasts of white water shooting up the faces of the cliffs, like twenty-foot waterfalls flowing upwards.

Should we try for Margaree? Or should we just go on to Chéticamp? We studied the shoreline through the binoculars.

"Those look like pretty big breakers in there," Chris said.

"One of the fishermen said she'd be breaking a mile out from Margaree in a wind like this," said Sonja.

"Let's just go to Chéticamp," I said.

Had we but known, a touching ceremony had taken place in Margaree Harbour four days earlier: the rededication of Farley Mowat's *Happy Adventure*. Years earlier, Farley contributed her to the museum at River Bourgeois, where he lives. The museum left her rotting, which horrified Stephanie May. She and her husband, John, operate Schooner Village, a gift-shop complex attached to an old Lunenburg schooner, the *Marion Elizabeth*, which they have converted to a restaurant.

Stephanie persuaded Tourism Minister Roland Thornhill to help fund a restoration and moved the ship to Schooner Village. Since the planks had fallen off the port side, she had viewing windows installed. Tourists can see the vessel's log and compass, along with photographs of Mowat and his publisher, Jack McClelland, during the years when they believed themselves immortal and therefore felt brave enough to take her to sea.

At the dedication ceremonies, Farley said he was "pleased that the old lady has been brought back to a semblance of life and to where she has belonged since she was built—on land." McClelland sent a telegram expressing his pleasure that the boat would finally be in her proper environment. The thought of actually seeing her again made him lean towards bottles of rum. As a gesture to myth and history, *Silversark*'s rigging includes one galvanized shackle from *Happy Adventure*. But a gesture is enough. *Silversark* has never leaked a drop; her bilges actually get dusty. *Happy Adventure* leaked constantly. Had we known she was in Margaree Harbour, we would have planned to avoid the place, just in case the Mowat virus was infectious.

We swung a little offshore, steering for the faint, hazy point of land which was Chéticamp Island. The new course passed to seaward of Margaree Island, also known as Sea Wolf Island. Sailing fast, we reached the island at 10:30. Sixteen nautical miles in three hours is an average speed of 5.3 knots: good work for a small boat whose theoretical maximum speed is just 6.87 knots.

After Margaree, the wind dropped. As the pressure on her sails eased, *Silversark* rolled more and more easily. That made the crew seasick. Not just one or two of them, but all four.

Chris is fine on deck, but all he can do below is sleep. Lulu usually gains her sea legs after the first few days aboard, but strong rolling can make her sick again. (Lord Nelson, curiously, had the same problem.) Mark and Sonja have fairly steady stomachs, but both of them felt sluggish and queasy. But not me. I have been seasick only twice: once in the cuddy cabin of a fishing boat bobbing aimlessly off Canso, and once aboard *Bluenose II*, which kept me nauseated for three days.

Chris and Sonja went below and squirmed into the two quarter berths. Mark and Lulu dozed on the cockpit seats. I sailed on alone, like the Ancient Mariner, surrounded by the prostrate bodies of the crew, musing about boats and boatbuilding, about knowledge, death and love.

If you want to see me perfectly happy, put me in the shop for a long, sunny afternoon with Lulu, Chris, Peter, Edwin or Jerry. Leave the door open, so the sea breeze can sweep in across the fields and the woods. Let us shape a rudder, install a portlight, redesign the galley. Let us reconvene the Nine-Year Seminar on Boatbuilding and Life.

Inside the little old barn, the nose of the half-built boat probes the dusty air. Her long sweeping lines are countered by the diagonal thrust of her mahogany plywood planking. She seems very tangible and solid, but she is not really made of mahogany, epoxy, bronze and stainless steel. She is made of thought, learning and experiment. She is a structure of knowledge.

Originally, *Silversark* was a Bruce Roberts design called the Adventure 25. In 1976, I visited Roberts, then in Vancouver. I told him I was interested in building his 25.

"But I'd like to make a few changes," I said.

"What sorts of changes?"

"Well, a longer keel, and a cutter rig. And a raised flush deck. I'd want the transom raked aft, rather than forward . . ."

"I see," said Roberts drily. "What was it that you *liked* about the boat?"

I felt myself flushing. I hadn't meant to insult him.

"Actually, those are very sensible modifications," Roberts said. "They'd give you a boat rather like my 36."

"Yes," I said. "And if I could afford that much boat, your 36 is what I'd build."

"All right," Roberts said. "I'll draw those modifications for you."

Back home, I drew out her lines on the shop floor. Roberts did eventually send the new drawings, but by then I had already built the basic hull, and his 25-footer had grown to 27 feet. A boat's plans are only a skeleton anyway; the builder always fleshes them out to his own taste.

Before I started to build, I visited Second Peninsula, outside Lunenburg, to see David Stevens and his son Murray. David was best known as the builder of the schooner *Atlantica* at the Atlantic Provinces Pavilion at Expo 67. He was "retired" when I knew him, which meant he was building 50-foot racing schooners for his own amusement, not for sale. Murray had taken over the business, and he and his wife, Florence, sold us most of the materials for *Silversark*. Murray's cousin, Arthur Dauphinee, provided the varnished blocks. When we were baffled, we called David or Murray, or David's brother Harold, who eventually made our sails.

When Chris and I worked out the exact size and shape of the lead ballast for the bottom of the keel, for instance, we used mock-ups, drawings and endless calculations. Then we called Murray, who told us to check our work by carving an accurate model of the boat below the waterline and setting the model on the edge of a knife. Where the model balanced on the knife, there the boat would balance in the water. And there we should put the centre of the lead weight.

Though they were 250 miles away, the Stevenses were part of the building team. So was the elfin Morris Allen, who rigged both *Silversark* and *Bluenose II*: "Rigger Morris," as he was known in Lunenburg. Chris was always on the team, and Lulu had been dreaming in parallel while she studied biochemistry in Denmark. When she came home, sailing brought us together.

Lulu and Edwin DeWolfe grew up next door to one another. Edwin quit school in Grade 7 and developed into a fine carpenter—the man I called when I needed a new roof, a dormer, new storm doors. A gentle, humorous man, he is also a good teacher. Inevitably, Edwin was drawn into the project. Peter joined us when his business foundered. Jerry Jones came along in 1985 to help us get the boat launched that season.

None of us had ever attempted anything like *Silversark*. We learned how to build her by building her.

Get the rhythm, first. Steady, persistent, patient, unhurried. Think what you're going to do, and why. Think out loud. Plan it, draw it out on paper, make a template of scrap plywood or hardboard. Measure twice, cut once. Don't glue it down till you're sure.

Building a boat is a process of thinking, knowing and doing— of learning and creating, which are the two most important of all human activities. It is not a single big job; it is a thousand little jobs, some of them done over and over and over. What you learn is not just a matter of technique, of handling wood and metal.

The hand and eye can sand the hull while large tracts of the mind are free to talk, to speculate, to hear Stan Rogers on the shop stereo or an *Ideas* show on the CBC. The hands move steadily, filling hollows and boring holes, cutting off and gluing on, driving screws and chiselling wood—

"This chisel's dull."

"Let's have a look," said Peter. "Mmm—it's not too bad. Use my Japanese water stone, the medium one . . ."

Among Peter's many Japanese tools is a huge power plane designed to smooth and true the columns for temples. Building temples is a recognized branch of Japanese woodcraft: carpentry to honour the gods. But think about this boat, on which we lavish such care. What gods does it honour? The gods of wind and sea?

We imagined *Silversark* clawed by gales, buffeted by gigantic seas, rolled down on her beam ends with tons of water tumbling across her deck. Was that bulkhead strong enough? Were her crew well protected? Such thoughts make boatbuilders and sailors deeply conservative. If an innovation fails, the cost will be measured not in money but in lives. If in doubt, don't do it. Use methods ripened by the centuries.

"I thought that table-top was finished," Lulu said sorrowfully. "But it's going to need another coat. I'll have to sand the whole thing again."

Workmanship. When is it good enough? The professional knows; the amateur doesn't. Lulu simply knew she wasn't satisfied. That's why an amateur's boat is sometimes more finished than a professional's. Amateur: the word means "lover," which the non-professional shipwright must be.

How many clients, after all, are willing to pay for the time it takes to get things right? Our economic system rewards quick, shabby work. We had to battle those reflexes and learn to do things properly.

Edwin and I splined floorboards together, cutting grooves in their edges and gluing strips of plywood into the grooves. Then we planed their edges to fit the constantly changing curves inside the hull. The floorboards are afrormosia, a brown and yellow tropical hardwood which yields a sweet perfume when you cut it. As we worked, Edwin shared the knowledge buried in his hands and eyes. A shaving here. A bit more there. Now she'll fit.

The Seminar lived in conversations that often ripened over weeks. Periods of talk were followed by silence, or by noise: the whines and screams of router, saw and sander. Time to think, ruminate on the last conversation, file it for later attention.

We talked about politics, art, business management, music. We followed *Canada I* at the America's Cup. We discussed the relationships between men and women. Edwin had been married for twenty years—the only one of us still with his original partner. How did they manage this? Edwin had kept out of debt, too. He said it wasn't difficult, but the rest of us never mastered it.

The Seminar drew on solid knowledge of the world we live in and how it is made. Both Chris and Peter are full of curiosity. They read anything and everything. When Chris finds himself at loose ends near a library, he goes in and tries to read at least one article in each of half a dozen periodicals he's never seen before. Peter is an encyclopaedia of tools: how they work, how pressures are applied, how the body must be used to produce the result. He and Chris both know an amazing amount about the behaviour of wood, metal, plastic, electricity, fluids, about heat and geography and natural history.

Working with wood, for instance, means understanding trees. Peter points out that tropical woods don't have the familiar growth rings you find in a northern log, because the tree grows all year long without a dormant winter period. Instead, the fibres run in a spiral through the tree. That means the grain will run both upwards and downwards in the same board. That's what puts ribbons in ribbon mahogany. Planing it requires a sharp blade, and a thin shaving.

The team in the shop performed experiments. We developed specialized tools for awkward, difficult jobs. We designed a galley, mocked it up, didn't like it, tore it out and tried again. We found ourselves theorizing about good design, the delicate interplay of gracious form with efficient function.

We learned new things about ourselves. Edwin confessed one day that originally he had been doubtful whether he could do the fine work which the project required. But he did it well, which improved his opinion of himself. Then he realized that he had done it partly because everyone else assumed he could. Our faith in him was an injection of confidence.

I learned about myself, too. The project was much more demanding than I expected, partly because of "the escalation factor." Still, if I took my time, I could do it. If I lacked a skill, I could practise on scrap wood till I had mastered it. I am a much more patient person than I thought I was.

"The escalation factor" was the growing severity of the demands we made on ourselves. My schooner *Hirondelle* was built to fishermen's standards. It contained no exotic woods, it was fastened with galvanized nails, and its interior was cramped and awkward. I loved that schooner, but not her boxy, flimsy cabin, her thin glass windows, her huge open cockpit. In building my own boat, I wanted to improve on the materials and the design—but I never thought of improving on the workmanship.

As we learned more, though, we increased our demands on ourselves. Paint can be brushed on, yes, but we learned to spray it. We replaced the bald plastic rings around the portlights with afrormosia. We covered the ventilating holes in the lockers with wicker and mahogany, and inlaid strips of oak and white ash in the dark floorboards. We sealed every single piece of wood with two or three coats of epoxy resin.

Time-consuming? Yes—but those things felt indefinably *right*—and the curse of a wooden boat is maintenance. By building quality into her, we were building maintenance out of her. We have drawn the benefits ever since. In 1990, we did no maintenance at all. We launched her, rigged her, and sailed away.

Boatbuilding was joy, not work. People were always stopping by the shop—friends, neighbours, even tourists and film crews. More than one evening ended with an impromptu party. The boat was built upside down, and the keel was laminated from heavy planks, held together by long threaded rods while the glue set. One night, Chris accidentally struck a rod with his wrench—and the boat emitted a deep, round BONGGGGG! The hull had become a phenomenal resonating chamber, a 27-foot wooden bell. Chris hit another rod and got a different note. Lulu and I scrambled under the hull. There must have been twenty rods, and for half an hour we serenaded the village with something that sounded like the big brother of Mike Oldfield's *Tubular Bells* album.

Escalation, and the human interruptions of work, marriage, politics, friendship, family—that's how it became a nine-year seminar. Looming over it were large questions which occupied many a happy hour, while the busy fingers scraped, marked, cut and painted. Why would a person devote such time, such love, such energy, to building a boat? To be sure that the boat could safely travel to any place touched by salt water. Why would one go there? Because the world is a vast, fascinating place, and we know only small corners of it. What about the risks? Life itself is a risk, and it seems sweetest when it is least predictable.

I was trained in the arts; the Seminar massively increased my appreciation of science, which had given me the new, forgiving products and techniques that made the project possible. Watching my scientifically trained friends solve problems, working with products like epoxy, urethane and polycarbonate, I began to understand the fascination of scientific endeavour.

But there is another kind of knowledge—the kind of knowledge St. Thomas Aquinas had in mind when he declared that "the slenderest knowledge that may be obtained of the highest things is more desirable than the most certain knowledge obtained of lesser things." These are the questions we asked as we came to know one another well, as late evening flowed into early morning. What is the nature of reality? What is goodness? What is our purpose? How do we know what is true? How should we live?

"Knowledge of the highest things" is variable and fluid, a flickering illumination gained by introspection, meditation, talk and prayer. A person skilled at negotiating these uncertainties is not just knowledgeable, but wise—and the more we learn, the more clearly we see that the object of knowledge is to gain wisdom. With wisdom comes humility, Leonard Pertus's understanding that "you do the best you can, it's all you can do."

The Seminar began with tools and wood and working hands, but again and again it made its way home to philosophy, as every human activity ultimately must. If, as I believe, our purpose in this life is to learn who we are, what we are and how we are related to the world and to one another, then perhaps the boat was only an occasion, and the Nine-Year Seminar on Boatbuilding and Life was the thing we were really doing.

"I have a favourite Zen parable," said Chris late one night in the boatshop. He was wearing cockeyed broken spectacles, and his coveralls were coated in white epoxy dust. A paper dust mask, perched on his head, looked like half of a big white egg.

"A man falls off a cliff," Chris said. "Halfway down, he breaks his fall by grabbing a vine. On the vine is one perfect strawberry. He eats the strawberry, and then, as the vine starts to let go, he cries, 'How sweet it is!'"

Sailing *Silversark* down the Cape Breton coast, I was glad to have Chris aboard for his competence as a sailor, but even more for his well-filled mind, his spirit and his insight.

Lulu woke up. I was humming to myself.

"I've never seen you so relaxed and happy at sea," said Lulu.

"Chris is here," I said.

While the crew slept, the good westerly faded. Now Margaree Island was far behind and Chéticamp Island was close ahead, with the silver spire of the village church thrusting up behind it. ("You can see the steeple for ten miles," Donald Rankin had said.) The south end of the island is connected to the mainland by a beach. The harbour is formed by the beach and the island. To enter the harbour from the south, you have to sail the full length of the island and come in from the north.

The crew revived as we floated slowly by the island. The breeze kept easing. We bobbed along, a few inches closer with each passing wave.

Slowly, slowly, we passed Point Enragée, at the northern tip of the island. On the mainland shore, range beacons mark the approach channel. As the beacons came into line, we turned. As we crept towards the entrance, the range opened again the other way.

"There must be a current," I said.

"Yes, and it's carrying us past the entrance," said Chris.

An alarming thought. Between Chéticamp and the northern tip of Cape Breton, the only harbour is Pleasant Bay, another small river, but much narrower and tighter than Mabou. And after that? The North Shore of Quebec, or Newfoundland.

"Let's row," said Lulu.

"Give me an oar," said Sonja.

We rowed. Steering well to starboard of the range, we gradually closed it again.

We rowed into the shelter of the island, and the current lost its strength.

Spelling one another at the oars, we rowed.

At the red light buoy inside the island, we turned again. It was a big, open harbour. By now we were only a hundred yards from the shore, close enough to watch cars and trucks passing and to read the signs on the shops.

"Where's the government wharf?" Lulu asked.

"Up by the church," I said.

"Is there anywhere else to moor?"

"Just private wharves, according to the pilot book."

"Let's get those sails down. They're not helping anyway."

We rowed. A big pleasure cruiser came by, with a man on the afterdeck taking photos. How many vessels enter Chéticamp under oars? I imagined the old Acadian skippers sitting on their porches, looking out over the harbour.

By d'Chris', are dey usin' h'oars on dat vessel?

I t'ink so, me.

Dis day and age, you'd t'ink dey could afford a motor.

We rowed.

The wharf took shape. It was lined with fishing boats.

But what fishing boats! Mabou fishing boats might be 30 feet long and 10 or 12 feet in the beam, with low sterns for hauling nets and traps. These Chéticamp boats were twice that size — regular ships, with sides like walls rising out of the water. One or two were handsome, and an old wooden dragger from Caraquet, New Brunswick had a sweeping sheerline and a well-proportioned house aft. But most of them were as graceful as apartment blocks.

We rowed on, around the end of the wharf. On the south face, two or three smaller boats lay moored near the wharf. One bore the name *Bonnie and Maureen*. She had two men aboard.

"Can we moor up beside you?"

"Sure! Come on in!"

One of the men aboard *Bonnie and Maureen* was Bill Crawford, who teaches school in the winter and runs the whale-watching tours all summer. Business was brisk, and his main boat was fully booked, so he had launched *Bonnie and Maureen* to take the overflow. Neither his voice nor his name was Acadian: how had he come to be here? Crawford laughed. He had spent most of his early life in Moncton and Montreal, he said, but he got fed up with it. His mother was from Chéticamp, and he moved down to get out of the rat-race.

"Happy about it?"

"Oh, yeah. I love it here. I'd never go back."

Back aboard *Silversark*, Chris and Sonja rummaged in the cooler, dug out vegetables and made a salad. Lulu arranged cold cuts and bread. We found we were very hungry. We had eaten only snacks since leaving Mabou more than twelve hours before.

After wolfing down our food, we headed up the main street.

We were in Acadia, *bien sûr*. It was not just the language, but the whole style of the village: the colours of the houses, the lofty church, the clusters of people deep in animated conversations all up and down the long harbourside street. It was the bumper-to-bumper traffic on the street, young bucks in muscle cars and fancy trucks burbling slowly past knots of young girls. It was a whole sense of life being lived intensely, collectively, out in the open.

"This feels like Quebec," said Sonja. Completely bilingual, Sonja practises psychology in Montreal in both English and French — and in Serbo-Croatian, too, if need be.

"Everybody on the move, everybody on the street," said Chris.

"I really feel at home here," said Sonja.

Having passed the Restaurant Evangeline, we went into Le Gabriel, a large, dimly lit restaurant, for dessert. Lovers as competitors: curious that Longfellow, who may never even have met an Acadian, has given an enduring symbol of love and fidelity to Atlantic Canada's francophones. Better yet, the symbol is commercially useful. Most of Cape Breton's tourists are Americans, and many of them read *Evangeline* in school.

Mark and I ordered lemon meringue pie. Lulu, Chris and Sonja ordered the house special, an Acadian strawberry-rhubarb pie.

"Oh, this is really *excellent*," said Sonja. "I'm going to get the recipe."

We drank huge glasses of ice water and ordered more. We were all parched from the sun and wind.

"And rowing," said Mark.

"Right," said Chris. "I wonder how far we rowed."

"I measured it on the chart," I said.

"And—?"

"Five miles."

PARTONS, LA MER EST BELLE

Alfred LeBlanc was on the wharf in the morning. In Mabou, where he works with Frazer Hunter at Incor, Albert had buttonholed me. "When you get to Chéticamp, you call me," he had said. "Anything I can do for you, I'll do it." We needed to get to Mabou, to pick up Chris's car. Albert's car was waiting on the wharf.

"Bring her back when you're done," said Albert.

A Chéticamp patriot, Albert is a sailor himself. He was selling the 20-foot Nordica in which he used to sail back and forth between Chéticamp and the Magdalen Islands, 45 miles away. His new boat was a 45-foot pilot-house sloop built to sail the south coast of Newfoundland. She was sitting in a cradle at

Chéticamp Boat Builders. Albert proposed to rebuild her, sell his house and move aboard.

I drove Chris and Sonja to Mabou, stopping to view the little harbours we had missed: Grand Étang, Margaree, Inverness. Friar's Head Boat Harbour, no longer in use, must be the ultimate gunkhole: a jagged rock ledge parallel to the shore, about 150 feet out, its gaps filled with concrete. To enter, you sail almost into the surf, then turn sharply to port. Inside is a broken-down concrete landing stage and a dirt track switch-backing up the 80-foot cliff. In bad weather, combers must break clean across the whole affair.

Across the road is one of Cape Breton's oddest tourist sites. Joe Delaney's scarecrow farm began in 1983, when Delaney, then sixty-seven, planted a garden.

"The neighbours told me, Joe, it's no use because of the deer, the crows, the foxes and the seagulls," he said later. With old clothes and Hallowe'en masks, he built three scarecrows. But they didn't just stand in the field. They *did* things. Two of them, for example, were sawing away with a crosscut saw.

People were delighted. Delaney built more scarecrows— scarecrows fiddling, dancing, waving at passersby. A military scarecrow hobbled on one leg. Scarecrow kids danced in a circle while a loafing scarecrow snoozed nearby. By 1986, the community numbered forty-six scarecrows. But vandals attacked the farm that November. The scarecrows were massacred.

"Everything was down," said Delaney. "Crisscrossed. Broken in two. Arms off. Masks ripped off and everything. That was a real heartbreaker. Every man who has wealth, he has to lose some. My wealth was my scarecrows, and I lost them."

But not for long. The next summer, Delaney's field sprouted seventy-five scarecrows, plus a snack bar and a gift shop. The whole venture won him an Innovation Award from the Cape Breton Tourist Association and a place on the honour roll of the Tourist Industry Association of Nova Scotia as "a man whose achievement is truly out of the ordinary."

We crossed the broad, shallow valley of the Margaree. Five or six miles further on, we saw an old International Scout parked across a culvert. A tourist in a battered cloth hat sat on the roof, his feet on the hood, his lunch box open beside him. He was gazing across the road at a farmhouse, a sloping field and the offshore hump of Margaree Island.

"Great place for a picnic," said Sonja.

"Great chair," said Chris.

In Mabou we talked with Donald and Mary, retrieved the Volvo and left. Two hours later, driving back, I found the tourist was still sitting atop his Scout, still eating his lunch.

Double-take! That's not a tourist: it's George Thomas, painting a watercolour.

"I've spoiled it," said George, holding the painting out for inspection. "I had it right an hour or two ago. I kept fiddling with it, and it's getting worse now. Come on down for a coffee."

George is a painter, a photographer and a sailor; his wife, Lynn Zimmerman, is a writer. They came up from the States twenty years ago, settling in an old house right beside the Margaree Harbour lighthouse. George took tourists on day trips in a 30-foot schooner. Together they published *Margaree*, a book of text and photographs. Not long ago, they moved back to Nantucket, where they now spend their winters, primarily because they felt their children would get a better education in New England.

George and Lynn are not alone in this. Education in rural Nova Scotia has been savagely cut in recent years, and the cutting is not finished. The result is long bus rides, poor labs and libraries, overcrowding, few extracurricular activities—and parents who now go to great trouble and expense to have their children educated elsewhere. We ourselves had spent the previous three winters in Halifax—for business reasons, partly, but also in the interests of Mark's education.

George and Lynn remain bewildered by the passiveness of Canadians in the face of such issues.

"The government takes all these facilities away from people, and they just seem to *accept* it," George said. "All the things that make up a rural community, the things people really need if they're going to live in the country—the wharf, the post office, the schools, the trains, the lighthouses—how can people just let these things go?"

George is right. For a century, the cities have been draining the country, and somehow these issues—like so many others—

have been reduced to a numbers game. Such expensive services, so few rural people. But we once thought that all Canadians were entitled to the same basic services, wherever they lived. Cost was only one factor among many. In those distant, golden days, we even seemed to feel there was a kind of social ecology at play, that a nation was enriched by self-reliant, knowledgeable people who produced things like wheat, eggs, wool, hides, milk, fish, coal, lumber.

For me, the country still offers a better life than the city. I appreciate the vitality and variety of a city: the music, the restaurants, the libraries, the shops. I enjoy the company of people who produce films, design publications, program computers, run government departments, render legal judgments, study the ocean floor. Really big cities make me uneasy, but I love compact, complex, gossipy little cities like Halifax, Charlottetown and St. John's.

But the country offers a different kind of wealth. The urbanite may have disposable income; the country family has disposable *time*. For most of my years in the country, I didn't even have a mortgage. Survival required hard work—but Lulu and I had time to sail, time to visit, time to travel, time to build a boat. In Halifax, I have no time to build anything.

I was rich in the country. I am poor in the city. And that has nothing to do with numbers.

With those sad and bitter thoughts, I drove to Belle Côte to pick up Henry and Lucy Doucet, who immediately improved my mood.

Henry is a retired stonemason, a one-time fisherman and merchant seaman. He turned ninety last spring. His young bride is nearing eighty herself. Their son, Father Dan Doucet, is my friend, a priest who gracefully bridges the space between Catholic orthodoxy and New Age sensibility.

Lucy is an encyclopaedia of song. She knows traditional songs, pop songs dating back as far as the 1920s, comic songs, love songs, plangent Acadian melodies. She always had a true, clear voice; she claims old age has spoiled it. Maybe. Another time we'll drink more rum and get her singing again.

Fifteen years ago, when we first met, Henry Doucet gave me a searching oral examination on seamanship.

"On that schooner of yours, now, when it comes to blow, what do you do first? Hah?"

Lower the foresail, probably.

"Ah-hah! And if it blows some more?"

Reef the main, and possibly the jumbo too.

"Yah, and then?"

Pull 'em both down, and put the foresail back up.

"That's right! That's right!" He clapped me on the back. "I just wanted to see if you knew what you were doin' or if you were full of bullshit. Have a drink, now, have a drink."

Henry had seen *Silversark* in the building shed, but never in the water. In Chéticamp, he scampered down over the wharf, gave Lucy a hand, crossed the side decks and cockpit of *Bonny and Maureen*, and swung across the lifelines onto *Silversark*.

"You made a great job of her," said Henry, seated below, looking around at the glossy woodwork. "Hah! She looks *great!*"

Henry went to sea at the age of fourteen, when his father bought a small fishing schooner in Tancook Island, near Lunenburg, built by David Stevens's grandfather, Amos.

"Amos Stevens, that's the man that built her," Henry nodded. "And Mister Man, that thing could plough. My father and I went down to get her—just the two of us. Foggy! We never saw the land at all. My father only had compass and dividers to navigate with. I don't know how he did it. When he said, 'Well, we'll turn now and run into the Strait of Canso,' that's just where we were."

But he had charts, of course?

"He had only one chart for the whole coast, right from Tancook to Mulgrave," said Henry. "Of course, after we got to Mulgrave we didn't need a chart. We knew where we were then.

"We blew through the Strait of Canso in a gale from the south'ard. A big schooner came too close to us. She was an American, the American ships used to fish in the Gulf all the time—mackerel, herring, they'd use it for bait.

"Well, this big Banker took the wind from our sails and left us dead in the water. We couldn't do anything. He could see he was going to hit us. So he bore away, hah? Nearly missed us, too, but his boom hooked on our mainmast and nearly broke it. But it bent, and then it sprung away—and the cursing that came out of my father then—well, well!"

Henry travelled the world on cargo vessels. In Tahiti, in the 1920s, he thought he was in paradise.

"If you wanted food, it grew on trees," he recalls. "You didn't need a house, it was warm all the time. All you needed was a pair of dungarees. What a place to live!" With some friends, Henry jumped ship. The skipper had to bring them back by force.

He was shipwrecked on Sable Island in 1935.

"It was a Sunday in October, two in the morning. We were coming home from the Grand Banks with a load of fish. Everybody was tired—when the fishing is good you don't sleep very much. Well, the lookout fell asleep. When he woke up, we were heading straight for the light at the east point of Sable. The helmsman threw the wheel hard over, but it was too late. I was sleeping in the fo'c'sle, and I woke up when I felt her go *bump-bump-bump*. Next thing I knew, a sea came down the scuttle and soaked me.

"We got off some flares, and in the morning the rescue team came from the west point. They got us all off with a breeches buoy—fired a rocket out to the ship with a line on it, and then you got in this seat hanging from the line, and they pulled you ashore and sent the seat back out for the next fellow."

Henry didn't like the skipper on that vessel, an Icelander.

"We nearly lost him one time, but we didn't," he said regretfully. "We were coming out of Halifax in a sou'east gale. I was at the helm, and the seas were right on the nose. When my trick was over, the skipper and I were outside the wheelhouse going to the galley. I saw a big green one comin'. I grabbed the funnel shrouds and hung on for dear life. Boy, I barely hung on. When the wave passed over, I went into the galley and looked around, and I didn't see the skipper. I said, Okay, good!

"But after about five minutes the skipper came crawlin' in all broken up. He had been slammed against the taffrail, but he didn't go over." Henry laughed. "If I'd have been there, I'd have pushed him."

Silversark's interior is crowded for five, so Chris and Sonja went off to find a campground while I took the Doucets back to Belle Côte. I watched with joy as Henry scrambled up the ladder to the wharf. Ninety winters on his head, Yeats would have said, but Henry is not a paltry thing. Old clothes upon old sticks to scare a bird? Not Henry.

Acadian communities are often treeless, which gives them a shaven green look in summer, a bleak white aspect in winter. South of Chéticamp, the hills recede inland; further north, cliffs plummet straight into the sea. At Chéticamp itself, the landscape embodies dramatic contrasts: a steep rounded ridge like a wide green forehead, then a gently sloping plain thrusting like a pouting lip towards the sea. This is not a cozy, intimate landscape, with the sweep of land and sea broken by islands and distant shores. This is big, powerful country, open and strong.

The valleys which cleave those round hills create the district's dreaded southeasters. Five or six times a year, the southeast wind gathers on the Highlands and hurls itself down through the valleys with hurricane violence. The southeaster whips the roofs off buildings and shatters mobile homes. One winter, when the new school was just under construction, a southeaster picked up half a dozen steel I-beams and tossed them out onto the harbour ice like pick-up sticks. They were eighteen inches wide and fifty feet long. They weighed several tons each.

Such storms are bad enough on land; at sea they are killers. Larger vessels nuzzle up along the outside of Chéticamp Island, where the water is deep and the offshore wind has no fetch to build up a sea. The ships cower there, nosing into the wind with their engines running. Fishermen tell of epic voyages home, smashing forward at full throttle for twelve hours to cover a single mile. They reach the wharf with the wheelhouse windows smashed out, the deck swept clean, the electronics gone, and the helmsman wearing snowmobile goggles to protect his eyes from raindrops that strike like needles.

Chéticamp's Acadians are cheerful, blunt, mercurial, funny, generous. The Cabot Trail, Nova Scotia's premier tourist route, is a famous corniche road which winds through the Cape Breton Highlands. It is Chéticamp's main street. The southern boundary of Cape Breton Highlands National Park is the village's northern boundary. Tour buses, motor homes, trailers and bicycles stream through the village all summer long.

Chéticamp is the main service centre of this coast, with such facilities as a laundromat, bank, liquor store, bus service, ship chandler, pharmacy, restaurants. We did errands, often stopping at the Deli Marina, a delicatessen/café built on a wharf. Our crew was particularly fond of their homemade raisin toast. Though Hobie Cats and Lasers lie alongside it, the Deli Marina is not yet a marina, but the owners plan to put out moorings and offer a tender service.

Meanwhile, at the government wharf, we wrestled with big draggers and choppy water. The southwest wind whistles over the low sandbar connecting Chéticamp Island with the mainland, building up a fair chop by the time it reaches the wharf. The draggers ignore the chop, but a boat like *Silversark* rolls and swings, grinding herself against other boats and the wharf.

I awoke at five one morning to the *squaaak*! of our fenders being pinched between the boat and the wharf. Pulling on my pants, I went on deck. A fisherman was just casting off.

"Good morning, sir!" he cried, as he motored past *Silversark*. "You've slept in!"

I had not: I adjusted the mooring lines and went back to bed, satisfied that *Silversark* was not doing herself any damage. By eight, the wind was stronger. Lulu and I warped the boat into a corner of the wharf, alongside a heroically scruffy old dragger, all splinters, fish scales and rust. I laid planks across her fishpens so that we could traverse her without touching her—and we soon learned to cross her breadth without taking a breath.

Beside her, however, with her bow into the wind and waves, *Silversark* rode much more comfortably. Lulu and I left with a load of laundry. Halfway back, laden with bags, we met Mark, riding in a fisherman's car.

"Hurry!" he cried. "We have to move the boat! Someone else is coming in!"

It was the first day of the snow crab fishery, and a big crabber was due. The grubby dragger would have to move, and so would we. But the wind held us pinned where we were. We might perhaps have sailed out, but the manoeuvre would be tricky, and where would we go? Eventually I asked the good-natured skipper of the dragger where he would be going.

"Oh, just aroun' de wharf, dere."

"Couldn't we just stay where we are and go around with you?"

"Yeah, why not?"

He went aboard, and then, before his engine even started, his bow began swinging away from the wharf, blowing sideways and threatening to sandwich *Silversark* between the dragger and a husky crabber. The skipper cursed his deckhand: "What the hell's the matter wit' you, you don't know to keep dat bow line till you're told to cast off?"

Silversark's crew and a dozen fishermen sprang into action, holding off the dragger, easing *Silversark* backward out of harm's way, keeping her clear of the crabber's mooring lines, guarding her rudder from being smashed against the wharf. Swinging faster, the dragger finally brought up with a jolt against a small fishing boat moored alongside the crabber. Jammed in the corner, *Silversark* was held off the wharf by a dozen strong arms.

The dragger started his engine. He cast off and rumbled out into the harbour, then moored along the face of the wharf.

Breathing heavily, we worked *Silversark* back to the berth just vacated by the dragger. When the incoming crabber finally arrived, we hauled *Silversark* up to the windward face of the wharf and held her off with our hands while the crabber docked. Then we eased her back alongside.

The government wharf really is no place for small yachts. Willie Joe Chiasson showed me the alternative: La Digue, a busy little basin full of smaller fishing boats. Somehow we had rowed right past La Digue on the way in. There is also a fine basin on Chéticamp Island. We didn't know about that one, either, but it's too far from town for cruising sailors to walk.

Willie Joe is a thoroughly contemporary fisherman, with a solid grasp not only of fishing but also of economics, electronics and tax law. He proudly showed off his new boat, built to his specifications in New Brunswick. Her Caterpillar turbo diesel drives her at 16 knots. Her autopilot is linked to the Loran C electronic navigational system. When Willie Joe leaves the harbour, he types the exact location of the traps he wants to haul. The Loran instructs the autopilot, which steers the boat right to the buoy.

"Some of these guys don't understand depreciation," said Willie Joe, standing in the pilot house. "You can write off a new boat at so much a year. That's a big help with your taxes. My old boat, down the wharf there, she's in great shape, all fibreglassed, good electronics, a new Volvo diesel. She's good for another ten years—and I sold her for $14,000. But with the help you can get on a new boat, and the depreciation, you're away better off building a new boat than fixing up an old one."

Willie Joe is also a musician, with a cassette to his credit. *Ce Petit Coin de l'Acadie* might be described as Francophone Country and Eastern: ballads and folk songs in 4/4 time performed on acoustic guitar, fiddle and bass. One of them is the lovely, mournful *Partons, la mer est belle*—almost the anthem of Chéticamp, local people say.

> *Partons, la mer est belle;*
> *Embarquons nous, pêcheurs,*
> *Guidons notre nacelle,*
> *Ramons avec ardeur.*

Row with ardour? *Silversark*'s crew knew about that one.

Chéticamp's musical hot-spot is The Doryman tavern on a Saturday afternoon. It's a big tavern, but it was packed and rocking. Men in T-shirts and baseball caps, women in shorts and summer dresses, laughing waitresses threading their way through the tables with trays of beer held aloft.

Donny LeBlanc was playing when we arrived, a tall, angular young fiddler with a fiery, passionate style, accompanied by Hilda Chiasson on piano and Gélas Larade on bass guitar. When LeBlanc stepped down, he was replaced by Arthur Muise, a sweet, smooth player who is LeBlanc's second cousin. People from the audience, inspired by rhythm and beer, clambered up on the stage and stepdanced, arms and upper bodies held still, feet twinkling and tapping. The music went on all afternoon.

We had already made acquaintances in Chéticamp—a

woman Lulu had met in the laundromat, a couple of fishermen from the wharf, an old friend from New Waterford, a teacher named Tommy Larade who runs deep-sea fishing tours. Mark had gone with him the previous day, bringing back a nice cod for supper. It was a convivial scene; if a person lived in Chéticamp, it would be easy to make it a Saturday ritual.

But the afternoon was sullied by our pointless, puritanical liquor laws. In Canada, children are not allowed in taverns, period. In Holland, in Denmark, Mark simply goes with us. We drink beer and he drinks pop. Canadian taverns could provide segregated areas where families might sit together, or outside spaces like the terrace of a British pub. But no. Parents can't be trusted to guide children towards sane drinking habits. Only the provincial government can do that.

So we spent the afternoon ducking in and out of The Doryman, checking on Mark as he took photographs, talked with passersby and just sat on the steps outside, listening to the music. Albert and Marcelle LeBlanc came by and took him for a drive. After that, we tried to smuggle him into the back of the tavern, just inside the door, but a sharp-eyed waiter ejected him. Well, that's his job.

We left earlier than we intended. We had come to hear the music: we wound up playing hide-and-seek. The hell with it.

Église St. Pierre, the imposing stone church with its lofty silver spire, is just a few steps from the government wharf. The most popular mass is on Saturday night, which leaves Sunday clear for other activities. Mark and I arrived a few moments late, and saw no empty seats. A wiry little man in a flowered sports shirt jumped up and led us to a pew.

The interior is high and airy, decorated with elaborate murals and fine carving. The mass was entirely in French: *Notre Seigneur, le Saint Esprit, la Sainte Vierge.* Cape Breton's Acadian communities are clustered around Chéticamp and Isle Madame; many are almost assimilated, while the Acadians who migrated into the industrial towns around Sydney and Glace Bay have not even been granted an Acadian school. So a French mass is a rarity. Even in D'Escousse, the French mass draws only a minority; the big Saturday night mass is in English.

The Diocese also has a problem finding francophone priests. The priest in Chéticamp was Father Bill Burke. Father Bill comes from Main-à-Dieu, an Acadian village near Louisbourg, and spent some years in Isle Madame. He has worked hard to recover his French, and that night his words rang out strong and certain. He has a clear, strong singing voice and a good sense of humour; his repertoire of comic songs has enlivened many a party.

After church, we talked on the steps. I remarked on the splendour of the church.

"They're very proud of the church, which is a mixed blessing," said Bill. He laughed. "You have to go on bent and bleeding knee to get money for adult religious education around here—but if it's for the church building you've got it in two weeks, no problem.

"It used to be cream-coloured inside, and quite dark. You had to be right up against things to see them. People from Quebec supervised the redecoration, a firm that specializes in old churches. They recommended four shades of grey, and they were absolutely right. All the details come right out now."

I was struck by the fact that it was absolutely full, and the congregation looked prosperous—like the town itself.

"It's generally full on a Saturday night," Bill said. "Chéticamp is an extraordinary place, you know, and it's not just the Acadian factor. They make big money from fishing, yes, but they've also made fortunes in tourism. That's just an extension of their natural hospitality, and they do it really well."

He reached out to stop two women who were passing by.

"Do you know Flora's Gift Shop?" asked Bill.

"Of course," I said. René LeFort has made an extraordinary success of Flora's, featuring the hooked rugs which are Chéticamp's special form of folk art.

"Well," said Bill, "this is René LeFort's wife, Marie, and this is his mother-in-law, Flora. She started the business, and she still makes rugs."

"And don't you call me an old hooker, neither!" said Flora.

"How long are you going to be in Chéticamp?" asked Bill.
"I think we're sailing in the morning," I said.
Partons, la mer est belle . . .
But it was still blowing hard.

NEWFOUNDLAND

TO

LEEWARD

The wind was whistling at bedtime. It was still whistling at six A.M. In the cockpit, we listened to the forecast.

Strong southwesterlies dropping to moderate and then veering to moderate westerlies. All right: let's go.

I went to the bow to take the bag off the jib. Good Lord!

"What's wrong?" called Lulu.

"The jib stay's come adrift."

Had the turnbuckle been tightened properly in the first place? Maybe not. Three days of constant vibration had shaken it apart, leaving the stay disconnected at the deck.

"I'll slack the backstays," said Chris.

To connect the stay, we had to bend the mast forward until

the threads on the two ends of the turnbuckle engaged again. We tightened it up and took stock.

The wind remained blustery, but it was a clear, bright summer morning. Casting off forward, we let *Silversark*'s bow blow away from the wharf. As she fell away, we pushed off the stern. Taking the wind, she heeled to port, heading towards the rocky shore by the church.

"Ready about!" called Lulu. "Hard a-lee!"

With a snap of canvas, the little cutter wheeled around, heeled to starboard and tacked out into the harbour.

"Ease sheets!"

With the wind behind her, *Silversark* ran down the harbour, her bow wave roaring, a long creamy wake streaming astern.

"We're going out a lot faster than we came in," said Sonja.

"With a lot less effort, too," said Lulu.

Swinging past Point Enragée, we reached out to sea. Beyond Chéticamp Island, tall, steep seas began rolling in, lifting the boat and lowering her bodily as she ran along their spines.

"When we turn downwind again," I said, "she's going to roll. If we put her under the two headsails, we won't have to worry about the main boom swinging across."

"Let's try it," said Lulu.

Chris and I hoisted the jumbo, released the main halyard and pulled the sail down. Seven feet above the boom, it stopped.

"What the hell—?" I said, looking up. "Oh, *damn*! The halyard's jumped the sheave!"

Chris squinted aloft. The main halyard runs over a six-inch bronze sheave in a slot at the masthead. As the boat tossed, the halyard had slipped sideways, jamming itself between the sheave and the mast. The mainsail couldn't be raised or lowered.

My fault. You rig things like that jackass arrangement at the masthead when you're in a rush to launch, as we were in 1985. It's temporary, you say. But it works—and you never get around to fixing it up.

Well, now we would pay for it. Without the mainsail, we couldn't beat back to Chéticamp. Downwind, the only available harbours were Pleasant Bay—a really tight little river estuary— and Bay St. Lawrence, our destination, 35 miles away. Both would be difficult without the mainsail, perhaps impossible. The other downwind options were Newfoundland, maybe the Magdalen Islands, the North Shore of Quebec.

These thoughts raced through my mind in a flash. But I was also working on a solution. So was Lulu.

"Don," she said, "that topping lift was designed for this."

"Right," I said. "If we can get the sail free from the halyard, we can hoist it on the topping lift."

"How much line have you got aboard?" said Chris.

"Quite a bit. Why?"

"We could reeve two lines through two blocks and send them aloft on the topping lift," he said. "Then we'd have a new halyard, and we'd still have a topping lift."

"Terrific."

"How should I steer?" said Lulu.

"Just try to keep her from rolling," I said.

While Chris and Sonja rigged up the blocks and lines, I stood on the boom, clinging to the mast while I undid the shackle from the headboard of the sail, lurching heavily from side to side as the boat rolled. Don't complain, I told myself. You're unbelievably lucky. The sail was almost down when it jammed, so you don't have to go up the mast. It's a fine summer day. Chris is here. Imagine doing this in the fog, with just the three of us, the wind blowing hard and a rocky shore to leeward . . .

By the time I had the sail free and the halyard tied off against the mast, Chris and Sonja had the blocks and two lines ready to go aloft. Chris hoisted while Sonja and I paid out line. The two blocks rose smoothly to the masthead. We tied one line to the mainsail, the other to the end of the boom.

"We'll have to reef the main," I said. "That block's a good deal lower than the original sheave."

We tied in the reef.

"Back in business," said Chris. "Hoist away."

Nothing ever looked more beautiful than that broad tanbark mainsail, soaring up against the deep blue of the sky. *Silversark* heeled a little farther and shot forward.

"Swing her back on course," I said.

"What's the course?" Lulu asked, grinning.

I looked around and glanced at my watch. The repairs had

taken over an hour. Jogging offshore under the headsails, *Silversark* had travelled four or five miles. The coast was a broad smudge on the eastern horizon.

"Steer to clear that northern point of land," I said. "I'm going below to see if I can't figure out that Loran C."

"Good idea," said Lulu. "About time we used it."

Lulu bore off on a boisterous, rolling charge to the end of Cape Breton. I went below to study our newest electronic helper.

We had installed the Loran C the previous year for a trip to the Magdalens; we had never used it. In part, that was a matter of habit. Lulu and I both learned to navigate by dead reckoning, steering careful compass courses, estimating speeds, towing a taffrail log to get our distance run, and taking frequent bearings. That worked perfectly well for Eric the Red, Columbus and Leonard Pertus, and it worked for us, too.

Now I read the Loran C manual, and in half an hour it changed everything.

A Loran C receiver gathers signals from three or four widely separated transmitters and notes its magnetic bearing from each of them. Those bearing lines can cross in only one position. The Loran computes that position and flashes it on the screen. It is not always dead accurate, because radio waves travel at different rates across land and water and can be somewhat bent or refracted by mountains and other obstacles. But even a poor Loran fix will place the navigator within a few hundred yards of the true position.

Loran can also tell you how to get where you want to go. The navigator punches in the co-ordinates for a destination. That position is called a waypoint. Now the Loran calculates and announces the distance from the present position to the waypoint, the course to steer, the vessel's present speed and the time it will take to get there at that speed. When we are a tenth of a mile from a waypoint, our Loran beeps anxiously.

Loran does not replace the evidence of the eyes, the ears, the nose and common sense. But it is a powerful source of new evidence—and sometimes it provides the only hard evidence available. Unlike most navigators, Loran is just as happy—and just as accurate—in the fog as in the sunlight.

Looking at the chart, I noted the latitude and longitude of a point north of Cape St. Lawrence where we could turn south-eastward for the harbour of Bay St. Lawrence. I typed the co-ordinates into the Loran, and pressed GO. Bingo! Distance: 22 miles. Course to steer: 010 Magnetic. Present speed: 6.3 knots. Time to go: 3.5 hours. No: 21 miles now, and 3.3 hours to go. The Loran updates itself constantly. I checked the chart. The Loran agreed quite closely with my own calculations.

I came on deck and announced my findings.

"Steer 010. Twenty-one miles till we clear Cape St. Lawrence. We're doing 6.3 knots."

I felt like Merlin the Magician.

"Look," said Chris, pointing aloft. "Eagle." A bald eagle was circling in a thermal updraft, wings extended and motionless— "president," as Sam Slick said, "of all he surveys."

"When I was a kid, I thought they were in the Lord's Prayer," said Chris. "Deliver us from eagles."

Silversark drew closer to the round, abraded mountains which contain the most ancient rock in the province: Precambrian gabbros and gneisses, slivers of the Canadian Shield. North of Pleasant Bay, the mountains drop sheer into the sea; a shore road passes through a handful of houses at the hamlet of Red River, clinging to the cliffs for a dozen miles before it peters out. From there to Cape St. Lawrence and beyond, for twenty miles, there is no human habitation whatsoever.

Near the end of the road is a unique institution: Gampo Abbey, the only Tibetan Buddhist monastery in North America. The abbey sits on a shelf of land high above the sea: a dramatic setting conducive to contemplation, meditation and study. A Buddhist from Oregon calls it "Big Sur—but colder."

The abbess, Pema Chodron, is middle-aged, American-born, quiet and calm. Nova Scotia's five-hundred-odd Buddhists, based mainly in Halifax, are followers of the late Chogyam Trungpa, Rinpoche—a Tibetan who took it as his mission to meld Buddhism with Western lifestyles. The Rinpoche, then based in Colorado, apparently had a vision, says Pema, "of a really good place, not just for Buddhism, but a place where wisdom could flourish. He asked people to try and find this place, and someone suggested Nova Scotia. He came to see, and said, Yes, it's Nova Scotia.

"It really is a very special place. The people are very open-minded and of the earth; they're not prejudiced, their attitude is live and let live. Lots of places would really freak out to have this foreign religion sort of plunking down in the middle of them, but here they just judge you by what you do. There doesn't seem to be a lot of fear."

Silversark was still flying, though the breeze was losing power. Chris was experimenting and designing again, pointing out a hook in the leech of the staysail, thinking about the gossamer sail *Silversark* needed for light air. We went over the boat together with a notepad, noting possible improvements.

"What do you think of her, overall?" I asked.

"She's great. She feels really solid, she's easy to handle, she sails really well, and she leaves a clean wake," he said. "She's turned out to be exactly what you wanted her to be."

Once again, the crew was slathering suntan lotion and feeling mildly unwell. Chris, in particular, was tired: the previous night, he had driven to Bay St. Lawrence with his bicycle on the roof of the Volvo and left the car with a lobsterman named Fred Lawrence. Fred would keep an eye out for us and tow us through the narrow entrance if necessary.

Then Chris cycled back—55 miles of mountain riding at night, through switchbacks and gorges, against a punishing wind. He got back at 11:30, just half an hour later than he predicted. By midday he was bagged, and he went below for a nap.

The wind eased further. The boat moved more and more slowly. The lighter the wind, the more erratically the boat rolls. People get sick in light winds more than in heavy ones, and the crew was feeling queasy as we closed the coast again at Cape St. Lawrence.

"Look at that cove," said Lulu. "What a spot! I wonder why there isn't a village there." The spot, we later learned, was Lowland Cove—and there once was a village there.

As we rolled slowly past the tip of Cape Breton Island, out of the Gulf and into Cabot Strait, the Loran beeped. Time to turn into St. Lawrence Bay, the crescent of coastline which defines Cape Breton's short northern coastline. I got out the binoculars and scanned the shoreline.

"What are you looking for?"

"There's supposed to be a lighthouse on Cape St. Lawrence."

"Well, there's no lighthouse over there."

"Then maybe we're not where we think we are."

"There's nowhere else we could be."

"I know, but—aha! Some bloody lighthouse! Look!"

Nobody else could see it: I was the only one with binoculars. It was another wretched skeleton tower.

At two o'clock we jibed and sailed slowly into St. Lawrence Bay, peering ahead for the entrance to Deadman's Cove, the harbour of Bay St. Lawrence. The wind came back from the south, building quickly and steadily. A mile into the bay, and *Silversark* was foaming along. Another mile, and we lowered the jumbo.

"That wind's blowing straight out of the entrance," I muttered. "We're not going to be able to sail in there."

"Fred should be looking for us," Chris said.

"Be nice not to trouble him, though. I just wish I knew for sure how that wind's blowing in the gut."

"What about the VHF?" said Lulu.

Ah! The handheld VHF radio was another unfamiliar modern convenience—partly, no doubt, because we had never been able to talk to anyone on it. VHF is the standard marine radio system for commercial traffic, but boaters in our area rely on CB. Since we never used the VHF, we often forgot that we had it aboard.

I fished it out, and Lulu started calling.

"Any stations, any stations—this is *Silversark*, Victor Oscar 3460. *Silversark*, Victor Oscar 3460. Do you read me?"

Crackling, and static, and a faint voice.

"This is *Silversark*," said Lulu. "I can't make you out."

"This is *Bonny Susan*," said the crackling voice. "We're a whale-watching boat."

"Can you tell me whether the wind in Bay St. Lawrence is blowing out of the gut?"

"Come back on that?"

"Is the wind at the entrance blowing out of the gut?"

Bonny Susan didn't get it. Lulu explained: in an engineless sailboat, we couldn't sail dead to windward in a narrow channel.

"But there's a big white fishing boat right behind us now," Lulu said. "Maybe we can get a tow from him, if we need one."

"That's me," said *Bonny Susan*, with a chuckle. The skipper steered right up beside us. He was a lanky, long-haired man in a shapeless Greek fisherman's cap. A boatload of tourists snapped pictures.

"If you need a tow when we come back in, we'll pick you up," said the skipper. "Right now we're gonna go find some whales." He wheeled around and went back towards Cape St. Lawrence. *Silversark* charged on towards the harbour.

The northern tip of Cape Breton is big country, too, but deceptive: it doesn't look as big as it is. Westward are the high bluffs of Cape St. Lawrence, eastward the cliffs and crags of Cape North. The bay recedes in a long, shallow curve between these headlands. At the centre of its arc, the highlands slope down to low green hills along the shore. This is where the village of Bay St. Lawrence is located, and the hills look bucolic and gentle until you see that the houses are mere dots on their faces. Things are out of scale; the hills are twice as big as they seem to be, like a gigantic man so well proportioned that he looks normal until you stand beside him.

Silversark bowled along—and then sailed right out of the wind, half a mile from the entrance. We could see the wind behind us, a band of ruffled water stretching seaward.

Becalmed. No matter how we jigged with the sails, the ship turned idly this way and that, a plaything of stray currents.

"Let's row," said Sonja.

Singing "The Volga Boatmen", we shipped the oars again. On the rounded hill beside the entrance stood a gigantic crucifix. An ominous portent. We were close enough to see the steel cladding on the east wall of the channel and the rock breakwater on the west. A fish plant stood just inside, and beyond the fish plant was a house and barn. Fred's place, said Chris. With the binoculars we could identify the Volvo. An orange boat cleared the entrance and steered towards us.

"I think that's Fred," said Chris.

The open boat was *Suzie Q*, a 20-footer driven by a big black

Mercury outboard. The sunburnt man at the wheel wore shorts, a T-shirt and a ponytail.

"That's Fred," said Chris.

Suzie Q circled and came alongside.

"Hi, Chris," said Fred. "Give me a bow and stern line. I'll tow you alongside."

THE QUICK

AND

THE

DEAD

"**N**obody really sees this shore except the lobstermen," said Marg Lawrence. "It's fantastic. I'd like to make a film of it. I'd use classical music for the sound track, and I'd show the shapes and colours of the cliffs. There are caves and arches, rock pinnacles, bird colonies—and nobody sees it except the lobstermen."

"I should go out with someone," I said.

"Come with me if you like," said Fred.

"When?"

"Tomorrow. You'll get a feed of lobster out of it, anyway."

"Don't worry about that."

Fred smiled. "Oh, you're gonna earn 'em."

Marg had come to the wharf with her two young daughters,

Ria and Carmen. Chris and Sonja had tossed their gear on the wharf, packed the Volvo, hugged and kissed and roared off towards Montreal, leaving a big lonely gap behind them. We toasted our arrival and then went up to the Lawrences' home for a shower.

Here, too, the southeaster is the dreaded wind, battering the village several times a year.

"See that skiff out there?" Fred said. "One time I had it tied to the shop, and I saw it flapping like a flag at the end of the rope. Marg said, 'What are you going to do about that?' '*Do?*' I said. *Do?* I'm not going to do *anything*.'

"You can tell when a southeaster's coming by the clouds. The clouds lie right on the mountain tops, and they come pouring down the face of the mountain like smoke from dry ice. The farther down the clouds come, the worse the blow is going to be. It's the same in South Africa, at Table Mountain, before a bad blow. They say the table-cloth is set."

The barn we saw from seaward is actually Fred's boatshop. Inside is a replica of Joshua Slocum's famous *Spray*, the oyster boat in which Slocum—a Nova Scotian—made the first single-handed circumnavigation of the world between 1895 and 1898.

The hull of Fred's *Spray* was built by Chéticamp Boat-builders to traditional standards, like Slocum's. Balks of birch and oak, thick pine planking, hanging and lodging knees. Fred had installed a diesel, built the deck, shaped the bowsprit. He had been at it for more than six years. He hoped to finish in two more years and take his family sailing. Shipbuilding is in his blood: he is distantly related to W.D. Lawrence, the builder and owner of the largest wooden ship ever built in Atlantic Canada.

"It's good to have people come along who did build their own boat and got it finished and went sailing," Fred said, latching the shed door. "It's kind of . . . reassuring."

At dawn, it's cool—even in July. I wore a sweater, wool socks and insulated coveralls. That was just right: the weather stayed windy and cold all day.

Lobster traps are laid out in "strings," each trap marked by distinctively painted floats which distinguish one person's traps from another's. With his small, handy boat, Fred sets his traps close in, ducking among the rocks and reefs. As he reaches each float, he throws the engine in neutral, gaffs the buoy and hauls it aboard. He flips its line onto an overhead pulley and then down around the hauler, where a grooved disc catches the line and hauls it in. Up comes the trap, dripping and kelp-covered. Fred flips it sideways onto the boat's rail.

Fred opens the top and clears out the contents—lobsters, crabs, sculpins, flounders. In one trap we found a wolffish, the first I ever saw—an ugly monster, with bulging eyes and a mouth bristling with sharp, pointed teeth. Fish go into the fresh bait pail and lobsters onto a wooden counter partitioned into small boxes. Crabs go overboard.

A surprising number of lobsters go back overboard, too. Why? Fred holds one out and turns it over, revealing it as a "berried" hen. Under the tail, fastened to the small appendages known as swimmerets, are black, spongelike masses of up to 100,000 eggs. That's the future harvest. Don't disturb it.

My job is to measure the lobsters, bind their claws with elastics, and drop them through one of two holes into a bin filled with circulating salt water. The gauge is a bronze plate shaped like a wide, shallow H. One end of the gauge goes in the lobster's eye, the other down the back of the carapace, the hard shell of the body.

"Don't worry about hurting him," says Fred, "his eye just rotates out of the way. Look." Sure enough, the eye just swivels.

If the carapace is too long for the gauge, he's a keeper. A big one which "makes the gauge" on the wide side is a valuable "market" lobster; those who make the gauge on the other side are "canners." A lobster which fits in the gauge so tightly that you can pick him up by lifting the gauge is a "hanger." You can keep him.

To band a lobster, hold it from the top and bring its foreclaws together. Lobsters have plenty of strength to close their pincers, but virtually no power to open them. Slip the band pliers into a thick, fat elastic, slide the band over the claw and release the pliers. For a big market lobster, use two bands.

During the day, I band dozens of lobsters. Every one is different. Some thrash their tails furiously, or arch their backs and brandish their foreclaws, like angry swan-divers. Others lie motionless, resigned. Some are preparing to moult, and sharp lines down their carapaces mark the place where the shell will split. Cocks moult annually; hens moult in alternate years. With each moult, the animal grows 10 to 15 per cent.

Every lobster has one claw which is heavy and blunt, shaped to hold or crush, while the other is sharper and slimmer, designed for ripping and tearing. Some are right-handed, others left-handed. Some have claws missing; others have one tiny stublike claw, regenerated after the loss of the original claw.

While I size and band the lobsters, Fred tosses the old bait in a pail—soft, blanched fish skulls and skeletons. When the pail is full, he dumps it on the beach. If he dumped it overboard, it would foul the bottom. He baits the trap with herring, mackerel, hake heads from the fish plant, whatever is cheap and available.

This shore is bold, dramatic, fractured and unforgiving. Sharp pinnacle rocks rise sheer from the water. The cliffs tower above us, grass and moss and tiny spruces clinging to their faces. Sea-caves, eroded by the waves, vanish into darkness at the base of the cliffs. Tiny beaches lie in deep clefts of rock.

The rocks have a tortured appearance: abrupt, sharp shapes, angled striations, rapid shifts of colour from pink to white, rust, green, grey, black. The geology looks like frozen violence: layers of rock bent, twisted, broken, folded, thrust upward, knocked sideways, pressed downward.

The impression of violence is accurate. The geology of northern Cape Breton is convoluted, and this little stretch of coast bears the record of ancient volcanoes, mighty glaciers, up-tilted seafloors. On a geological map of the province, great reaches of the mainland are pink, taupe and yellow: Devonian granite, Ordovician slate, Early Carboniferous sandstones, shales and conglomerates. Cape Breton, by contrast, is a riot of colour: tuffs and gneisses and schists, basalt, andesite, rhyolite, coal, shale, marble, quartzite . . . Between Money Point and Bay St. Lawrence, at least four regimes of rock are visible: metamorphic and volcanic formations at Money Point, pink granite at Cape North, a 130-foot-thick strip of marble, and the sandstones and shales on which Bay St. Lawrence itself is built.

To a newcomer, the rocks are spectacular, colourful, wildly

varied, but essentially anonymous. For the lobsterman, each spot has a name. Grassy, The Shark's Nose, MacIntosh's. The vein of marble—which runs northeastward to Newfoundland and on through Cape Breton to mainland Nova Scotia—is called White Rock. Shag's Roost is a precipice on which cormorants nest. The whole rock face below them is stained white with their guano.

Out to seaward is the misty profile of a killer island. St. Paul sits in the fogs and tide-races of Cabot Strait, a trap for unwary shipping, rising like a sunken peak from depths of 120 and 130 fathoms. The great stream of the St. Lawrence flows around it, alternately aided and opposed by the tides and flayed by the winds. The water is as tumultuous as the geology.

"Look, you can steam out there for eight miles in calm water," says fisherman Paul Bonin, "and then all of a sudden you find yourself in fifteen or twenty-foot seas. You might get that for a mile, and then it's calm again right out to the island."

A gift-shop map of St. Paul Island shows more than sixty shipwrecks. Local people put the number nearer two hundred. Scuba divers say that wrecked ships lie stacked on the steep underwater cliffs. As recently as December 1989, a savage winter storm sank three vessels in these waters, with the loss of forty-seven men.

Just beyond Money Point, the eastern boundary of this little cusp of north-facing coast, the bows of two ships lie rusting on the rocks. The point itself was named for a French pay ship lost there; people used to go out carrying long poles armed with tallow, probing the bottom and bringing up French coins. Lumber Cove commemorates the loss of a lumber vessel whose cargo helped the villagers build homes and outbuildings. The cross on the hilltop at the harbour entrance marks the graves of several seamen drowned when a vessel was lost at Wreck Cove.

The shores remember death, but the sea is full of life. Loons, terns, shags, gulls and guillemots fly past the boat. Eagles circle overhead. Pilot whales browse in the distance, heaving through the water like synchronized swimmers. Fred often sees deer on the cliffs, and occasionally moose and bear.

By midmorning, Fred has hauled the traps in his outside strings all the way to Money Point. He works his way back closer to the shore—close enough that his outboard motor sometimes rubs on the rocks. Near the Shark's Nose, he puts the engine in neutral, drifting while we eat lunch. With his ponytail and his tabouli salad, this fisherman is very much his own man. We've talked all morning, in that sparse, thoughtful, intermittent fashion that goes with shared labour. Fred has become a trusted, familiar companion, though our friendship isn't twenty-four hours old.

Fred was raised in Eliot, Maine, the son of a Nova Scotian father and a mother from Prince Edward Island. His brother drifted up to the tip of Cape Breton fifteen years ago on a holiday. After a memorable party in Meat Cove, he bought some land and called Fred and his father. The three of them built the house that Fred and Marg live in. The other two later returned to the States; Fred bought a lobster license and settled in.

Marg's father was a Swiss Guard from Vatican City who emigrated to Canada and sired nine children on an Ontario farm. Marg thus has three citizenships: Swiss, Canadian and Popish, if not Polish. Until the children came along, Marg had her own lobster license and fished commercially herself. *Suzie Q* was originally her boat, not Fred's.

"Marg was written up in the Toronto *Star* and places like that," Fred recalls. "But that caused some problems in the community. It's not all that unusual for a woman to go fishing here. A couple of women fish their own boats out of Bay St. Lawrence. Lots of women here fish with their husbands, too." Families fish together as well; we often saw boats heading out with husband, wife and a couple of children aboard.

Our lunches finished, we go back to catching lobsters.

Despite its importance, the lobster remains a somewhat mysterious crustacean. The North American lobster can grow to as much as 45 pounds, in record cases, and live to hoary old ages. Loretta, a recently famous specimen, was caught off Lockeport in June 1987 and shipped to Vancouver. She weighed 21 pounds, and fisheries biologists estimated her age at 150 years. Moved by her uniqueness, Vancouver fish dealer Wylie Costain flew back to Nova Scotia with her and returned her to the sea.

Biologists describe lobsters as "opportunistic" feeders, a polite way of describing the garbagemen of the ocean floor. They eat whatever comes along, alive or dead, plant or animal, including clams, crabs, starfish, sea urchins, sponges and even occasional stones and nails. They live in any depth of water from the low-tide mark to 1,300 feet. They seem to migrate between deeper and shallower water at various points in their life cycle. Little is known about these migrations, but they may be related to breeding cycles.

The hen is sexually active just after moulting, and if a cock approaches her at that season she whips him with her antennae until he flips her on her back and mounts her — "face to face, just like people," as one old fisherman put it. A cock lobster's foremost swimmerets are grooved; placed together, they make a channel through which sperm can flow into a chamber called the spermatheca near the base of the hen's tail.

The sperm stay there until the hen ovulates, as much as a year later. As the eggs pass backward along her body towards her swimmerets, she releases some of the stored sperm to fertilize them. The eggs may remain glued to her swimmerets for another year. Eventually she rises on the tips of her walking legs and fans her tail, hatching the eggs and releasing the larvae.

The larvae, about the size of a mosquito, swim to the surface, feed on plankton, and moult four times in their first three to six weeks of life. They are attractive prey for birds and fish, and only 1 to 5 per cent survive. After six weeks, the survivors migrate to the bottom for good.

Historically, lobster has been available only during the actual lobster seasons, which vary somewhat from district to district. Scarcity alternated with oversupply, creating a chaotic market, and keeping fishermen poor. Today, however, the industry provides premium-quality live lobster all year long. Only ten miles from our home on Isle Madame is the development which makes this possible: a high-tech "dryland pound," based on a new understanding of lobsters and of markets.

Lobsters react dramatically to water temperature. At a steady 18 to 20 degrees Celsius, they can grow to market size in twenty-six months; in the cold Atlantic, they may take up to twelve years. Spawning, too, is governed by temperature. And when Clearwater Lobsters Ltd. discovered that lobsters essentially go dormant in icy water, they had the key to a world market.

In Clearwater's $12-million plant near Arichat, prime live lobsters are sorted into shallow plastic trays, each lobster in its own individual compartment. The trays go into huge racks which reach clear to the ceilings of the cavernous holding rooms. Clean sea-water—24,000 gallons per hour, chilled almost to the freezing point—flows constantly through the trays. At that temperature, lobsters do not eat, grow or moult, but they retain their weight, their texture and their taste, drawing only on the nutrients in their blood. Suspended in this way, a robust lobster can be kept fresh for up to a year.

Assured of a steady supply of lobsters, Clearwater began airlifting lobster to customers everywhere from Amsterdam to Tokyo. Today, Maritime lobster is a Christmas tradition in Paris and a regular menu item in Frankfurt and Seoul.

Clearwater grew from a single roadside lobster stand operated by president John Risley to become a corporate empire with 1987 sales around $350 million. With plants in Newfoundland, Nova Scotia, Quebec, Georgia, Britain and France, Clearwater was processing a variety of seafood and employing more than three thousand people. It has since encountered choppy financial waters, but in the Maritimes it stands second only to the venerable giant of the industry, National Sea Products, and it is the undisputed leader of the lobster business.

In the shelter of the cliffs, the southeasterly breeze had scarcely touched us. Off the low sandstone hills near the harbour, the wind was screeching. Up above, the clouds were pouring down the face of the mountains, like a slow, misty waterfall. A southeaster in the making?

"The clouds aren't very far down," said Fred. "We'll get a good breeze, but nothing to worry about."

By midafternoon we were back at the Victoria Co-op Fisheries plant, filling the fuel tanks and unloading our lobsters. Fred reached in the bin, selected eight lobsters and dropped them into a pail.

"Here."

"Fred, that's far too many. One for each of us is plenty."

"Go ahead, take 'em. You earned 'em."

Could *you* resist a determined man forcing lobsters on you?

The wind was shrieking through *Silversark*'s rigging. She was practically woven to the end of the wharf with heavy lines.

"I was worried," said Lulu. "No. I wasn't worried, I was *terrified*. After what Fred said about the southeasters—and when I saw the clouds pouring down the mountains—and you were out in that little boat with Fred—and I thought, I'm going to lose my boat and my husband all in the same afternoon—"

"She was *freakin'*," said Mark. "She made me go and ask one of the fishermen how bad it was going to be."

"He was really nice," Lulu said. "He came over and told me not to worry, it was just going to be a gale. And then he sent over a whole feed of snow crab legs."

"No," said Mark. "That was another guy."

"I wish I knew who to thank," said Lulu.

"I rode a horse," said Mark.

"What?"

"Lori Cox took us out to their place," said Lulu. "Her husband, Dennis, is the skipper of the whale-watching boat. They've got a little farm halfway to Meat Cove, right beside a creek. Mark rode one of their horses."

"He ran right in the barn," said Mark. "If I hadn't ducked my head—boy! I'd have been dead meat."

Lobster for dinner. While the water boiled, Mark hypnotized the lobsters, which makes the dinner party much more comfortable for the lobster. He held each lobster upside down, with the pincers and the head on the cockpit seat. Then he slowly stroked them, moving his fingers upward along the back and over the curve of the tail. In a matter of minutes, he had all eight lobsters standing on their heads, blissed out, motionless, entranced.

We popped them into the boiling water, and they were dead and cooking before they even awoke. We steamed them all, ate four, and put four in the cooler. *Un embarras d'homard*, the French might call it: an embarrassment of lobster. I remembered a Cape Breton professor sitting in his elegant dining room, eating lobsters and strawberries and drinking white wine.

"I love living in a depressed region," he smiled. "One lives so well."

Next morning, Fred and I hoisted Lulu to the masthead, where she rove the main halyard through a block shackled to the masthead and fed a length of yellow polypropylene rope through the original sheave as a spare halyard. Later, up on the wharf, we met a stocky, ruddy-faced man climbing off a boat called *Hell's Angel*.

"I hear you're from Isle Madame," he said.

"That's right."

"So am I." He put out his hand. "Paul Bonin. You know my brother Frank."

"You're Frankie's brother?" I said.

"You must be Cecilia Poirier's brother, too," said Lulu.

"That's right."

In Halifax, you might identify yourself by saying, "I'm George Smith; I'm a lawyer with Trix and Squeezum." In Cape Breton you say, "I'm John MacNeil; I'm Red MacNeil's son from Rear Barra Glen." Your new acquaintance says, "Oh, you must be Theresa's nephew, then!" Cape Bretoners identify themselves not by their occupations but by their location in a web of people and places. Occupations are slippery and variable: the same man may be a fisherman, a woodcutter, a carpenter, a lumber-yard clerk or a school-bus driver, depending on circumstances. He may be several of these at the same time. But he is always Red MacNeil's son: that, at least, never changes.

Paul Bonin is the current chairman of the Bay St. Lawrence Harbour Committee, which has transformed the port over the past ten years. In 1980, when Lulu and I were here on our honeymoon, Bay St. Lawrence didn't even have a wharf. Now it has a glorious one, which cost $1.7 million. Paul's committee is proposing a renewed electric system, plank cladding and an extension of the cribbing down the shore towards the Co-op.

"We got the wharf through Allan J.," Paul says. ("Allan J." is Allan J. MacEachen, who represented this riding for a generation.) "This little place lands a hell of a lot of fish—seven million pounds of groundfish and three million of shellfish last year. Allan J. got onto the Minister of Fisheries, and his assistant called down to see if there was a road in here. Can you imagine that? They thought they'd have to come by helicopter. Yes, I told him, we've got a road—and electric lights and indoor plumbing too, boy, we've got everything but a wharf.

"Well, the Minister came down and he was amazed at the activity he found here. There's fifty-four boats fishing out of here. That's what got us the wharf. There's fishermen here that are millionaires, you know."

Millionaires?

"Oh, yeah. And that Co-op over there, that's got $2 million in assets, $7 million in sales, and it don't owe a cent to anyone. We've got a blast freezer over there, and a cutting line. We've got plants and buying stations in other harbours, and we pay a good dividend to our members. We own our own tractor-trailers and everything. We had to buy a new truck this year, $195,000, and we paid cash for it. Just wrote a cheque. We can have fish from here on a supermarket shelf in Arizona in twenty-two hours after landing it. You going to be around here long?"

Couple of days, likely.

"Why don't you come up to the house tonight for supper?"

"Well, we're going to Dennis and Lori's."

"Tomorrow night, then," said Paul. "I'll pick you up."

Dennis Cox loves the individuality and the strength of character of his neighbours—and he has a fine ear for accent and word play. A neighbour once claimed to have "a horse so skinny we had to tie a knot in his tail to keep him from slipping through the collar, so skinny we had to put a blanket on him to keep his heart from gettin' sunburned." Another said it was ten miles to Sydney "but maybe only eight in a big car like the one you got there."

He tells about Billy, a local fishing skipper who speaks like a machine gun. One morning a shore-bound kibitzer called Billy on the radio, asking how the fishing was going.

Billy politely replied that there had been some mackerel around earlier, but they had disappeared. "Wuzsome-mackr'lherezmornin'but'eyregone."

"What's that, Billy?"

"Wuzsomemackr'lherezmornin'but'eyre*gone*," Billy repeated.

"Come back on that, Billy?" said the kibitzer.

"Why...don't...you...clean...the...shit...out...of ...your...ears?" said Billy.

Dennis laughs and passes food. Dinner is lobster, crab legs, spaghetti with a tangy sauce and a fresh garden salad with cheese. The Coxes live at the mouth of the tiny Salmon River, in the kind of homesteader's house that was erected in the 1970s by people who read *Harrowsmith* and *The Mother Earth News* and took courses at The Shelter Institute. An open plan centred on a massive stone chimney. Glass on the south wall, thick insulation in the north wall. Green plants, open shelves, natural pine.

"A fellow came in out of a winter storm into a glebe house where three priests were sitting around the fire talking," says Dennis. "He was kind of a nobody, this fellow, and the priests didn't pay too much attention to him. Finally one of them turned to him and said, 'Well, now, where have you come from tonight?'

" 'From Hell, Father,' said the fellow.

" 'I see', said the priest, not really hearing him. 'And how are things there?'

" 'Same as here, Father,' says the fellow. 'So many priests at the fire I couldn't get close enough to get warm.' "

After supper, Dennis gets out his flat-top and sings with Lori—Appalachian songs, Woody Guthrie songs, comic songs. Hah! Do they know the words to a parody Mark and I know only in fragments?

> Oh, dear, what can the matter be?
> Seven old ladies got stuck in the lavatory
> They were there from Sunday to Saturday
> Nobody knew they were there.

Lori knows the man who would know the words: Dennis Ryan of Ryan's Fancy, now a money manager with Central Guaranty Trust in Halifax. But she knows another song which delights Mark:

> There were five, five, constipated men

In the Bible's Book of Moses . . .

The first constipated man was Moses, who "took the tablets." The second was Balaam, who couldn't move his ass, and the third was Joseph: "they wouldn't let him go." The fourth was Job, who couldn't do the job. We sang the song at sea throughout the rest of the voyage. If you passed us in the fog off Scatarie Island, you could have identified us by the singing:

Oh, the fifth, fifth, constipated man
Was Solomon: he sat for forty years . . .

The Coxes have toured professionally as a folk duo and made a record which includes several of their own songs.

I've lived in your cities and I've lived in your schemes,
It's a long road winding to the land of my dreams,
But I'll make it back to your country streams
Walking down freedom trail.

Their own freedom trail was the Trans-Canada Highway, which brought them across the Canso Causeway in 1971. Their 1955 Jeep pick-up contained pregnant goats, pregnant rabbits, a pregnant dog and a pregnant Lori. They lived in a wood-floored tent the first couple of winters. Then they built a barn and moved into that. They did all the rural things — clearing land, gardening, raising animals, cutting wood, building, fishing.

After a few years, Dennis bought a lobster boat and a license. The boat was supposedly eleven years old. It was in Dingwall, on the eastern side of Money Point.

"We got it launched and tried to start the engine," Dennis remembers. "Before we got it started, it drained the battery. So I got it jump-started from my truck battery and just took off into a northwest wind. I never reflected that nobody was looking for me, and if the engine stalled I couldn't restart it. It was quite a trip, right into the wind and the waves, spray flying back over the boat. But I made it." He laughs.

"God must love fools. A couple of years later the whole side fell out of the boat just after I'd bought another one. The good metal left in the nails was no thicker than a diaper pin. It was a good twenty years old and more."

Not all the idealistic homesteaders of the 1960s and 1970s succeeded, as the Coxes did. Across the Salmon River is a bizarre little castle made of wood and stone, looking out over Cabot Strait. It was built by a dreamy hipoid couple named Jim and Darcy. David Rasmussen, another incomer who now teaches at the high school in Dingwall, rented them a cottage in Meat Cove and helped them to buy the land. They built the castle out of odds and ends. The entire roof came from another building and was pinched together to fit on the little castle.

The couple eventually went back to the States and split up. Jim returned early one June, and David learned that he had commenced a fast in mid-May, seeking spiritual purification.

He was already very weak. David moved him to the Meat Cove cottage and consulted doctors, including a psychiatrist. Eventually he began eating — but only nuts and dates. He died in the third week of July. He is buried in North Sydney. Fred Lawrence, who is a stonemason, carved a headstone.

But for every such demented pilgrim there were a dozen other settlers for whom the move to places like rural Cape Breton worked out very well. After twenty years on their farms and in their villages, the young homesteaders of the 1960s and 1970s have really become a distinct layer of immigration, like the Scots, the Irish, the Loyalists, the Newfoundlanders, the postwar Dutch farmers. Now they are middle-aged, and their children are native Cape Bretoners. Yesterday's hippies are today's teachers, carpenters, weavers, school-bus drivers, authors, contractors, consultants, sculptors. They operate craft shops, nurseries, boatyards, sawmills. A surprising number are fishermen, farmers or forestry workers — just as they set out to be.

And the settlers have had a disproportionate influence on rural Cape Breton. Many of them brought new and unexpected skills with them; equally important, they filled a demographic gap. Rural Maritimers have normally been obliged to leave their communities to find work, and have returned only to retire. The result is a double-humped demographic profile: lots of children, lots of senior citizens, relatively few people in the age group between twenty and sixty, which normally dominates economic and political activity. The settlers slipped right into that gap. The Cape Breton ethos is both generous and tolerant, and in general, Cape Bretoners have made the newcomers welcome. The relationship has been a good one all around.

Like some others, Lori and Dennis now winter in Halifax, where Lori is doing graduate work in sociology, with a thesis on the depopulation of Cape Breton coastal communities. They return to Bay St. Lawrence each summer. The whale-watching business is recent, but it fits well with the lobster fishing. Dennis hauls his traps early and is back at the wharf in time for a 10:00 whale trip. He does two more trips during the afternoon. His clients see whales on more than 95 per cent of his trips; if they don't, their next trip is free.

Fred Lawrence shakes his head in admiration: to establish the whale-watching business, Dennis had to obtain a master mariner's ticket, and he has to equip and maintain his boat to Canadian Steamship Inspection standards. None of this is cheap, but a steady stream of tourists finds its way to the wharf.

Mark went out twice without seeing a whale. Dennis was chagrined. To be skunked twice was almost unprecedented. Lulu went with Mark the third time. Steaming from the harbour and turning east, towards Money Point, they encountered a large pod of pilot whales, browsing near the surface and surging headfirst out of the water in groups of two and three, "spy-hopping," as Dennis called it. But one group of whales stayed together, focussed on something in the water. They came closer and closer. Dennis inched the boat nearer.

In the middle of the group of whales was a young whale, deeply gashed—by a propeller, perhaps—and unconscious, possibly dead already. The other whales nosed up underneath it, raising it to the life-giving air. The whales were talking, too, with sonarlike beeps and whistles. They showed no fear of the boat; indeed, they almost seemed to be looking for help.

The people on the boat had no help to offer, only their heartsick sympathy, expressed in reverent whispers. And so the event became a strange kind of funeral, whales and people gathered around the dying calf. Two species, meeting at the junction of air and water, full of sorrow and wonder, contemplating the end of a life.

When he first came to Bay St. Lawrence, Dennis Cox fished

with Joe Curtis. Joe doesn't fish any more, not since his heart attack. He is a short, cheerful man in his sixties, wearing a baseball cap. He owns the rounded, grassy hill with the big cross on it. His house and workshop are built on a shelf cut from the hillside, looking southward over the harbour towards the village.

Down below the workshop, three husky fishing boats are tied to a substantial wharf. Is it his?

"Well, it's ours," he says. "My sons and I built it."

How do you do that? I'd like to build one in D'Escousse.

"We did it in the winter," Joe says. "Cut holes in the ice and poked the poles down through them—35-foot creosote poles. We used the winch on one of the boats to haul a good heavy weight up a trestle and drove the poles right down in the mud with that. Then we bolted the cross-bars on 'em and put the deck on."

It made a good job.

"Oh, yes, although I think we might have put a few more poles down. You can see it's settling a little bit, there in that corner. Some of those poles, we didn't find any bottom, you know. That mud just goes down and down and down."

The harbour used to be silted shut, didn't it?

"Yes, it was. They dredge it every year. It's only been open since the 1940s. I've driven across there myself in a dozer and never even got the treads wet."

Fred Lawrence told me that three sailors' coffins worked their way out of the eroding seaward bluff, and Joe reburied them further back in the field. That's true, says Joe. Would we like to go up there?

We would. Joe's K-car goes flying skyward up the steep grassy track, rising over the crest of the hill like a boat breasting a swell. Close up, the cross is huge, surrounded by a rectangle of stones. The village's first cemetery was here, Joe explains, and also the first church—a shared community church, used alternately by Protestants and Catholics. A few feet away, a cairn marks the occasion in 1853 when a visiting bishop confirmed 150 candidates. The windy hilltop commands a sweeping view from Cape North almost to Cape St. Lawrence. Out in the bay a few fishing boats are working, and far out to sea a tiny white triangle marks a yacht bowling along before the westerly breeze.

"I make my garden up here," says Joe. "I took up gardening after I had to quit fishing. This isn't really a good place for a garden—too exposed, really—but I get good potatoes and beets. Most things'd do a lot better down by the house. But I like to work up here—I can look out to seaward and see the boats and see everything that's going on, you know."

You can't see the town from here; you would see it from the other side of the hill. For Joe, though, "everything" is going on at sea, not in the town.

Joe picks a few vegetables for dinner. He looks around before he climbs back in the car.

"Yes, sir," he says. "This is a great spot."

It is. And out on the edge of the seaward view is St. Paul Island, which Joe, at least, should view with some warmth—for it was there that Helen Dunphy met Jimmy Curtis. He was a lifeboat man, she cooked for the lighthouse crew, and they would become Joe Curtis's parents.

Jimmy and Helen Curtis were famous for singing—and though Jimmy is dead, Helen is very much alive at ninety-three, still living in her little house opposite the Co-op grocery store. She was raised in White Point, a little nook in the rocks much favoured by Newfoundland fishermen who based themselves there during a whole summer of fishing. Her family home was right above the wharf, and her parents loved music, so the house became a social centre.

"In the early morning, they'd leave to go fishing," Helen remembers. "When they'd be hoisting up their anchor, they'd be singing, having a nice song, and I could hear it coming in through my bedroom window. It was beautiful."

Helen worked at various jobs—in a lobster cannery, in a Sydney hotel—and then, one summer, she got a job helping the wife of the superintendent at St. Paul Island.

"That superintendent, he was cranky," Helen remembers, "but his wife was a lovely woman. There were two lighthouse keepers and their families, and five or six men. There was a lot of work to do—they had to fill the lamps with oil and wind up the clockwork mechanism, and when the supply boat came they had to row out and get the supplies. It was bare bold cliffs, you know. No shoreline, or no beach or anything that you could land at."

Jimmy Curtis was always singing, and it was singing that brought them together.

"He'd be always singing around his work. Whatever he'd be doing, he'd be singing or whistling a tune. And he asked me if I could sing, and I said, 'Oh, yes, I can sing a bit.' We used to sit out on the verandah and sing. He was a sweetheart."

They were married in 1923, and their singing household became a magnet in Bay St. Lawrence. People would come to the house, perhaps with a bottle, and the Curtises would sing. Or the party would be elsewhere, and they'd send for the Curtises—"and you'd sing there," says Helen, "and perhaps three o'clock in the morning you'd get home.

"It was entertainment—you know, there were no TVs or no radios or nothing. And there wouldn't be a word when those songs were sung. You could hear a pin fall." On Christmas Eve, when people would come in from the countryside for midnight Mass, the Curtis house would get so crowded that the family would have to bring in blocks of firewood for people to sit on.

Over the years, the Curtis family amassed a vast repertoire of songs. The children wanted them written down, and Jimmy Curtis filled up four or five scribblers with the words. In the 1960s, Rose Curtis Burton and Charlotte Curtis MacNeil went through the scribblers and typed them out. By then, the seven children were grown and gone. In the afternoon, just before or after they took a nap together, Jimmy and Helen would get down the songbooks and the two of them would sit and sing, all by themselves, just for their own enjoyment. Jimmy died in 1977.

"You're not going to believe this," Helen Curtis told Ron Caplan of *Cape Breton's Magazine*. "Yesterday was my husband's anniversary. And I took down this songbook, and I sang ten of his songs yesterday.

"He was such a sweet man. My God, he was a good person. Everyone loved him. He loved everybody. And I sure loved him."

I spent a lot of the summer thinking about wealth. Robert Campeau's empire was crashing. Michael Milken, the Drexel Lambert junk-bond king, was going to prison for fraud and market manipulation. Bankruptcies were soaring, interest rates were punitive, the hot air was leaking fast from the golden balloon of the 1980s.

I thought about Jimmy and Helen Curtis, the big man and the small woman, deeply in love after decades of marriage, sitting together and singing.

What's wealth? Who's wealthy?

Paul and Annette Bonin live in a trailer near the church, not far from Helen Curtis. This is actually a separate community called St. Margaret's Village—though if you don't know, you can't tell. Set among the wild rose bushes and the stunted spruce trees, the trailer looks temporary. It *is* temporary, Paul says. When he retires, they're moving to the Yukon.

The Yukon? For retirement? Well, yes. Paul lived in the Yukon for several years, hunting, fishing, prospecting. He loved it. He still owns a sluice mine there.

Temporary though it is, the Bonins' trailer signals an economical and rewarding approach to living. A fisherman has no shortage of fish, Paul notes, and the apple trees around the trailer are already bearing fruit. Add the high-bush cranberries, deer, moose and the produce of a garden, and your food bill becomes very modest. When the fishery is as lucrative as it has been—a good fisherman should gross around $200,000 a year, Paul says—one can live well in Bay St. Lawrence.

As we talk, Paul shucks lobsters and wraps a fillet of grey sole around the meat from the tails and claws. He purees the remaining odds and ends of lobster meat and blends it with undiluted tinned mushroom soup. He pours the soup over the rolls of sole and lobster, and bakes the whole thing. Annette, meanwhile, has made scalloped potatoes and broccoli.

This is the most unbelievably wonderful meal of the voyage. Even in memory, it makes the mouth water. Paul gives the leftovers to the dog, and laughs.

"The freezer's full of lobster and grey sole," he says. "It's nothing special here."

I love living in a depressed region, I thought. *One lives so well.*

After supper, Paul talks about the fishery. The local fishermen are moving beyond the usual species—cod, haddock, pollock, flounder, sole, swordfish, crab, lobster—into new fisheries. Shark, for instance.

"We started with dogfish," Paul says. "They have to be skinned as well as filleted, but we're doing all right with them. We've just started on the bigger sharks. There's three licenses issued—one to Donnie Hinkley in Pleasant Bay, one in Arichat, and one to me. It's expensive to get set up for it. It costs $2,300 for two miles of longline gear—one-eighth wire cable, with stainless steel hooks every forty to sixty feet. We can set five miles of gear in one string, and I think we can catch four to ten tons a trip.

"There's good money in it. Mako and porbeagle, what they call mackerel shark, those are the valuable ones. They run from six to eighteen feet, and you can get 'em up to nine hundred pounds. They're worth $2.50 a pound—but the jaws are worth $200 to $500 a set, and the fins are $17 a pound and the livers $5 to $7 a pound.

"We're lookin' at whelks and sea urchins, too. We got to do something about the sea urchins anyway. We're losin' our bottom to them. There's a pile of 'em out there, and they're eating the kelp, and the groundfish like the kelp."

Is there a market for them?

"Oh, I guess there is! Sea urchins, they're gettin' $15 a pound for 'em in Newfoundland. A diver can get a thousand pounds a day. Use a pump, bring 'em up into a tank. January to April is the best time, that's when they're full of roe for sushi. They pay $100 a pound for that roe in Japan."

What would the Japanese pay, I wonder, for a meal like the one we had just eaten?

We begin our last day in Bay St. Lawrence at five o'clock, intending to sail to Dingwall or Ingonish. But the forecast calls for moderate to strong southwesterlies with coastal gusts to 35 knots, plus fogs and thunder showers. Who wants to fight that?

Strolling on the dock at 5:30, I meet Lori and Dennis with Father Peter MacDonald, the priest from Dingwall whose parish includes Bay St. Lawrence. Father Peter introduces Gilles Richard, a retired military photographer from Quebec who lives

Carl Vilas

When I brought *Hirondelle* to the Cape Breton village of
D'Escousse in 1973, she was the first schooner to make her home
there since Leonard Pertus laid up his trading schooner in 1928. At
83, Leonard taught me to sail *Hirondelle* in Lennox Passage.

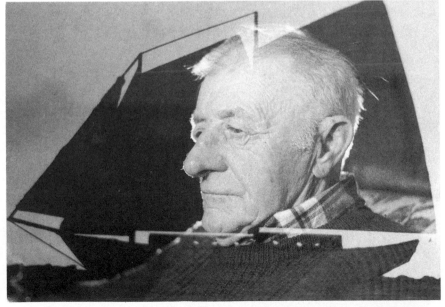

Silver Donald Cameron

Leonard was famous for being calm in a crisis. "When you're caught, you're caught,"
he'd shrug. "No point getting excited, you'd only discourage the crew. You do the best
you can, it's all you can do."

Shirley Macnamara

I built *Silversark* over a nine-year period — with Lulu, who married me early in the project, and with much help from friends such as Edwin DeWolf (below, working on the fore-peak.) Lulu's father Arthur Terrio (left) with Claude Poirier (right) pitched in when the hull was ready to be rolled right-side up.

Silver Donald Cameron

Lulu Terrio-Cameron

Richard Mayes lives on Lennox Passage and builds husky vessels ranging in size from his dory *St. Mary Magdalen* (shown here) up to the 52-foot trading ketch *Star of Bethlehem*. A modern Noah with a proper ark, he serenely awaits a divine catastrophe.

The Great Paper Boat Race of the World took place on July 1, 1984, in Port Hawkesbury, on the Strait of Canso. *The Papal Boat* (bottom left) was paddled by Bob Delaney and Bud McIntyre; coxswain Bill MacInnis wore blue shorts, a white shirt and an orange tie "so I could be seen on the bottom if I fell overboard." *Mean Machine* (bottom right) carried a crew of eight.

Courtesy Mulgrave Machine

Courtesy Mulgrave Machine

Courtesy James Organ

The triumphant crew of *Stora Viking* rowed like Norsemen bent on pillage. The crew, from left to right: Jimmie-Joe Organ, Tommy MacDonald, Ralph Keefe, George Ryan, Freddie Snow and the designer, shipwright and skipper, Jim Organ.

Silver Donald Cameron

The ferry to Port Hood Island is Bertie Smith's fishing boat. Bertie and Shirley are the last year-round residents of the island. The ferry pulled in one evening with a white wicker sofa on the cabin roof. The owners were sitting in it.

Lulu Terrio-Cameron

I spent a cold day in July lobstering with Fred Lawrence (right) in *Suzie Q*, out of Bay St. Lawrence.

Silver Donald Cameron

While the water boiled, Mark hypnotized the lobsters. He held each one upside down, with the pincers and the head on the cockpit seat. Then he slowly stroked them, moving his fingers upward along the back and over the curve of the tail. In a matter of minutes, he had all eight lobsters standing on their heads, blissed out.

Owen Fitzgerald

Dory Tuvim came from
Montreal to North Sydney.
He bought the 140-year-
old North Sydney Marine
Railway, renamed it Good
People Sea and Shore
Services and helped
revitalize the local
economy.

Chris Latchem

Auxiliary engines are foul-smelling, unreliable, explosive devices which lull you into
trusting them. Then they fail. *Silversark*'s auxiliary power is a pair of 10-foot oars clipped
to the rigging — quite sufficient for one or two people to move her short distances in calm
weather.

Silver Donald Cameron

At the end of the experiment we threw the still overboard, because none of us could afford six months and $500. So there's no still, no moonshine. We're law-abiding citizens who drink government booze. But, as they say in Waterford, whether you believe that is entirely up to yourself.

Lulu Terrio-Cameron

Harold Fudge is a Newfoundlander who fished out of Louisbourg for more than twenty years before he joined the Coast Guard lifeboat crew in 1974. He was a reassuring presence when we had to feel our way into Louisbourg in dense fog.

Sonja Susijnar

Chris Latchem (left) was a charter member of the Nine Year Seminar on Boatbuilding and Life — but he never saw *Silversark* completed and never sailed aboard her until the summer of 1990.

We eased past the beach at the tip of Bernard Island and on into the harbour. One last tack to the wharf. We could see our own house on the shore. "We've seen everything!" cried Mark, but we had seen nothing more welcome than this. I took a deep breath and savoured the harbour of home.

in Dingwall with two sons. Four more people are walking down the wharf: Archie Doucet, a student from Ingonish, and a sorrowful-looking middle-aged woman with an adult son and daughter.

This is a funeral, says Father Peter, for one of the thirty-nine men lost on those two freighters last winter. Michel Pellerin was only thirty-four when he died, and his mother, his sister and his brother have flown halfway around the world to say prayers in his memory and to cast flowers into Cabot Strait.

May I come?

Gilles asks Madame Pellerin, who nods. We board *Bonny Susan* and motor out of the harbour in the pale dawn.

By 6:15, the motor is shut off and the boat is rolling heavily three miles off Cape North. The foghorn at Money Point brays monotonously, although our patch of the ocean lies in bright sunlight. To the northeast, faintly limned against an offshore fogbank, is the rocky silhouette of St. Paul Island.

In the photographs which his brother and sister show to the little knot of Canadian mourners who never knew him, Michel Pellerin looks youthful and handsome. The background is tropical. The photos were taken on New Caledonia, 800 miles east-northeast of Australia, where the Pellerins make their home.

Michel Pellerin was a member of the twenty-three-man crew of the freighter *Capitain Torres*, which developed engine trouble just as a savage winter storm struck Cabot Strait in early December, 1989. Her skipper radioed for help, but his crew managed to deal with the problem, and he cancelled the call. Then the storm worsened, and the problem recurred. By Thursday, December 8, *Capitain Torres* found herself in a desperate fight for survival, engineless and drifting, swept by towering seas. Sixty miles east, the Philippine freighter *Johanna B* was also disabled and sinking; off Newfoundland, the Shelburne longliner *Johnny and Sisters II* had disappeared.

Capitain Torres battled overnight, her struggle tensely reported in regional newscasts. In the fishing villages, men watched the bright blip of the *Capitain Torres* on their radar screens, listened to the voices on the marine radio. As their situation grew hopeless, the seamen called home, patched through the phone lines around the world, saying farewells to wives, lovers, parents, children. The seas, said the master of *Capitain Torres*, were "monumentale." It was "impossible de sortir." There was no way out.

And then, between one moment and the next, the voices ceased. The radios ashore yielded only static. The bright blips vanished from the radar screens. On Friday morning, the Coast Guard cutter *Sir Wilfred Grenfell* spotted a liferaft with survivors, but while she was manoeuvring into position, the captain "saw two horrible breakers tumble the raft." When the *Grenfell* came alongside, no survivors remained.

"It hit us very hard because we're of the sea ourselves," Fred Lawrence told me later. "The people who had been listening on the radio had to go and talk it out. It just shook them. Outside our house you couldn't look down over the cliff without goggles. The wind was blowing 60 or 70 knots, it was 20 below, and the waves were 50 feet high—solid walls of water.

"Marg and I and some others walked the beaches every day for a week and a half, looking for bodies, wreckage, anything. We didn't find a thing. Not a trace."

Father Peter says prayers of intercession, which Gilles translates into French. Tears run down Madame Pellerin's face, as they have since the boat left the wharf, as they will till it returns. Dennis and Lori sing a lilting, melancholy carol. Wave-caps slap against the boat. In a powerful baritone, Gilles sings "Amazing Grace".

The Pellerins place a wreath of flowers over the side. It is tied to a concrete block. Father Peter commends it to the ocean. They lower the concrete block into the water and release it. The wreath falls through the water and is lost in the darkness below.

Everyone throws flowers overboard. Each of the Pellerins empties a vial of water, carried all the way from the South Pacific—a little piece of home to leave with Michel. They dip the vials in the chill waters and recork them. They will take these tiny samples of Cabot Strait back to New Caledonia.

Father Peter says a benediction. Dennis starts the engine and turns the boat back towards Bay St. Lawrence.

As the boat moves off, everyone looks back. St. Paul Island has vanished behind the fogbank. Far to the eastward, gleaming gold in the sunlight, a cargo ship emerges from the fog, heading directly towards us. It stands high and proud, like a square building on the water. Nobody points it out to Madame Pellerin.

Michel Pellerin's brother shakes his head.

"La mer," he says. "La mer ne pardonne pas."

The sea is unforgiving.

Amen.

CAPE BRETON'S

PLAYGROUND

We sailed from Bay St. Lawrence on another golden morning, with a riffle of southwesterly breeze on the indigo water.

Fred Lawrence motored slowly by, heading for his traps.

"Want a tow out?" he called.

"We can sail out, I think. Thanks."

"Beautiful morning for it."

Normally, Cape Breton has plenty of dirty grey cloud, raw wind, cold rain and snow. Sydney records the highest average winds of any weather station in Canada. I once spent three weeks writing in a secluded cove, watching the rain run down the portlights. But the summer of 1990 was magnificent.

Dennis Cox motored past the end of the wharf.

"Want a tow?" he called.

"No, we can sail."

"You're sure, now?"

We lingered briefly over coffee, reluctant to leave this extraordinary place. But only a fool wastes a favourable breeze. At 6:30 we cast off and ran swiftly out the narrow entrance. At the inner fairway buoy we hardened in the sails, shaping a course for Money Point.

We planned to stay a mile or so off the land, clear of the gusts and williwaws which might blow down from the cliffs but well inside the first tide-race, four miles out. But—I have seen this happen innumerable times, and I still don't understand it— even with the wind blowing off the land, *Silversark* edged steadily closer to the cliffs. There is a factor here like parallax: the sensation that you *are* sailing parallel to the coast, coupled with the undeniable fact that you are steadily closing the shore, as though the current were setting you in.

Fishing vessels speckled the sea right out to the horizon. Off White Rock, we saw Fred Lawrence's little orange *Suzy Q* in among the rocks. We waved. *Silversark* sailed quickly on.

The wind was building, and the air was chill, the opalescent quality of the light reminiscent of the morning of Michel Pellerin's funeral. When we reached Money Point an hour later, we were close enough in to see the foundations of what used to be the lightkeeper's house, and his assistant's. A husky blue vessel lay anchored beyond the point, her crew lined up along the rail, jigging for mackerel.

A blast of wind roared down the cliffs. *Silversark* heeled abruptly, and I scrambled forward to douse the jib. As we passed the point, the sea opened before us to the eastward, fading to an indistinct boundary between sky and water, the long high coastline running southward and evaporating in the distance. The wind hauled a little to the westward, and we hardened up again for Cape Egmont, sailing almost to windward now across the wide crescent of Aspy Bay, with its long, deserted beaches. John and Sebastian Cabot landed here in 1497, an event which is reenacted every year on June 24. (The point is vigorously disputed by Newfoundlanders and others, but Cabot's landing is an article of faith in Cape Breton.)

The bay is shallow and sandy, with only two small, difficult harbours: Dingwall, midway along the shore, and White Point, near Cape Egmont. We thought of sailing into Dingwall to see the stained-glass windows in the new church, crafted by Lieutenant Commander Bernard Grover and dedicated to the memory of his parents.

"I told Bernie, I don't want the old saints and angels," Father Peter told me. "I want three windows: Life, Death and Resurrection. Well, you should see what he did. It's all Cape Breton images. You should go take a look."

We saw those glowing windows later. In the Life window, Grover shows mallards, bulrushes, an old Scottish shieling and a Celtic cross. In the Death window, surmounted by the cross of Golgotha, an overturned lifeboat is clutched by a drowning hand as the ferry *Caribou* sinks in the background. The Resurrection window features *Bluenose II*, the beginning of a fishing season, and a glorious sunrise beneath the Alpha-Omega cross, the cross of Easter.

We also wanted to visit Gilles Richard, who lives with his sons Alain and Pierre in a little rough-and-tumble house in the woods behind Dingwall, surrounded by a workshop, a truck, a boat, diesel engines and other interesting tools and artifacts. Alain and Pierre fish with a much-modified 28-foot Newfoundland trap skiff called *Home Brew*. They raised the topsides of her lean and graceful hull and added a mast, sails and a tall wheelhouse as well as a four-cylinder Volvo diesel. The result is a handy, frugal and idiosyncratic vessel which looks like a Fisher yacht or an old North Sea dragger. They were planning to do a similar conversion on a bigger hull the following winter.

Alain thought we should install a diesel in *Silversark*, a notion we had begun to consider.

"But then we wouldn't be purists," Lulu said sadly.

"True, true," said Alain, with a regretful Gallic shrug. "But purists on the rocks—it's not so good."

Still, Dingwall was upwind, and the summer was passing quickly. We decided to sail on to Neils Harbour, and possibly to Ingonish, the next important town, passing up White Point, where mutual friends had instructed us to visit Senator Lowell Murray.

The senator is a native of New Waterford, Cape Breton. He is married to Helen Curtis's grand-daughter, and in the summer of 1990 he was no doubt glad of a vacation. He had just put in a strenuous spring wrestling with the Meech Lake accord; he was about to face a strenuous autumn wrestling the Grab and Snatch Tax through the Senate. His main opponent there would be Senator Allan J. MacEachen, our former MP, who summers at Lake Ainslie, near Mabou. MacEachen has generated his very own cliché: reporters almost invariably describe him as "the wily Cape Bretoner."

When two Cape Bretoners fight, the earth shakes. That fall, all Canadians were to feel the shaking.

We did later visit Murray's hilltop retreat. The Murrays were gone, but the climb to their eyrie was worthwhile anyway. The weathered contemporary house stands on a rocky pinnacle, with its back in the trees. The largest of several sun-decks thrusts out like the bow of a ship, high above Aspy Bay. The sweeping view takes in Sugarloaf Mountain, Money Point, a great stretch of open sea, and the White Point shore. It may be the most magnificently situated house in all of Cape Breton.

If Lowell Murray had been sitting outside with his breakfast coffee one July morning, he might have spied a little wine-sailed speck sailing across the bay far below. It would have caught his attention: sailing vessels are rare in Aspy Bay. He might have wondered, idly, who was sailing her, and where they were bound.

Now he will know.

The wind eased as we crossed the bay, and we put the jib up again. The land was still attracting us: by the time we reached Cape Egmont we were not offshore but sailing close along the rocky coast. Beyond the cape the land receded again. We passed fishing boats along the shore and tall fairway buoys off New Haven—once known by the grim name of Hungry Cove—and Neils Harbour. Both villages are little more than dimples in the rocky shoreline, improved by the addition of massive rock breakwaters. As the accents of their people will tell you, they are populated largely by Newfoundland families. Along the shore they are actually known as "the Newfoundlanders," although many—perhaps most—were born and raised in Cape Breton.

The wind remained puffy and unsteady, laying us over on our ear and then abandoning us almost completely. After putting the jib up and down a couple of times, I gave up and stayed on the foredeck, ready for action, jumping below from time to time for a peek at the chart and the Loran.

Speed 4.6 knots, course 210 magnetic, 6.7 miles to Waypoint 16, off Ingonish Island.

Here the land slopes gradually back from the shore, terminating in what Chart 4363 calls a "featureless plateau about 1,550 ft. high." An old chart: antique, pre-metric, like the skipper. But the sea and the land have not changed much since it was new, and the current *Sailing Directions* and *List of Lights* tell us about today's aids to navigation. All the authorities tell the sailor to carry new charts—but not how to pay for them. When I started sailing, Canadian government charts cost $1.00. Admittedly, a dollar was worth something in 1973—but nowhere near as much as $13.20 (tax included) is worth today. The forty-odd charts needed for a voyage like ours would add $500 to the budget, which is more than we spent on food. I concede that yes, indeed, we should use new charts. I should also exercise, floss and stop swearing. Perhaps someday I will.

By one o'clock we were passing the 200-foot-high round hill of Ingonish Island, with its abandoned lightkeeper's residence, its clouds of gulls and its cliffs streaked with guano. Again, the land had drawn us towards it—too close, according to the chart, for the island is guarded by off-lying rocks. We bore off and entered the twin bays of Ingonish.

On the chart, the two bays look like two perfect bites in a slice of bread, separated by the slender peninsula of Middle Head. Both bays enclose sandy beaches, and both are completely open to the east. On the north side of North Bay, a breakwater runs out from a spit to form a small harbour; in South Bay, a narrow opening in the beach leads to a spacious anchorage, with a government wharf on one side and a sheltered creek on the other.

On this breezy afternoon, we chose the creek in South Bay. As we crossed North Bay, the wind piped up, then faded slightly under the lee of Middle Head. Along the crest of Middle Head stood a white ruff of buildings, like a nurse's headpiece: Keltic Lodge, one of the Maritimes' fanciest resorts.

We beat up into South Bay against a stiff and gusty wind, using just the main and jumbo. Because both sails are on booms, they swing across the vessel on their own when we tack. Nobody has to handle anything, an ideal arrangement in a situation like the one we now confronted.

On the south side of the bay, two lines of buoys mark a narrow channel leading to the gut through the beach. By now the wind was blowing hard — and directly out of the gut. In a strong puff, a sailboat will nose up closer into the wind; when the wind eases, she falls away. At the helm, Lulu was playing the tiller like a fisherman playing a fish, "eatin' up" into the puffs. At the sounder, Mark called out depths. I stood on the foredeck, peering down into the water, looking for the bottom. There —

"Tack!" I called. *Silversark* swung her nose up through the wind and fell away on the other tack, hesitated, gathered momentum and began to sail.

"Too narrow!" called Lulu. "Can we do it?"

"I think so!" I called. There was no real danger; even if we *did* go aground, there was no sea running, and the strong wind would only blow us into deeper water.

Tack. Tack. Tack. Foot by foot, we gnawed our way up into the gut, the bottom coming closer and closer, the boat barely gathering steerage way before we had to tack again. But now we were in the gut, with the bottom coming up fast —

"Tack!" I called. "And right after this tack, *tack!*"

Lulu steered a quick, sinuous S-turn, right in the eye of the wind. *Give us a puff,* she muttered through her teeth. *Come on, a nice little puff to carry us through.*

Blow, I breathed tensely, gazing downward from the bow. *Blow. Blow. Blow!*

A gust of wind came rattling down the mountainside, filled the sails, laid the boat over. Lulu steered a touch to windward. *Silversark* slipped inside the harbour, passing the gravel beach with perhaps six feet to spare.

"Whoo!"

"*Yahoo!*"

But the harbour is ringed with high mountains—at the head of the harbour we could see the green slashes of downhill ski runs—and, says the *Pilot*, "the squalls from these high lands are very violent at times."

The wind suddenly doubled in strength, forcing the boat over and tearing at our clothing. We tucked a quick reef in the main and looked around. We were far enough in to make a run for the sheltered creek to starboard. We bore away and eased the sheets. The sails ran out, and *Silversark* took off like a thoroughbred, racing for the creek—far too fast for an approach to the small wharf ahead of us.

We dropped the main, gathering it in bunches on the boom. Under the jumbo alone, *Silversark* charged forward—

—and slipped into the lee of a high bluff—

—and nearly stopped.

Amazing. Once we were in the shelter of the creek, the wind dropped to nothing. A hundred yards astern the wind was screeching down the harbour, blowing the tops off the white-caps. Inside the creek, carrying just the little jumbo, we barely had enough wind to sail.

We coasted slowly to the wharf and jumped ashore with the dock lines.

The wharf is privately owned and leased to National Sea Products; its noisy refrigeration unit started and stopped twenty-four-hours a day. But there is no public wharf on that side of the harbour, so we were grateful to be allowed to stay.

The creek was placid, sheltered by bluffs and trees. A prosperous-looking house with a substantial wharf proved to be the home of a successful lobsterman. Just beyond our own berth was a complete marine railway and repair shop, where a steady succession of fishing boats came to be hauled, serviced and painted. In a pool past the next bend, a fibreglass daysailer drifted idly around her mooring.

We went looking for a telephone. It was a long walk—perhaps a mile and a half—to the Cabot Trail, which here becomes the main street of Ingonish Beach. Service stations, motels, restaurants. Post office. Bank. Liquor store. Small diners and convenience stores.

Ingonish is not so much a town as a ribbon of buildings strewn along five miles of beach: Ingonish, Ingonish Centre, Ingonish Beach, Ingonish Harbour and Ingonish Ferry. Summer and winter, Ingonish is much favoured by the well heeled, including prosperous Cape Bretoners. Keltic Lodge is a genteel old resort—shuffleboard, perfect flowerbeds, walking trails. The ski hill and the golf course are among the best in the region.

Somewhere in the district were three of Lulu's brothers' families. Chris's family and Pat's were in one of the Parks Canada campgrounds; Terry was visiting Dingwall. We tracked them down by phone and walked back to the boat. While his parents read and wrote, Mark caught two big flounders for dinner. In the evening, a car pulled up with three high-spirited young men and a cheerful girl. One of the young men worked for National Sea; they had come down for a few shovelsful of crushed ice for a beach party.

"Want a beer?"

"Sure. Come on aboard."

The four of them piled over the wharf, passing out bottles of Moosehead Dry.

"Some nice boat, b'y. Where'd you get her?"

"Built her."

"G'wan! Did you? How long d'you take on it?"

"Nearly nine years."

"Jesus. She's some pretty."

"Take a look below."

"Jeez, you got everything down here. Look, stove and toilet and everything. Like a little house."

"We've been living aboard for nearly a month."

"Never been aboard a yacht before, b'y. I'd love to know how to sail one of these."

"Listen, we gotta go. See ya, buddy. Thanks for the tour."

"Thanks for the beer."

Terry arrived early in the morning with a pailful of mail. He,

too, is one of *Silversark*'s people, having welded most of the
stainless steel on the boat, most notably the "pushpit," the fence
around the stern. After coffee he drove us to Broad Cove, where
the others were camping. We borrowed a car and left Mark to
swim and play with his cousins while we spent the day shopping, washing and doing other errands.

Telephoning, for instance. Chris Zimmer had hired Cordell
Wynne to direct "Peggy", and Cord had some questions. Living
on a boat makes such things as phone calls very difficult. You
trudge a mile to a pay phone and hope your party is in. If not,
then what? Wait in the rain? Trudge back and forth again?

We ate at the campground—Danick's spaghetti, our lobsters—and drove back to the boat. The magazines and newspapers made us depressed: films like *Gremlins*, Don Blenkarn
braying at Clyde Wells, the invisible Jean Chrétien, the standoff
at Oka, Dan Quayle's latest gaffes—

I don't read the news when we're sailing, and I don't miss it, I
wrote grumpily in my notebook. *Seen from here, the news is
mostly a long saga of greed, squalor, small minds and large egos.*

The antidote arrived next day in the shape of Hugh Gauntlett, Carole MacDonald and Ron Caplan. Once the head of CBC
Television Variety, Hugh moved to Halifax as regional head of
program development—in effect, ambassador to Toronto for
Atlantic producers and writers. "Peggy" began over lunch with
Hugh. Carole, his wife, operates Goose Cove Pottery near their
summer home on St. Ann's Bay.

Ron Caplan is the founder, editor, publisher, owner and sole
reporter of *Cape Breton's Magazine*, an eclectic homespun publication devoted, says its banner, to "the history, natural history
and future of Cape Breton Island." Caplan drifted from Pitts-
burg to Wreck Cove, pop. 38, in 1971. He was twenty-nine. He
started the magazine a year later, focussing on transcribed
interviews with elderly people well rooted in Island traditions.
Eighty per cent of the contents are in English, the balance in
French, Gaelic and Micmac.

After fifty-three issues, Caplan has confounded the skeptics
and become a Cape Breton institution himself. The best of the
material has been collected in two books: *Down North* and *Cape*

Breton Lives. It also prompted a powerful evening of theatre by the St. Ann's Bay Players, an outstanding amateur troupe.

Hugh Gauntlett and I thought *Down North* would make unique and wonderful television. We had failed to persuade the ice-eyed TV executives in Toronto—but we had placed it as a CBC radio series for "Morningside". Caplan and Gauntlett live just a few miles apart, but they first met aboard *Silversark*. At six-foot-six, Ron overwhelmed the boat, so we sat in the cockpit. Mark immortalized the moment by shinnying to the spreaders and photographing all our upturned faces.

Carole confirmed what others had told us: in the middle of a glorious summer, tourism was down in Cape Breton. Why? Nobody really knew: the high Canadian dollar, the prices of gasoline and liquor, the sense of domestic discord spread by Meech Lake and Oka. But Carole's own work—created in Halifax during the winter, trucked home to the Cape Breton shop for the summer—was selling well all the same.

Hugh and I still agreed that *Down North* should be done for television, and we talked with Ron about his concern for the integrity of the voices in the radio plays. Thus far, Ron has been more a collector than a writer, eschewing selection or shaping or imagination in favour of an exact and literal record of just what was said—an approach which makes it hard to create a drama except in the fluid, poetic fashion of a play like *Under Milk Wood*.

"Well," said Hugh, rising from his seat, "we'll just keep plugging away at the network. We'll try them again after we've got the radio version. Good to meet you at last . . ."

After Hugh and Carole had gone, Ron settled back in his seat—carefully, making allowances for his bad back.

"You know," he said, "I'd like to do some books—not collections from the magazine, but books about that material, books I'd write myself."

"I have a theme for you," I said.

"What's that?"

"Well, I was talking with an architect about the construction of our first house—the one you had to stoop in—and he referred to its 'mediaeval framing.' That startled me, but then I realized he was right. It's framed the same as the fourteenth century house I lived in once in England. Big posts and beams all mortised and pegged together.

"And you know, for the people you've been recording, life really *was* much the same as it was for Chaucer. They heated and cooked with wood, they ploughed with horses, they raised animals, they made their own music and stories, they fished with hooks and lines. They travelled on horseback or cart or under sail —"

"Or walked," said Ron. "It's unbelievable, the distances they walked. Fourteen-year-old boys walking from Cape North to Glace Bay to get work in the mines."

"Well, exactly. And that whole way of life has disappeared in one generation. When people like Henry Doucet and Helen Curtis are gone, things that people knew for a thousand years will be gone forever. All that ancient knowledge is vanishing."

"Yes, and so is the tradition of people being involved in what they do," said Ron. "Like the *Silversark* people you talk about, building a voyaging yacht—the involvement in design, all that thought and care and love. Today people buy a fibreglass yacht off the shelf and it means nothing."

"Very few people in our generation really know what it was like on the other side of that change," I said. "But you've spent twenty years listening to their voices."

"The old people had a sense of work as sacred," Ron said. "That's really the root of craftsmanship. And it ties back into their attitude towards the sea and the natural world."

"You know those wood-and-stone anchors the fishermen use in Little Anse?" I said.

"Killicks," said Ron. "Lovely things. Not too many of 'em left, either."

"Those are Norse anchors," I said. "And that's the Norse word for them."

"That's a big theme," said Ron. "I'll think about it."

"You've been thinking about it for years," I said.

After Ron left, Mark finally had his way: we went to the beach, as he had wanted to do all day long. It turned out to be one of those pure, simple, joyful moments, shimmering in memory, which will eventually be all that remains of parenthood.

What made that evening so special? Where does joy come from, anyway? A mellow summer evening, with the slanting yellow light of an approaching sunset. An arc of sand rimming the water, a dune of stony beach blocking the sea from a freshwater lagoon. Wildflowers painting splashes of yellow and magenta against the infinite greys of the rounded beach stones. Lulu plucked a couple of daisies and tucked them in the band of her hat.

The slight, lean brown body of our boy-man, racing along the sand and capering in the waves, the breeze blowing his hair back; the two of us, happy together in the enjoyment of his enjoyment. He found an elaborate sandcastle, decorated with stones and twigs and feathers, abandoned by some child whose day had already ended. Right beside it, as though in reply, Mark built his own castle, and drew his signature in the sand with his toes, a fivelined supergraphic scrawl.

A middle-aged German couple came marching by: robust, red-cheeked, sensible, fit. *Goot eefening.* We walked on down the sand, picking up bits of debris. I tucked an insouciant feather into my own hat. Up on the beach stones lay a long, straight piece of driftwood with a sharp bend at one end, like a 20-foot hockey stick. It took a moment to see what it was: the spine of a vanished boat, the keel and the stem still joined together.

Far down the beach, near Keltic Lodge, a lifeguard's tower loomed above a group of giggling teenagers. We soon saw why: a head protruded from the sand, wearing a hat and spectacles, talking and laughing. The rest of the girl's body was entirely buried, and the sand was smoothed out all around her. It was an oddly eerie spectacle.

As we walked back along the beach, the dusk stole out from the black crevices between the rocks, staining the day with patches of darkness. The German couple marched towards us out of the dim distance, nodding again: *Goote nacht.* We helped one another up the dune of rolling stones and stood at the top with the lagoon on one side, the sea on the other, Middle Head behind us and the massive bulk of Cape Smokey ahead of us. The sun dropped behind the green ski hill. The day was over.

Time to sail to Sydney, but the forecast called for southerly head winds with fog and showers. We slept late and came on deck to discover a perfectly acceptable sailing day, with high overcast and a fine breeze from the *west*. Typical: the forecast winds had been consistently wrong. I remembered an old fisherman in Louisbourg: "Forecast? Forecast? Them fellers couldn't forecast a fart s'posin' they *smelt* it."

We ate fast and made sail at 10:30, skimming out quickly through the gap in the beach and on down South Bay under the looming wall of Smokey. When we cleared the bay, the wind went southerly and faded to a whisper, leaving us rolling and plunging in a disorderly chop. After creeping to seaward for an hour, we had made no progress towards Sydney.

The hell with this. We swung our stern into the light breeze and squared away for the breakwater harbour in North Bay, behind Ingonish Island. It took us two hours to cover those three miles. Inside the breakwater we found a dozen small boats at moorings, with another dozen tied along the inner face of the breakwater itself. We dropped the sails and coasted alongside, making fast to a baby-blue Cape Islander called *Bluegill*.

It had become a volatile, dramatic day, brilliant sunshine mixed with towering black clouds and pelting rain showers. The squalls rose behind the mountains and funnelled down the valleys, their dark veils of rain streaming below them, transforming and reshaping themselves. Some of them soaked us; others bypassed us altogether, leaving us in the sun on the sandy beach.

Late in the afternoon, a tanned, fit-looking older man came to the wharf and looked at the boat. Rollie MacLean owns a new chalet-style house just across the cove, and he was building a 16-foot rowing wherry in his old grey barn. A native of Ingonish, he had retired after a construction career in Halifax. Among his neighbours in suburban Fall River had been Leonard Pertus's daughter Jeanette: in fact, Rollie had known The Skipper himself. So we were friends, and we went off to look at his lovely little wherry, meet his wife, Anne, drink some rum and talk about boats.

"Will you be here tomorrow?" Rollie asked.

"Not if we get a fair wind," I said. "Why?"

"My daughter and her family are coming," said Rollie. "I thought Mark might enjoy the kids."

"All right!" said Mark.

"We'll see," I said.

"That means No," Mark pouted.

Bluegill belonged to a bald, brown, virile-looking crab fisherman named Ian Best. Ian's brother Dave haunted the wharf, like the spirit of the place. He was there during the great gale of 1983. In Ingonish Harbour, the gale carried away wharves and buildings and flung fishing vessels up into the trees on the bluffs, twenty feet above the high-water mark.

"We were down here savin' a friend's boat," Dave said. "It was a super-high tide along with the gale, and the seas were breakin' right over the wharf. My buddy was a Newfoundlander—tough, b'y, the only thing tougher than a Newfoundlander is two of 'em. He was down in the boat. I looked out to seaward and I saw four big ones comin'. I shouted *Hang on!* and I wrapped my arms and legs around a light pole. I was right under water. Good thing for me that pole stayed put. I saw another pole ripped right off and fired right through a bait shed.

"Afterwards there was rocks the size of a man's body in the field over there by the tourist cabins. The seas were pourin' right across that little neck of land, right across the road. We saved the boat all right—but there was an awful pile of boats smashed and gone when it was all over."

In the morning we found the harbour glassy calm. "Good," said Mark, "we're staying." But at ten a light southwesterly sprang up. We cast off and tried again for Sydney. Mark was in a snit, expressing insolence and rebellion just in the way he handled the lines. Midget mutiny. We took a long tack out of North Bay, but we were forced to the eastward as the wind freshened. By the time we reached Middle Head, the wind had gone around to the southeast, blowing hard—and straight from Sydney. We eased the sheets and ran back to the breakwater.

And now, suddenly, we were the best of parents, the finest of friends.

Mary MacLean had arrived with her children, David and Amy, and her happy husband, Tad Kikuchi. Tad and Mary are athletes; Tad immigrated from Japan to teach gymnastics in Halifax. He coaches the Canadian boys' gymnastic team, which had just won a gold medal at the Pan American Games in Tallahassee.

David knew a nearby cave full of rock crystals, so he and Mark took hammers in hand and went off to get some samples. By now the wind was whipping across the bay from the southeast, and a couple of windsurfers were screaming along, half vanishing in the troughs and flying off the wave-caps.

Lulu and I walked down the road in the blazing sun to find Lynn's Craft Shop and Art Gallery, which is owned by Christopher Gorey, a fine painter and a moving force in Cape Breton cultural affairs. Gorey was out, but he came to visit us later, with his two small sons: a thoughtful, soft-spoken man with a trim black beard, younger than I expected given the serene maturity of his paintings, not to mention his success with the Royal Canadian Mint, for whom he designed silver dollars in 1981 and 1987. The gallery generates 75 per cent of his income. If he sells a piece through a Nova Scotia dealer, the dealer takes 40 per cent. In the U.S., the commission is 50 per cent, and in New York City it can be 60 per cent. In Ingonish, Gorey keeps 100 per cent.

Mark and David had rock crystals spread out all across the front steps. Amethyst, they said; salt, said Rollie, though it didn't taste salty; quartz, said someone else. Perhaps it was amethyst, after all; Chris Gorey says there is supposed to be amethyst in the district, though he has never seen it.

Anne MacLean had macaroni cooking: would we stay? Yes, but only if we could contribute the six huge crabs we had bought earlier in the day. It made an eccentric feast: macaroni, home-baked bread, crab legs. Tad's nephew Hisachi Tobe, a tall, lithe young man who was studying English, proved himself a heroic trencherman. He mowed down the crab legs with the efficiency of an automated production line: precision cutting, accurate disassembly, just-in-time delivery. Wiping his lips, he declared that the meal would have cost him $50 in Japan.

Learning that Mark had been home-schooled till the age of nine, Tad and Mary bombarded us with questions. How had the school system reacted? How had Mark adapted? What about his social life? They wanted to home-school David and Amy, emphasizing Japanese language and culture. Neither Mary nor the children speak much Japanese. But no wonder. Daddy aside, with whom would they speak it? A Japanese-Canadian friend tells me that there are exactly forty-two Japanese people in Halifax.

Back at the boat, we found John and Helen Nicholson standing on the wharf.

"John Nick" has white hair, bushy black eyebrows, a shrewd mind and a wide toothy grin. He is semi-retired now, but I remember meeting him in 1985, just off the plane from Buenos Aires and having spoken the preceding week in Atlanta. In the previous two months, he had spent thirty-six nights away from home.

John is, if such a thing is possible, a *co-operative* jet-setter, a credit union volunteer of international reputation. When he was an undergraduate at St. Francis Xavier, he was fired with enthusiasm by Moses Coady himself. He became a professor of sociology and joined the board of Sydney Credit Union. He became chairman of the local, provincial and national boards, eventually chairing the World Council of Credit Unions. The job of the World Council is "to assist in developing credit unions in the underdeveloped world." On that mission, he visited thirty-seven countries—while teaching full-time and raising six children.

What was he doing in Ingonish? He laughed.

"We've been spending our summers here for sixteen years. We heard you were here, so we thought we'd come and say hello. You're sailing right around the island? Marvellous."

"Are you going to write about it?" Helen asked.

"Absolutely."

"Did you hear Bobby McVeigh had a heart attack?" said John.

McVeigh was principal of the Nova Scotia Community College in Sydney, mayor of Dominion and president of Credit Union Central of Nova Scotia. Another tireless volunteer. Is volunteer work worth the stress?

"Oh, sure," said John. "It's given me a vision not only of the co-operative and credit union movement all over the world but actually of the world itself. It's a very complex world, and my credit union work has allowed me to see a lot of it.

"Mind you, you can't do it unless you have the support of your family. I've had wonderful support from Helen and the kids. I think that's where the whole problem of volunteerism is going to arise in the next ten or fifteen years—not just in credit unions but any volunteer organization. I don't know whether there's going to be that kind of support system for volunteers.

"I hope there will be. It's important, and it's fantastically rewarding."

THE WEE SHIPS,

THE

BONNY SHIPS

Westerly, 15 to 20 knots, said the forecast, *veering to northerly and then backing to southwesterly.* Westerly would be fine, northerly grand, southwesterly tolerable—particularly if we had crossed Sydney Bight before it backed to the west. We cast off at 5:30, rowing into another gilded, pastel morning. Fifty feet from the wharf we found a zephyr and shipped the oars.

At Middle Head we caught a gust of breeze—westerly, as promised—from South Bay. After carrying us across the bay, it let us drift for two hours off Cape Smokey. Smokey is an important boundary: "north of Smokey" is almost considered a separate principality. Evidently its ruler wanted us to stay.

We waited. In the hushed calm, we could hear the engines of

the fishing boats on the horizon, see the dark lines inscribed on the water by their wakes. The sunlight was weak, masking distances in a thin mist like vapour or smoke. Far to the south-east, we saw the outlines of two towers, grey on grey, like the uprights of a suspension bridge: the coal-fired power plants at Lingan, east of Sydney.

We had scarcely seen a yacht all summer, but now a tall sloop emerged from the northern haze before dissolving slowly in the smoky east. Another sloop emerged from behind Smokey, out-ward-bound from Ingonish Harbour, and slowly dwindled into the northeast, heading for Newfoundland. Before these two were out of sight, a husky ketch flying the Stars and Stripes slipped out past Smokey and swung around us in a broad arc, bound for the Great Bras d'Or and the Bras d'Or Lakes. Like the others, she had her sails up, but she was motoring.

As a result, her crew missed almost everything.

When the sea is cut up by sharp-edged waves and hollows, you can see very little on the surface. When you drift in a flat calm, the life of the ocean reveals itself.

Far off, a cloud of gulls hung over a boat, eager for fish scraps and offal. Black-and-white guillemots skittered over the water. Cormorants skimmed the surface with their fast, energetic wingbeats. Terns flew past the crosstrees, emitting their high-pitched cry—*pip-pip-pip!*—and circling restlessly over the water, then rearing back and fanning their wings as they hovered in the air. When they see a fish, they fold their wings and plunge into the sea like grey arrowheads. *Zzzzzunk!* Then up they come, swallowing their prey and resuming their ceaseless, circular patrols.

Seals popped up out of the water here and there, wet black doglike faces looking at us curiously. There were whales all around us, and we found them not by looking but by listening. *Puh-phoo!* Turning quickly towards the sound, we would see a sleek black back and a dorsal fin arching through the surface, sometimes nearby, sometimes off in the distance.

Clouds and rain showers wandered along the ridge of the mountains and spilled down the clefts of the valleys. Mark gazed through the binoculars, then inverted them and examined the top of his leg. He looked up with a grimace.

"Ugh," he said. "Looking through the wrong end of the binoculars is enough to discourage you from having skin."

Driven by vagrant puffs of wind, we worked our way slowly offshore.

"I'm going below for a nap," said Lulu.

"All right," I said.

To the south lay St. Ann's Bay, a spacious basin embraced by steep wooded hills and almost closed by a sandy finger of land. We wanted to explore St. Ann's, but the long run down into the bay and back out again was too time-consuming—which is exactly why there has never been an important town on this enviable harbour. The French established their headquarters here in 1713—the headland at the entrance is still called Cape Dauphin—but the trek in and out was too long for the fishermen. They moved to Havre à l'Anglois, which became Louisbourg. Since the fishery was the main reason for the colony, the garrison soon followed. Under the French, this coast became a refuge for free spirits who found Louisbourg bureaucratic and stuffy.

St. Ann's was the home of Angus MacAskill, the seven-foot-nine "Cape Breton giant" featured by the P.T. Barnum Circus in the 1850s. Famous though he once was, MacAskill would be forgotten today had he not captured the interest of an eccentric biographer named James D. Gillis. *The Cape Breton Giant*, published in 1898, is still in print. The literary critic W.A. Deacon considered it "the most remarkable prose work ever composed on Canadian soil." He may be right.

Gillis tells us very little about MacAskill, and what he does tell us is questionable. Gillis, for example, was a temperance man; MacAskill liked a drink. But, says Gillis, had MacAskill lived in more enlightened days, he *would have* been a temperance man, too. The book brims with moral precepts, scenic descriptions, historical detours and similar curiosities. Among Gillis's own qualifications, he notes, is that "I was twice to the United States: I do not say so for the sake of boast."

A genuine original who spent most of his life teaching in one-room schools, Gillis also wrote *The Canadian Grammar*—which, says Deacon sadly, "has never been adopted by the department of education in any province." Gillis was also the

bold geographer who pinpointed the West Pole in South Amer-
ica and the East Pole—which he modestly dubbed Gillis's
Pole—in Borneo. He was a poet, too, and his collection, *The
Great Election*, contains some stunning performances:

> I thought I was gone in the days of arrival
> To find that again
> We had met with ourselves.

As Deacon notes, this insight anticipates Einstein and relativity.
But Gillis can also be lyrical:

> And lovely girls
> In pink ado
> With costumes swell
> Enrich the view.

Not everyone can write like that.

On a bluff above St. Ann's Bay is North America's only Gaelic
College, which offers summer courses in piping, singing, weaving, Highland lore and history and Gaelic language and literature. The college is also the site of the Gaelic Mod, a festival of
Celtic culture held in early August.

The Gaelic College stands on land originally granted to the
charismatic preacher Norman MacLeod. Born in Suth-
erlandshire in 1780, MacLeod emigrated with some followers to
Pictou, on the Nova Scotia mainland. In 1820, dismayed by
Pictou's ungodliness, his congregation built six vessels—Mac-
Leod's was called *The Ark*—and sailed for the United States.
After they were scattered by a storm in St. Georges Bay, they
made their way to St. Ann's Bay, where they stayed.

MacLeod ruled the community like a sulphurous rustic pope,
though he would certainly have been enraged by the analogy.
He was the community's school teacher and judge as well as its
spiritual dictator, and in every role he was severe; he once
ordered the tip of a boy's ear clipped off on suspicion of theft.

Around 1850, MacLeod was inspired to shift his flock to
Australia, and in the fall of 1851—aged seventy-two—he sailed
away with 130 followers. Some months later, 131 people landed

in Australia; no one had died, and a baby had been born en route. Despite his severity, MacLeod was much loved; one of his St. Ann's followers nailed his front door shut after MacLeod left his house for the last time, vowing that no lesser man would ever pass through it.

The "Normanites" eventually settled not in Australia but in Waipu, New Zealand, where the Highland Moses died at eighty-six. Today, Scottish New Zealanders regularly visit St. Ann's, to see where their people came from, and Allan Mac-Eachen, when he was Minister of External Affairs, made a point of visiting Waipu. Nearly a century after the migration, Mona Innes Tracy—the grand-daughter of a Normanite couple who had made the voyage—wrote about the Cape Breton-built ships which travelled so far:

> In vision I see them
> As valiantly they come,
> The wee ships, the bonny ships
> That brought our clansmen home.

Puh-phoo!
Another whale, far to port. And another—no, that was a seal. A puff of wind, too, and we were moving right along—
Puh-phoo!
I looked around. Whale, but where? Somewhere astern?
Oh, my God—!
"Mark! Look!"
Just ten feet behind the boat, crossing our track, was the rounded black back of a whale. A big one, too, with a high square dorsal fin—and close enough that we could see the white speckles of barnacles on its back—
"*Lulu!*"
Lulu hurried on deck just in time to see the whale vanish.
—and then up it came again, relaxed, massive, lifting its head right beside the cockpit, 30 feet long, possibly more. I found myself looking right into a black eye the size of a softball, surrounded by wrinkles which gave it the appearance of amusement. It was too big, too close, to take in all at once. I saw the eye, Mark saw the baleen, Lulu saw the fin.
The whale cruised beside us for one frozen, unforgettable

instant. We gazed at each other. Then it flexed its massive back, lowered its head and dived. A little later, we saw a calf about 75 feet away. Mother and child? We never saw either one again.

Alone once more, we found ourselves shaking with excitement.

"I am extremely happy," said Mark solemnly. "We are *part* of the ocean. The whale thought we were like an island to explore."

Despite the faint and fickle breezes, we were creeping down the coast. A cargo ship appeared on the eastern horizon, and vanished. A very soft westerly filled in, not enough to ruffle the water but enough to heel the boat slightly to port and send her along. There is always some noise at sea—ropes slapping, wind humming, rain pattering. But not now. Total silence, except for the snapping of the flag.

"Ahhh!" I whispered.

"Wow," said Mark.

"Look," Lulu smiled and pointed. She had taken her hand off the tiller. *Silversark* was silently sailing herself.

For fifteen charmed minutes, we sat and listened as *Silversark* slid through the smooth water. We whispered, as though a loud word might break the spell. No gurgle from the wake, no chuckling at the bow, no creaking of the rigging. Just the flag.

The wind died. The boat straightened up. The stainless-steel gooseneck clanked. Somewhere, a hypnotist had clapped his hands.

"Amazing," said Lulu, in her normal voice.

"Never seen anything like it," I said.

Look, that little bird sitting on the gently heaving water, what's that? Binoculars—

Short, stout, with a parrot-shaped technicolour beak—a puffin! It broke into a strange little circular dance on the water, pattering with its wing-tips, and then suddenly plunged below the surface. A few moments later it emerged, cruised briefly on the surface, then repeated the whole performance.

A puffin is enough to make one believe in the Creator's sense of humour. Puffins are a Cape Breton icon—the Tourist Association issues MacPuffin dollars, which can be spent only on the island—but puffins are relatively rare. Only a few dozen pairs breed in Cape Breton, on Hertford and Ciboux islands, just outside St. Ann's Bay.

By now we were a mile from the Bird Islands, as they are known, and the puffins became more frequent. The islands are nesting sites for murres and razorbills as well as gulls, terns, puffins and other species. The islands belong to the Nova Scotia Bird Society, which correctly prohibits landing on them. As one reads through Robie Tufts's beautiful *Birds of Nova Scotia*, a pattern emerges: like the walrus and the woodland caribou, the birds have suffered for our presence in this wrenchingly beautiful land. Laughing gull, common murre, black-billed cuckoo, great auk, passenger pigeon, great horned owl—they were all Nova Scotian birds, and they are gone. Boat tours cruise close to the Bird Islands, which is fine—but we should not land on them.

If we had more wind and felt sure we could sail out, we might have gone closer, but by now it was getting late in the afternoon, no time to be among rocky islets without a motor.

True, but if we had a motor we would simply have motored to Sydney. And we would have missed everything that mattered.

The wind arrived at five o'clock that evening—a steady sea-wind from the northeast, where it was not supposed to be. *Silversark* lay into it, while Mark relaxed below, chanting the speed and distance to Cranberry Point, the portal of Sydney Harbour.

"5.6 miles, 6.4 knots—5.5, 6.4 knots—5.3, 5.9 knots—"

Fine sailing, parallel to the shore, looking through the glasses at the entrance to Little Bras d'Or, the scattered houses, the spires of churches and lighthouses. A hulking blue-and-white vessel emerged from behind Cranberry Point and cruised rapidly into the smoky northern distance: the *Caribou*, the newest, finest and fastest of the Marine Atlantic ferries between North Sydney and Port-aux-Basques, Newfoundland.

Having covered 15 miles in a dozen hours, *Silversark* now reeled off five miles in an hour, bringing us to Cranberry Point at sunset. We passed a raft of three power cruisers and headed up into the harbour, slowing down as the wind faded, edging along under coal-streaked cliffs capped by the houses of Sydney Mines.

"Can I go up the mast?" asked Mark.

"Okay. Let us know if you see anything special."

He shinnied to the crosstrees and peered into the gathering dusk. The wind died, and we rowed for a few minutes. Then the wind revived, light but steady, quietly pressing us forward.

Sydney Harbour is shaped like a tooth, with one root, the South Arm, running into Sydney itself. The other root lies west of south and is called the North West Arm. Don't ask me why. The North West Arm runs past North Sydney to the Northern Yacht Club and eventually vanishes under the Trans-Canada Highway and the railway track.

North Sydney lay just ahead, to starboard. Sydney was two or three miles further, off the port bow. In the gathering darkness, the harbour was a mass of streetlights, shop windows, winking buoys and steady range lights.

"Where should we go?" asked Lulu. "The yacht club?"

"Too far," I said. "We don't have a detail chart of the harbour. Let's go to Good People Sea and Shore."

"What's that?"

"The old North Sydney Marine Railway. Just past the ferry terminal. Dory Tuvim's place — you remember, I wrote a magazine piece about him."

"Mmmm," said Lulu doubtfully. "That red flasher, there, away out in the harbour — do I steer around it?"

I ducked below and looked at the chart.

"It looks like that light's for the ferries," I said. "Should be enough water if we go along the shore."

"Are you sure?"

"Yeah, yeah, carry on."

On we went, staring into the inky shadows along the water's edge. *Silversark* edged closer and closer to the ferry terminal —

— and stopped, gently.

"Woh-oh!" cried Mark from the darkness overhead.

"We're aground!" I said.

"Aground?" said Lulu. "We're still sailing!"

"We're not moving!" I said.

"He's right, Mom," called Mark. "We're stopped."

Lulu quickly put the helm over. *Silversark* leaned over a little and turned out towards the deeper water—slowly at first, then faster, twisting sideways in the soft sand. A little puff, and she started to move.

"She's off! She's sailing!"

"Head out into the harbour."

"Around the red light buoy."

"It wasn't just for big ships."

"Thank God the bottom was only sand."

"Amen."

Out around the buoy we went, then past the terminal, and then back in towards the shore again.

"We're going too fast," said Lulu. "I can't see anything."

"Right. Let's get the main off her. Mark, come down."

"But—"

"Come *down. Now.*"

With the main off, *Silversark* slowed to a crawl. I got out the hand spotlight and swept the waterfront.

"What are we looking for?"

"A big concrete wharf. Probably with a 120-foot oceangoing tug alongside."

A concrete wall loomed up ahead of us. Grass growing on top of it. Massive tractor tires for fenders. No tug, but it looked right. Lulu steered alongside, and Mark dropped the sails. With a mooring line in my teeth and a flashlight in my pocket, I swarmed up a massive rusty chain and made fast.

2200. Secured at Good People wharf, North Sydney.

GOOD PEOPLE

IN

BAD TIMES

On that evening in July, anyone walking down Commercial Street in North Sydney—the main street, opposite Herald Stationers, the Venice Pizzeria, Munchee's Sub and Donair—would have been startled to see three burglars breaking *out* of a deserted shipyard. The skinny little fellow scaled the gates like a monkey, ponderously followed by the grey-haired chap and his short, dark-haired sidekick. Then the three of them went directly to the police station.

"I wanted you to know what's going on," I told the officer. "And I need a phone."

"Right on the corner. Thanks for coming in."

Dory Tuvim was surprised but hospitable.

"I've got a night watchman coming on at twelve," he said. "Make yourselves comfortable. I'll see you in the morning."

We had a snack at the Canton Restaurant, and then, at 11:30, found ourselves exhausted. We had climbed out; couldn't we simply climb back in and go to bed?

Mark wriggled under the gate. I scrambled over. Lulu stood pondering. A chunky young man in a baseball cap issued from a shack by the office building. He walked straight to Lulu.

"I don't know why they're doing that when the gate's unlocked," said the watchman, shaking his head and opening the gate. His name was Art Francis. He ushered us to the boat with his powerful flashlight.

"I'll be around all night, makin' me rounds," he said. "If you hear someone on the wharf, 's only me. If you hear someone adjustin' your lines, 's only me. If you hear someone fall overboard, 's not me: I don't like the water."

In the morning, I looked over the silent shipyard. Three years before, there was an oceangoing tug at the wharf, a ship on the marine railway, a busy machine shop. Now there was a travel-lift, a new wharf, a new carriage on the marine railway, new buildings—but no people, no ships, no action. When Dory Tuvim arrived, we got some coffee and I asked what was wrong.

"The dream doesn't look very good right now," he said sadly.

Dory is a sailor turned businessman, and his dream had galvanized the whole town. Its roots lay in his childhood in Haifa, then a small city. Dory grew up on a hilltop farm looking over the town and down to his father's shipyard. In 1950, when Dory was fourteen, his father died in a car accident. His mother took over the shipyard, and Dory went to sea as a deck boy in the Israeli merchant marine and later served in the Israeli navy.

Born in 1936, having experienced the Second World War and three Arab-Israeli conflicts, Dory had little first-hand experience of peace, but he divined that it was preferable to war. In 1967, after the Six Day War, he emigrated to Montreal and joined Canadian Vickers. Two years later, he took his life's savings—$500—and established Dory Home Repairs. A customer asked whether he could repair shipping containers. Sure, said Dory. The customer was an executive of CTI, the largest container-leasing company in the world. Dory Home Repairs gave way to Marine Container Services, whose first office was an abandoned shipping container. A decade later, with a workforce of thirty, MCS was doing $1 million a year refurbishing containers.

"The moment it started to make money I got bored with it," says Dory. "No more challenge." He contemplated an expansion into the U.S., and a whole new range of uses for shipping containers as self-sufficient rooms. Fit them out, then pick them up by helicopter or load them on a ship. Take them where they're needed, set them down, open the doors. Presto: instant dental surgeries, construction offices, chapels, medical clinics.

In July 1983, mulling over these possibilities, Dory and his wife, Judy, took a Cape Breton vacation. They stopped overnight in North Sydney, a whipped, defeated town which "did not *have* an economy," as a Sydney consultant recalls. "The whole place was living on UIC, old age pensions, the New-foundland ferries and welfare." Dory went out for a walk. On the decrepit main street, he peered through the padlocked gates of the bankrupt 140-year-old North Sydney Marine Railway.

Ancient memories stirred. A shipyard, a hilltop farm . . . He talked to some bystanders. Canada had declared a 200-mile limit. The fishery was bustling. Multinationals were drilling for offshore oil. The trade of the Great Lakes and the St. Lawrence Seaway passed through Cabot Strait. With an oceangoing tug—

How could the yard have failed? Dory walked over to the town hall. The new mayor was a young teacher named David MacDonald. He was wearing sandals and a T-shirt. I want to make a bid for that shipyard, said Tuvim. I'm with you, said MacDonald. Dory went back to the hotel and told Judy there had been a change of plan.

Dory shocked the shipyard workers by signing their existing contract without reading it. "I want you guys," he said. "If you aren't coming with me, I won't buy the shipyard."

But, says Dory, "I couldn't believe the viciousness of the Cape Breton establishment." The bank and the receivers spurned the intruder from Montreal. Twice he bid on the shipyard; twice his bid was the highest; twice he was turned down. After the second bid was opened, the receivers sent for an auctioneer to break up the yard and sell off its assets. The workers set up picket lines at the bank and shipyard, called in the press and confronted the trustees in court. The judge reprimanded the trustees. Dory and Judy paid $225,000 for the industrial corpse. They renamed it Good People Sea and Shore Services.

The next spring, working sixteen and twenty hours a day, they demolished rotten buildings, renovated others, rebuilt antique machinery. Dory and Judy slept on a mattress in the abandoned office building with a stray puppy named Kushi. Six months and $1.8 million later, they had a functioning shipyard. Judy became general manager. They hauled their first ship—a dragger named *Must 'N' Tell*—in July. From September 1984 to June 1985, they turned over $1.2 million.

"But we didn't know the cycles." Dory winces. "The next winter was a total disaster. We lost $400,000 just to keep going." The establishment's hostility continued: one fish plant manager welcomed them warmly and then didn't send a ship for three years. He did make sure that Dory knew about each trawler he sent for refit, so they could watch it steam out of North Sydney bound for a competing yard in Newfoundland.

A subcontract for finish work on the new ferry *Caribou* allowed Good People to survive a second winter. Among the benefits of the contract were jobs for fifty workmen, a positive cash flow and a new devotion to marketing.

"Shipyards traditionally didn't have to sell," Dory points out. "To get the work done, you *had* to go to a shipyard." But modern shipyards are fiercely competitive. Each winter, yard manager Ross Thomas went home to Newfoundland and promoted Good People. To attract fishermen, Tuvim got his son Michael into an outfitting business serving the whole region. Michael's staff sent fishing gear and machine-shop work to southern Newfoundland and Labrador on the *Caribou* in just four and a half hours.

When Dory discovered that fishing boat repairs were going to the nearby National Sea plant because fishermen could also sell their catches there, he opened a fish plant. He knew nothing about fish, but his Good People did. By 1987, he had twenty-five workers cleaning and filleting for a retail fish market—"the first fish market here in twenty years," noted David MacDonald.

They still needed a tug. An oceangoing tug rescues crippled vessels far at sea—and delivers them to shipyards. Captain Don Tetrault had operated his 120-foot *Orion Expeditor* in the Beaufort Sea till Arctic exploration collapsed. He came to North Sydney scouting for work. He found a new base at Good People.

Dory and Judy bought a small farm high on a hill behind the town, looking down to the shipyard. Just like Haifa. By then, Good People was doing $1.5 million in sales and making modest profits. The yard should have been making 30 per cent gross profit on repairs, but the ancient equipment was killing it. With the original steam-powered marine railway, installed in 1866, eight men took half a day to haul or launch a ship. It should have been done by one man in an hour, with a push-button.

Dory borrowed more money, got some grants and modernized the business. Meanwhile, he and MacDonald and other activists had created a minor boom in North Sydney and Sydney Mines. In 1986, sixteen new businesses started in North Sydney, and the industrial park attracted such heavyweights as St. Clair Paint and Wallpaper and Magna International.

"But the shipyard was the first-born," said David MacDonald. "We learned our basic lessons here. The shipyard was proof that it could be done in Cape Breton—and that's what we needed more than anything."

So what went wrong?

"In 1984, the Tories killed the National Energy Program," Dory said. "That was the end of offshore oil. Then in 1989 the fishery collapsed. What's left? We got some industrial work— doing things for the Tar Ponds clean-up at Sydney Steel, things like that. But the basic problem is that we don't have enough work to service the debt. I went to Moscow to negotiate refit work with the Russians. I was surprised to find I could actually converse and negotiate in Russian—my parents were Russian-speakers, but I didn't think I knew that much Russian.

"I did manage to get a contract. We've had one ship, and we're supposed to have another in early August. I asked the people in North Sydney to make the Russians happy, and they lined the wharf cheering, invited them home for meals and all kinds of things. The Russians were amazed. It was only a dirty old fishing trawler, and they'd never had a reception like that anywhere.

"But even with the Russians it's not enough. We put $5.3 million in here, and if it goes down I'll lose $2 million personally."

I thought he seemed remarkably sanguine about it.

"I won't starve," said Dory. "I've still got the business in Montreal. But I'm sad about it, that's for sure."

We went to the yacht club for showers, visited friends, and found a laundromat a couple of blocks from the shipyard. Leaving Mark aboard, Lulu and I did the laundry. As we were folding the clothes, Mark appeared with Dory, who had steamed two huge bowls of mussels in wine broth and brought them down to the boat, along with two dozen eggs from his own henhouse. We poured some wine.

"The changes in one man's lifetime, it's just unbelievable," Dory said. "When I was young, I crossed the Atlantic, back and forth, for fifteen years with an old Italian mate—completely illiterate, so he couldn't get promoted to skipper. When he started, there was no such a thing as a license or a ticket. If you could do the job, the owner of the vessel hired you as captain and that was that."

A bell rang in my memory. Paul Bonin had said something similar: when he was a boy, there were no licenses for hunting, fishing, lobstering. If you needed a deer, you shot one. We hardly notice how much human activity *is* licensed and regulated today. Rightly or wrongly, we now accept a level of social control which would have seemed tyrannical to our ancestors. Lawyering, lobbying and administering will be growth industries for the foreseeable future.

"That old Italian, you wouldn't believe what he knew," Dory said. "Anywhere in the Atlantic, he always knew where he was. How? By the colour of the water, the birds, the patterns of the waves, whether there was seaweed, and whether it would rise or fall below the surface. He didn't reason it out. He just *knew*. It might be a beautiful day, not a cloud in sight, and he'd sniff the air and look off in the distance and say, 'In six hours we'll have a big breeze from the nor'west.' Six hours later, sure enough, there was the breeze.

"I used to watch him and listen, and after a while I developed a little bit of that myself. And I used to take sextant sights every half hour, just to be absolutely up to date in case we ran into overcast or fog. Every half hour! When I was sailing, the masters would come aboard with their own sextants. They were beautiful things, all brass inlaid with silver. They kept them in mahogany boxes lined with velvet. If you go on the bridge of a ship now, you'll still see a sextant, but I don't know if the young officers could take a sextant sight at all. They don't even take sextant sights as a back-up. It's all electronic."

Shipping is a tough, ruthless business, but it has its funny side. As a youth, Dory worked on a liner plying between Israel and Italy. The trip took sixty hours. The passengers would come aboard with picnic baskets, intent on avoiding the high-priced dining rooms. To thwart them, the master would withdraw the stabilizers after mealtime. The ship rolled violently for a couple of hours. Once the passengers had heaved their lunches into the sea, the stabilizers went back out. An hour later the passengers were hungry. The restaurants did a roaring business.

In the 1956 Arab-Israeli war, an old Egyptian warship cruised the Israeli coast, shelling settlements more or less at random — "for the sake of formality, really." Two Israeli destroyers went in pursuit.

"The normal practice in gunnery is to fire a round, note the range, adjust your sights, and fire again," Dory said. "But these two destroyers were each so anxious to get the kill that they fired overlapping broadsides. Well, then they couldn't tell whose shots went where — and they expended their entire magazines without *ever once hitting* the target vessel!

"So they called in the air force, who sent one jet, who used one shot. He just zoomed in and fired right down the stemhead. All the Egyptian sailors jumped overboard when they saw what was coming, and the shell blew up inside the ship and disabled her.

"Now the Israeli ships towed her back in triumph. Of course the whole thing was treated as a high-security matter, not ever to be discussed at all."

We left the boat with our Israeli friend while we stayed overnight with our Arab friend. Afra Kavanagh is a Moslem from Beirut who studied English literature at the University of Manitoba. She married a business student who eventually took her home to his native Cape Breton. Shrewd, effervescent and generous, Afra presides affably over a huge, lugubrious house reminiscent of Wuthering Heights. It will not be lugubrious forever, though its splendid dark wood panelling will always frown on frivolity. But already the walls between the pantry, the back porch and the primitive kitchen had been ripped out, and only a plastic sheet kept the rain out. Wuthering Heights would have a state-of-the-art kitchen by Christmas.

The literary Afra is a top real estate agent; the commercial Steve is a soft-spoken, retiring professor of marketing at the University College of Cape Breton. She is short, dark, intense; he is tall, silver-haired, laid-back. She is always on the move, on the phone, showing houses, entertaining guests, ferrying the two girls around town. Steve lingers over coffee. He smokes and thinks. He takes long hikes on remote coastlines and overgrown roads. He knows Cape Breton intimately.

We took coffee on their wide verandah, looking out over Sydney Harbour. The house is in Westmount, directly opposite City Hall, the Ramada, the Commerce Tower and the stacks of the blast furnaces at the steel mill, now silent and smokeless.

Sydney is the capital of Cape Breton Island in everything but law—and it was once the capital in law. About 130,000 of Cape Breton's 180,000 people live in Cape Breton County. When people say "Cape Breton"—as in "the troubled Cape Breton economy"—they usually mean *industrial* Cape Breton: Glace Bay, New Waterford and the various Sydneys. When I went to Sydney in 1978 as writer-in-residence at the University College of Cape Breton, one of the professors greeted me with a cheery "Welcome to Cape Breton!" I was nonplussed: I had been living in Cape Breton Island for seven years.

"Where will you go next?" asked Steve.

"We'd like to stop in Glace Bay, if we can," said Lulu.

"I wish I knew more about the alternatives," I said. "Morien, Lingan, little harbours like that."

"Why don't we go for a drive and look at them?" said Steve.

Afra recently sold a house on George Street in Sydney to Lulu's brother Bernie. We dropped Mark there for a visit with his cousins. Bernie Terrio's house faces Hardwood Hill Cemetery. To our surprise, Steve drove into the cemetery when we left.

"You get the best view of Sydney from here," he said.

You do. Though it has some charming neighbourhoods, Sydney is a grubby, warm-hearted, working man's town. From Hardwood Hill, you see the forest, not the trees. The western horizon is bounded by mountains, and the green V of rural Point Edward divides the two arms of the harbour. The sister communities lie sprinkled around it—Westmount, North Sydney, Sydney River. Sydney itself looks green and leafy, its rooftops nestled in a canopy of tossing trees.

Steve drove out on George Street, which eventually becomes the road to Louisbourg. I had expected him to follow the Sydney by-pass to Glace Bay.

"I'd like to see a book, or a series of books, called *The Cape Bretoner's Cape Breton*," he said. "Every Cape Bretoner knows places that the tourist never sees—really interesting places. Ever been to Broughton?"

No: I'd seen the name on a map, but that's all.

"Well, that's about all there is. It's a coal-mining town that never really got off the ground."

The story of Cape Breton County is about coal. The Sydney coalfield has 3 billion tons of proven reserves, a billion of which are recoverable with today's technology. Southwestern Newfoundland has outcroppings of similar coal, and the basin between the two islands may cover a prodigious body of coal, conceivably as much as 500 billion tons.

Cape Breton mining began in 1720, when the French pried coal from the seaside cliffs to heat the Fortress of Louisbourg. It mushroomed a century ago, when American industrialists realized that blast furnaces in Sydney could convert iron ore from Bell Island, Newfoundland, into steel for the markets of New England—which, then and now, had no steel plants of their own. During those turn-of-the-century boom years, people poured into industrial Cape Breton from all over the world: Italy, the Ukraine, the West Indies, Wales, Lebanon, Newfoundland, Poland. Catholic, African Orthodox, Jewish, Pentecostal, Greek Orthodox, Anglican, Mormon. Adversity and labour strife forged them into a cosmopolitan community unique in Atlantic Canada.

The fate of the steel plant may have been sealed as early as the federal election of 1911. The defeat of reciprocity — free trade — closed off the New England market and forced Maritime industries to compete in distant Ontario. But Ontario had coal and steel supplies much closer at hand. Absentee owners, aided by pliable governments, imposed appalling conditions on miners and steelworkers. The workers struck, and the companies, aided by the army, beat, shot and starved the men back to work. The result was the birth of the Canadian labour movement, and an electorate which has elected Labour, CCF and NDP members provincially and federally off and on since the 1920s.

All the same, Cape Breton steel and coal made healthy profits during the long expansion of the Canadian economy before 1970. Cape Breton produced 8.1 million tons of coal in 1913, and was still producing well over 7 million tons during World War II, when it was considered an essential defence industry.

But the mines and mills were never modernized, and by the 1960s they were capital-starved, obsolete, inefficient and uncompetitive. The coal faces in some of the older mines were eight miles out under the seabed; miners had to travel an hour and a half underground just to reach them. The last of the old mines, Number 26 in Glace Bay, employed about twelve hundred miners; the new mine at Lingan produces double the tonnage with only seven hundred men. In the end, the federal government took over the mines; the province took over the steel mill. Both have been searching ever since for a new and viable role.

Meanwhile, the Tar Ponds and the Coke Ovens associated with the steel plant are environmental disasters. The legacy of industry includes broken bones, crushed limbs and corrupted lungs. Until recently, the air in Sydney's Whitney Pier district was the dirtiest in Canada. Towns which grew up around a single mine lost their economic foundation when the mine closed. The slag heaps and abandoned railroad rights-of-way remain, along with the streets of "company houses" — cheap and antiquated duplexes slapped together by parsimonious corporations and now long past their intended lifespan.

Local government, too, is a mess. If industrial Cape Breton were a single city of 130,000, its problems would be far more tractable and its influence would be greater. But one city, six incorporated towns and countless smaller communities all lie within the county limits. Some municipal politicians jealously guard their turf; others abrade their spirits in endless negotiations. What can be shared in industrial Cape Breton: police departments, fire departments, hospitals, recreational facilities, planning policies, school boards? If there is to be a new university campus or shopping mall or hospital, where should it be located? Water pollution and sewage treatment are perennial problems. Halifax still flushes raw sewage into the harbour. So does Montreal. What can one expect of a dozen impoverished settlements scattered over several hundred square miles?

Confronting these facts, one might conclude that industrial Cape Breton is a horrible place.

One would be dead wrong.

Industrial Cape Breton is raucous and funny, full of music and theatre and satire. It is gossipy and anecdotal, tolerant of eccentricity, generous and co-operative. It is tenacious, disorderly, skeptical of authority, lethal to pomposity and pretension. It is fecund, unruly and affectionate.

It is a hard place to make a living, but it is a wonderful place to live.

Steve Kavanagh took a side road off a side road off the Louisbourg highway. After a couple of miles he slowed down, squinting into the alder bushes and scrub spruce.

"Right along here somewhere," he said. A narrow lane opened up, and he turned into the woods.

"Broughton," he said. The little Toyota station wagon bounced and hopped over the rocks and potholes. Other lanes ran off into the bushes on each side.

"This was the townsite," Steve said. "Those are surveyed streets. There was a mine administration building and a whole townsite laid out here."

"How come the roads aren't overgrown?"

"They're still in use."

"Who uses them? For what?"

"Oh . . . hunting. Snaring rabbits. Maybe other things, too."

We walked a few feet through the woods, up a gentle rise through the trees.

"The Broughton Hotel," Steve said.

At our feet was an elaborate concrete foundation with half-circles at each corner, notches for the cellar windows, a grand entrance. But it was lost in the forest. You might trip on it before you saw it. Forty- and fifty-foot trees were growing up right inside it, rooted in mounds of humus that once were joists, studs, hardwood floors. The forest inside the building and outside the building. Grand ambition reduced to a cement design in the forest floor.

"Look," said Steve, turning around. "It was all grass once."

In front of the hotel, the land fell gradually away to the shore of a lake. Something about the site suddenly evoked the hard bright elegance of the Jazz Age: Packards, pompadours, steamer chairs on the lawn. Imagery out of F. Scott Fitzgerald.

Sic transit gloria mundi.

We drove out through a bewildering skein of backwoods roads. Patches of clear-cut forest, gravel pits, a lonely little bungalow every now and then. We emerged on the pavement at the head of Morien Bay, wide open and lonely, with ranks of breakers building offshore and piling onto the wide beach.

"Shallow for a long way out," said Lulu.

"You wouldn't be coming anywhere near here," said Steve. "Port Morien is away up there on the left."

Another artificial cove between rock breakwaters, Port Morien was a busy little place, judging from the fleet of moored fishing boats and the substantial fish plant. The village looked brave but not cosy, a cluster of tidy houses on the bluff above the harbour—somehow frail and vulnerable, exposed to the sea before it and the low marshland behind it.

"Wasn't the Donkin-Morien mine supposed to be somewhere around here?" I asked, as we drove along the bluffs towards Glace Bay.

"Right over there," said Steve, pointing.

In the early 1980s, Devco proposed a series of new mines costing $2.5 billion. One was a second mine at Lingan, designed to exploit the low-sulphur Phalen seam for which Devco had ready export markets. But the largest was Donkin-Morien, a stupendous project, using the latest technology. Its most spectacular feature was a tunnel-boring machine, like a huge mechanical drill, which gnawed a shaft 25 feet in diameter through the solid rock down to the coal seam. It might have become the largest underground coal mine in North America.

These energy megaprojects had none of the glamour of oil and gas, and they drew surprisingly little comment. Yet Lingan-Phalen —which *was* built—will have a greater economic impact on Nova Scotia than the hyped and hypothetical Venture offshore gas field. Lingan-Phalen will produce $2 billion in household income, as opposed to Venture's $1.5 billion; it will operate for thirty years, Venture for only seventeen. Lingan-Phalen will create 50 per cent more man-years of employment, and its multiplier effects in the economy will be about ten times as large. And Lingan-Phalen represented only about 9 per cent of Devco's projected capital outlays for the 1980s.

At the time, it all made economic sense. In the 1960s, the price of coal hovered around $10 a tonne. In 1982, it went over $90. Devco's coal prices are linked to Canadian oil prices; if Canadians had been paying world prices for oil, says economist Roy George, Devco would have been making money as early as 1980 — and, with OPEC threatening oil embargoes, Cape Breton's massive reserves represented energy self-sufficiency for eastern Canada. Coal development would have slowed the outward flow of Canadian dollars; it would have guaranteed Nova Scotia's source of electricity; and its four-thousand-odd jobs were the backbone of industrial Cape Breton, which has been the real engine of the whole Maritime economy. Coal was also an export industry. By the early 1980s, Devco was selling a million tonnes a year to Sweden, Holland, Italy, Brazil, Korea and Japan. Capitalizing on coal, Devco's Industrial Development Division had catalyzed a whole cluster of mining-equipment companies, several of which were exporting across the country and abroad.

COAL! said a 1970s bumper sticker. NO FUEL LIKE AN OLD FUEL!

So why did Devco lose $46 million in 1983? Steve Rankin, then Devco's president, cited three reasons. First, Devco was locked into a money-losing contract with the provincially owned Nova Scotia Power Corporation. Second, the 1981-82 recession reduced world coal prices sharply, cutting Devco's revenues by $20 million. Finally, for political reasons, Devco could not respond by cutting production and laying off miners.

Devco was also paying for early-retirement plans dating from the mine closures of the 1960s. In addition, Nova Scotia's "automatic assumption" policy declares respiratory disease in miners with more than twenty years of experience to be an occupational disease unless proven otherwise. Automatic assumption cost Devco about $3 million in 1982.

These "social costs," notes a company document, "would not normally be borne by a commercial coal company." They *should* be paid, said economist Father John Capstick, but they should not be considered corporate operating costs. "It has pleased Ottawa and Halifax to make a fool of the corporation," noted Capstick drily, "and then to turn around and damn it for its performance. When the decisions have been political rather than economic, it's unfair to judge the results by economic standards."

Devco intended to finance about half of its $2.5 billion expansion out of earnings; Ottawa would have put up $1.2 billion, which Devco had pledged to repay. At the same time, CN proposed to spend $4.1 billion on its Western tracks, largely to move Western coal. Would it ever be repaid? In 1983, Devco lost $46 million—and Montreal's Canadair dropped $1.4 billion. Mirabel, the St. Lawrence Seaway, Massey Harris, Dome Petroleum . . . Maritimers have some trouble understanding why *we*, alone, are viewed as the nagging beggars of Confederation.

"Money going from Ottawa to Western Canada is considered an *investment*," Steve Rankin said wryly. "Money going from Ottawa to *Eastern* Canada is a subsidy. It doesn't make sense, but that's the way it's seen."

Devco's plans were slashed by the Tories, and Devco was dismantled: the Cape Breton Development Corporation is now a Crown-owned coal company, pure and simple, and its Industrial Development Division became Enterprise Cape Breton Corporation, a unit of the Atlantic Canada Opportunities Agency. Lingan-Phalen was built; Donkin-Morien was cancelled.

Well, coal has a bad name environmentally—but technology may yet convert it into a desirable replacement for expensive imported oil. And that vast treasurehouse of coal is still there.

As we drove into Glace Bay, we noticed bands of red, white and blue painted on the telephone poles.

"What are those?" asked Lulu.

"I can't tell you," said Steve. "I'm embarrassed."

"Come on."

In the end, he confessed: some civic organization had received a government grant to spruce up Glace Bay, and its members discovered they had no idea how to do it. They wound up hiring students to paint these rings on the poles.

Cape Bretoners and Newfoundlanders are the designated butts of much Canadian humour, and such episodes seem to justify our appointment as buffoons to the nation. The lens through which we look at the world is evidently not ground to the correct prescription. Our troubles with formal language don't help. One recently appointed provincial judge made it very clear to his secretary that he regarded Cape Bretoners as a barbarian sub-species of humanity. She objected—but then, in court, the judge asked some fellow what his occupation was.

"Oh, none, Your Honour," said the fellow. "I'm unoccupied."

"I'm a Cape Breton barbarian," sings Kenzie MacNeil:

> Well, we all are! Or didn't you know?
> Yes, I'm a hairy and scary one:
> That's how the mainland sayings go.
>
> Ah, but how much tax goes to Halifax?

And how much of it comes back?
How much coal and how much steel
Left on the west-bound train tracks?

Call a man a barbarian
Tell him he needs to have culture
Then make him your own beast of burden
And claim the spoils of the vulture.

We drove down to Glace Bay Harbour, another narrow estuary between massive stone breakwaters. This harbour, however, cut deep into the heart of the town, and it was lined from end to end with fish plants. It looked like the main street of a grubby industrial district—but in Venice, perhaps. It would not be easy to enter under sail.

Midway between Glace Bay and Sydney is Steve Kavanagh's employer, the University College of Cape Breton, which owes its very existence to Cape Breton tenacity. Twenty years ago, Nova Scotia had nine degree-granting universities. Six of them were in Halifax, led by proud Dalhousie, with its array of research laboratories and professional schools. With 20 per cent of the province's population, Cape Breton was served only by one junior college.

Cape Breton got its own university in 1974 over the violent objections of such mainland tribunes as Dalhousie president Senator Henry Hicks. Formed by the union of Xavier College with the Eastern Institute of Technology, the University College of Cape Breton began as a marriage of liberal arts and practical technology. Now that Devco has been dismembered, it is the most important institution on the island.

UCCB is home to the Cape Breton Archives, and it operates the island's leading public art gallery. Its press publishes fiction, poetry and historical works, and also produces albums and tapes of Cape Breton music, including fiddle music, rock and the sound tracks of satirical revues. The university has a whole collection of special-purpose institutes devoted to social development, co-operatives, coal and Cape Breton history.

Even more important, the university is a haven for mavericks and activists of various stripes: impresarios, critics, community organizers, internationalists, radical philosophers.

Take Greg MacLeod, for instance. (Some Nova Scotian authorities will urge you to take him far away and keep him there for a very long time.) An ordained priest, a spiritual descendant of Coady and Tompkins, a Ph.D. from the University of Louvain, Belgium, MacLeod teaches philosophy at UCCB. His father was a miner, his mother an Acadian. He is the compleat Cape Bretoner.

He is voluble, knowledgeable, impassioned, full of jokes, perpetually indignant. His teeth fit into his mouth more or less at random, he has a cast in one eye, and his forehead now rises smoothly back to a point well north of his ears. At an outdoor concert he seizes you by an arm and points indignantly at the sign over the stage.

"Look at that," he says. "Broad Cove *Scottish* Concert. One of those sanctimonious purists from Antigonish has gotten hold of these people and done that to them. We always called it a *Scotch* concert. That's what it always said on that sign. Why do people do that, make us embarrassed about our own culture, eh? Why? And why do we listen to them?"

Ashley MacIsaac, from Creignish, is stepdancing on the stage. A fine fiddler and dancer, he is sixteen years old.

"Oh, he's excellent," says Greg. "Look! Look! He's worked that Cape North drag in there! Say, I've got to meet that young fellow. He's really special, isn't he?"

Greg MacLeod is a student of co-operative economics, and in recent years he has spent much time in Spain, seeking to understand the process by which a depressed Basque district called Mondragon has become an economic powerhouse. As a result he is trilingual — English, French, Spanish. Not satisfied with that, he pretends to be quadrilingual. We once discussed Cape Breton issues together before a conference of educators.

"Do you speak Gaelic?" asked a woman in the audience.

"Oh, yes," said Greg. "I'm not really fluent, mind you."

"Could you speak a little Gaelic for us? Just so we can hear what it sounds like?"

"*Thig crioch an niall,*" said Greg. "*Pibroch na claddach, ceilidh, ciad mille failte.*"

"What does that mean?"

"It means, 'Here's a wee snatch of Gaelic for the charming young woman from the great western city'," said Greg.

The woman blushed prettily, and the audience applauded.

"I didn't know you could speak Gaelic," I whispered.

"I can't," hissed Greg. "But she doesn't know the difference. Look at her: she's delighted."

Greg is the founding chairman of New Dawn Enterprises, a remarkable community development corporation. Starting from scratch in 1973, New Dawn accumulated a real estate portfolio worth over $10 million by 1986, including houses, apartments, offices, a senior citizens' guest home, a group home for the post-mentally ill, a woodlot, two dental centres and a senior citizens' resource centre. It published music, sponsored concerts, provided consulting services, ran a construction company and sold used auto parts. Its aim is to ensure that Cape Breton becomes and remains a viable community. Greg MacLeod wrote the New Dawn story himself in a book called *New Age Business: Community Corporations That Work.*

"For me," he wrote, "a viable community is fundamentally one where people like to live, one which offers the opportunity for all its citizens to enjoy a full and abundant life. This includes social, cultural and spiritual considerations as well as economic."

That is the Cape Breton perspective on community life—and it reveals the island's fundamental strength. Socially, culturally and spiritually, Cape Breton is far stronger than most North American communities. All that is missing is economic strength—difficult enough, but by far the easiest defect to remedy among MacLeod's four considerations.

As a young man once said to me in a Sydney tavern, "Jesus, b'y, 's nothin' serious. 'S only *money!*"

ROOSTERS

AND

MOONSHINE

Back at the boat, we checked the forecast. Bad news: Hurricane Bertha would pound the Maritimes next day with gales of 50 to 55 knots from the southeast, straight into Dory's little haven. Instead of sailing for Glace Bay, we would move to a protected boat basin next door and wait it out.

There are old sailors, runs the proverb, and there are bold sailors—but there are no old, bold sailors.

But the morning forecast called only for southeast 15 to 25 knots, increasing to 25 to 35, and finally to gales of 40 to 55 sometime the following night. *Silversark* could sail in anything up to 35 knots—and we could turn and run back before a southeasterly.

We sailed at eight. The weather was overcast, drizzly and

warm. Despite the forecast, the southeasterly wind was lighter than it had been during the night, and it fell lighter and lighter as *Silversark* ambled out of Sydney Harbour. By 9:30 we had reached the Low Point buoy—the Farewell buoy, as it's known—and the wind had disappeared almost completely. We looked longingly down the coast to the town of New Waterford, perched on its coal-blackened bluffs, and the soaring twin chimneys of Lingan. Glace Bay was just a dozen miles away.

A sleepy Mark stuck his head out of the hatch.

"What's going on?"

"We're on our way to Glace Bay."

"You guys never tell me *anything*," he protested, pulling on his sweater and heading for the food bin.

"We just decided this morning," I said defensively.

"The milk's chocked in the sink," Lulu said.

A hulking blue vessel rumbled out of the harbour behind us and made a shallow turn to starboard: *Atlantic Freighter*, a Marine Atlantic cargo vessel bound for Argentia, Newfoundland. Ferries seem about as romantic as buses, but many a ship has been lost in this service, from the *Bruce* in 1911 to the *Patrick Morris* in 1970. Worst of all was the first *Caribou*, pride of the fleet, sunk by a German U-boat on her way from North Sydney to Port-aux-Basques, Newfoundland, in October 1942.

Even now, few Canadians realize the toll taken by the U-boats off the Atlantic coast. The German submarines sank scores of tankers, freighters and troopships, often within sight of American and Canadian ports. Haligonians still remember the ruddy glow in the eastern sky of ships torpedoed and burning just outside Halifax Harbour. By June, 1942, the U-boats were sinking a ship off the North American coast *every four hours*. They sank 2.5 million tons of shipping in six months.

The Battle of the St. Lawrence began that May, when U-533 appeared off southwestern Newfoundland. Two days later she torpedoed a British freighter near Anticosti Island—the first ship sunk by an enemy in Canadian inland waters since the War of 1812. In the next five months, the Allies lost twenty-three ships and seven hundred people in the St. Lawrence estuary—a larger death toll than the Canadian Army sustained in the battle for Sicily.

The last ship lost was the *Caribou*, torpedoed at 3:50 A.M. on October 14. Of the 238 people aboard, 137 died. The sinking is engraved in the collective memory of communities on both sides of Cabot Strait, captured in books, songs and stories. Most of the crew were from Port-aux-Basques. Twenty-one women were widowed in that small village that night, and fifty-one children lost their fathers. It was more than forty years before another *Caribou* entered the service, and the name still has a somewhat sombre ring.

I wonder whether mainlanders can ever really appreciate the extent to which the island provinces depend on ferries. During World War II, for instance, Prince Edward Island was linked to Canada only by one obsolete rail-car ferry, the *Prince Edward Island*, built in 1915 — and that noble old vessel also had an encounter with the U-boats during the Battle of the St. Lawrence.

The *Prince Edward Island* was in a convoy, returning from a refit in Quebec, when a Greek freighter was torpedoed just 400 feet away from her. The skipper called for full power and radio silence, left the convoy at 19 knots and zig-zagged his way home to Borden, P.E.I. It was the right decision. Canada's shipbuilding capacity was entirely committed to the war effort, and if the *Prince Edward Island* had been lost, Islanders would have been left to travel on manned ice-boats, tugboats and barges.

The *Atlantic Freighter* plodded into the distance. The southeast breeze returned, light at first and then building. *Silversark* heeled over and began butting almost at right angles into a steep chop. With her raised deck and flattened bow sections, she is a dry boat, throwing spray down and away. We sailed long boards and short: a long tack diverging gradually from the land, then a short tack in towards the shore.

The seaside mining towns slowly passed: New Victoria, New Waterford, Lingan. The wind increased, and the seas with it. How much wind would we get before Glace Bay? To seaward, fishing boats were still going about their errands, and a red-hulled vessel with a yellow superstructure was coming up fast from the east: a Coast Guard ship steaming parallel to the coast, steering to pass well inside us.

"Want to tack into Lingan Bay?" I said.

"Let's wait till that Coast Guard ship passes," Lulu said. "We don't want to cross in front of her."

When she was a mile away, the Coast Guard vessel suddenly altered course, steering directly towards *Silversark*.

"She's coming right at us," said Mark.

"I'll hold my course," said Lulu. "She'll still pass well astern of us."

The wind picked up. *Silversark* was plunging her stem heavily into the seas. After another half-mile, the ship altered course—and headed directly for us once again.

"What the hell is she doing?" I said.

"Maybe she wants to play tag," said Mark.

"She should play with someone her own size," Lulu said.

We both watched the ship, now only a few hundred yards away, looming over us on a collision course.

"Call them on the VHF," said Lulu. Right! I lunged into the cabin and grabbed the walkie-talkie.

"This is *Silversark*, Victor Oscar 3460, *Silversark*, Victor Oscar 3460, calling the Coast Guard vessel off Glace Bay, over."

The reply came back immediately.

"*Silversark*, this is *Mary Hitchens*. Go to Channel 19, over."

We switched to the working channel.

"*Mary Hitchens*, we were wondering what you're up to. You're a little big for us to play tag with, over."

"*Silversark*, we just wanted to know who you were and where you were bound. With these heavy wind warnings and everything, we wanted to make sure you were going to be somewhere safe before that hurricane gets here, over."

"*Mary Hitchens*, *Silversark*: we're heading into Glace Bay as fast as we can get there, over."

"That's fine, *Silversark*—didn't want to alarm you, but we'd rather talk to you now than come out here in the night and pick you up in the middle of a gale. Have a good cruise, now."

"Over and out."

Mary Hitchens swung away on her course. With her tall superstructure and low afterdeck, she looked like a big tug. Originally built to supply the offshore drilling rigs, she was bought by the Coast Guard when the exploration boom fizzled.

We bounced about in her wake, tacked twice more, and then

eased the sheets a trifle. *Silversark* took off at a canter, aimed straight at the narrow slot of Glace Bay Harbour. Mark and I readied the fenders and dock lines. Near the entrance we lowered the jib. *Silversark* slowed to a trot. We slipped between the two long fingers of broken rock into the wind shadow of the land. The boat slowed to a walk.

A quarter of a mile ahead, fishermen and plant workers were busily unloading a small trawler. Silent as a thought, *Silversark* slipped ahead. When we were 30 feet from the crew on the wharf, a man looked around, saw the tall red sails looming over him, did a cartoon double-take, and said, "What kind of a load of fish are you bringin' in?"

"Lot smaller than that," I said, pointing at the dragger.

Watched in near-silence by forty men, *Silversark* glided to the quay. We threw our lines ashore and peeled off our oilskins, suddenly stifling in the windless harbour. We dropped the sails. The wharf broke into chatter. Where were we from? Where bound?

"Not too many yachts comes into Glace Bay, b'y," said one.

"Can't stay there," said another. "Clearwater got a big dragger comin' in right where you are."

"Where can we tie up?"

"Prob'ly at Goldman's over there," said someone, pointing to an olive-drab building up the harbour on the opposite bank.

"Okay, let's go," said Mark, kicking an oar loose and carrying it to the cockpit. I freed the other one. The men threw our lines aboard. We pushed off with our oars and started to row.

"There's the answer to your question about the engine," said a voice on the wharf.

At Goldman's, we made fast and climbed on the wharf. Inside the dark, wet fish plant was a tiny glassed-in office. A man in a baseball cap was talking rapidly on the phone. Ray Goldman. When he set the phone down, I asked about tying up at the wharf.

"I know you," he said. "You're—aaaah! From down Arichat way. Wait, now. The writer. Cameron. You're Silver Donald Cameron. Right? I knew it. You had something about me in that newsletter. Sure you can use my wharf. Anything you like. Make yourself at home. It's an honour to have you here. My brother-in-law used to talk about you all the time."

"Who's your brother-in-law?"

"Newman Dubinsky."

"Newman!" I said. "You're Newman's brother-in-law?"

"Esther's my sister."

Newman Dubinsky—the late, and greatly lamented, Newman Dubinsky—owned and operated Sydney Ship Supply. Bald, portly and gregarious, Newman was a devout Cape Breton patriot. He and Esther also had a sheep farm at Englishtown, on St. Ann's Bay. They called it Sydney Sheep Supply. The lone Jewish householder on a bay of Scots, Newman had a tartan baseball cap made up for himself. It read *Newman MacDubinsky*.

The Dubinskys' children have made their marks in business, the professions and the arts. Newman's unforgettable birthday parties at Englishtown brought all their friends together for a family picnic-cum-Gathering-of-the-Clowns-cum-hootenanny. If Cape Breton had a society columnist—a boggling thought—she would certainly have considered Newman's birthday party to be the Event of the Summer Season.

Ray Goldman's fish plant is not just the usual cut 'em and freeze 'em and ship 'em operation, either. We featured him in *The Cape Breton Letter* for his innovative, high-quality mail-order business. D. Goldman and Sons has a live-lobster booth at the Sydney airport. They advertise—with an 800 number—in Yellow Pages across Canada. Recognizing that immigration has made Canada a cosmopolitan nation, they pack all sizes of special gourmet preparations for specific ethnic markets: smoked eel, special mackerel and rainbow trout.

"We make it easy for people to find us, and we offer a personalized service," Ray says proudly. "A satisfied customer is always directing friends to you. It's the best advertising you can get. Here, let me give you a piece of fish for your dinner. You like swordfish? Here, have some swordfish."

Readying *Silversark* for the hurricane, we borrowed more fenders from Kenny Muise, who owned a spiffy blue fibreglass fishing boat called *Figgy Duff*. With Kenny and a retired Newfoundlander named George Brown, we stitched *Silversark* to the wharf with breast lines and spring lines. We told them about our encounter with the Coast Guard.

"Comin' back from the drug bust, I guess," said Kenny.

Drug bust?

"At Baleine. The Navy was in on it, and the Coast Guard and the Mounties. I guess they got a whack of the stuff."

The lawmen had seized 20 tonnes of hash along with fourteen Nova Scotians, two Quebecers, an eighteen-wheeler, two five-ton trucks and two fishing boats. *Mary Hitchens* had played a prominent role in the operation. This was the year's second big catch: in May, 35 tonnes of hash were found floating in Puddle Pan Cove, near Shelburne. The Nova Scotia coast is a drug smuggler's delight, with all its thick fogs and deserted coves. The Mounties estimate that they intercept 10 per cent of the drugs entering the province, but most rural Nova Scotians believe that's wishful thinking.

"We all know which boats is into it," a South Shore fisherman once told me. "You take a feller that goes out every day but he don't land much fish — and yet he buys a new truck every year. Well, you don't have to be overly swift to figure out he's probably landin' somethin' else. But he might be your brother-in-law, too. It ain't your job to nail him, and he ain't troublin' you. So you might's well look the other way."

No wonder *Mary Hitchens* wanted to know who we were.

We walked up into the town and found a restaurant called, naturally, Wong's. Commercial Street looked bedraggled and sad. During the past decade, Glace Bay has taken a terrible pounding. By the 1970s it was reduced to one mine: Number 26. In 1979, an explosion killed a dozen miners, and in April 1984, a fire in Number 26 killed another man and closed the mine forever.

Meanwhile, the provincial government had assisted Deuterium of Canada Ltd. to build a plant to supply heavy water for Candu reactors which would be sold worldwide by Atomic Energy of Canada. But Candu captured the market only in Ontario, which had its own heavy-water plants. AECL took over the plant, and in 1986 the Tories closed it along with its sister plant in Port Hawkesbury. The town's third pillar, the fishing industry, lurched from crisis to crisis; the chief fish plant burned to the ground.

"What's the difference between a nagging wife, a broken-down car, and a house in Glace Bay?"

Dunno, b'y.

"You can get rid of a nagging wife or a broken-down car."

After supper we went to the Savoy Theatre, hoping to catch a show by the thriving musical theatre troupe, Festival on the Bay. All the important Maritime towns once had elaborate theatres, but few of them have survived. Sydney's Lyceum is now four floors of offices and craft school studios; in Fredericton, the onetime opera house became city council chambers and police headquarters. The Savoy, however, has been handsomely restored in rose and gilt, and all kinds of travelling shows play in it.

The show that night was "The Cape Breton Summertime Revue", a blend of comedy and song which delights Nova Scotian audiences every summer. (The musical director is Leon Dubinsky, Newman and Esther's son.) The "Revue" grew out of an earlier show, "The Rise and Follies of Cape Breton Island", presented four times between 1977 and 1985.

The recipe is deceptively simple. Start with a dozen of Cape Breton's best writers and performers. Stir in the best songs they've written during the past year, and some fiddle tunes. Add a few nostalgic choruses of such old favourites as Leon Dubinsky's "Rise Again", Allister MacGillivray's "Sea People", Matt Minglewood's "East Coast Blues", Rita MacNeil's "Working Man", Kenzie MacNeil's "The Island", Max MacDonald's "Working at the Woolco Manager Trainee Blues".

Then turn them loose to write satiric skits on the fitness fad, emigration to Calgary, the GST, regional airlines, the country store, the bureaucrats in the Unemployment Insurance offices, the loss of the passenger trains. Exercise good business sense, and tour the province with the show—first in May and early June, for local audiences, and again in midsummer for the tourists. The result is an audience of 24,000 and box office receipts of $250,000, plus tape and recording sales.

Some of the revue's characters have assumed a life of their own. One early contributor was Dave Harley, who has since built a whole career in comedy around the character of General John Cabot Trail of the Cape Breton Liberation Army. Then there's the fat, Hawaiian-shirted boor named Cecil, portrayed by Maynard Morrison, and the rumpsprung busybody played by Bette MacDonald. Both are grating, thick-skinned and manipulative; when they tangle, the battle is epic. Bette's complacent phrase of agreement—"Good, dear, good"—has become a comic refrain on the streets and in the taverns.

For all its irreverence, the revue is often poignant—notably in the 1986 show, which featured Rita MacNeil, and in this year's first-act curtain, a haunting Leon Dubinsky number called "They Took the Train Away Today", sung by Matt Minglewood. Minglewood, a Juno Award-winning singer, songwriter and guitarist, is not a regular with the revue; his rock band tours throughout North America and Europe, and two of his eight albums have been gold in Canada and abroad. This year he delivered the closing medley of Cape Breton favourites, concluding with a searing interpretation of Allister Mac-Gillivray's beloved "Song for the Mira":

> Can you imagine a piece of the universe
> More fit for princes and kings?
> I'll trade you ten of your cities
> For Marion Bridge, and the pleasures it brings.

On the sidewalk outside we met Ron Keough—an *homme du théâtre* who acts, directs and promotes as well as reviewing films and plays for CBC radio. This summer he was manufacturing mock Nova Scotia licence plates numbered 4U2 SEA, and marketing GOOD, DEAR, GOOD T-shirts. He was also writing a book on a complicated card game called tarabish, which is played only in industrial Cape Breton and may have come from Lebanon. In February 1990, he organized the first World Tarabish Championship, to the delight of Peter Gzowski and others. He and his henchpersons also created a special pack of tarabish cards, with miners for kings, Highland lassies for queens, and unisex jacks.

He was also raffling himself off.

"I'm selling tickets for $25. I give the money to my accountant. When I've sold forty tickets, he draws one, and I'll work for the winner for a week. I'm a writer, producer, speaker, broad-caster, entrepreneur. I have some knowledge of computers, I can empty your attic, clean up the basement, paint, do house-hold repairs, cook, shop, whatever. One woman wants me to spend the whole week teaching her to play tarabish, but her husband says that'd take more than forty hours."

The accountant would call the winner at the end of the week. If the winner was satisfied, he would pay Ron. It worked: a few months later a small item in *Maclean's* reported that at least sixty people had purchased tickets.

"Great idea," I said. "See you later."

"Good, dear, good."

A sultry, humid, breezy evening. Commercial Street was crowded with teenagers, talking, laughing, driving, eating snacks from a chip wagon. Who would these kids become? This tough old town produces plenty of despair, but it also produced the novelist Hugh MacLennan and the film director Dan Petrie.

Back on the boat, we checked the forecast. Hurricane Bertha was still down south. She would strike the coast late tomorrow.

Good, dear, good. We went to bed.

I lay awake in the delta berth thinking about the drug bust, Cape Breton folkways and the law. An old maxim holds that laws are made by those who have the power to enforce them. Cape Bretoners have never possessed that power, and they have often felt the sting of laws made by their enemies.

If the miners had obeyed the laws in the 1920s, their families would have starved. The British Empire Coal and Steel Company (BESCO) owned the coal mines, the steel mill and the shipyards of Halifax and Dartmouth. Steelworkers worked eleven-hour day shifts and thirteen-hour night shifts; every two weeks, at shift change, they worked twenty-four hours straight. There were no holidays, there was no overtime, and the pay was less than 35 cents an hour.

Senior miners earned $4.05 a day but often worked only two shifts a week. The deductions typically included $4.25 a week for their company houses, $2.50 for coal and 50 cents for medical coverage. Workers charged their groceries at company-owned stores, known as "pluck-me's," paying prices set by the company. A man might work a week and come home with no cash at all.

In 1922, BESCO announced a wage cut of 37.5 per cent. The miners went on strike. The company surrounded the mines with barbed wire, machine-gun nests and searchlights. Bombing planes were placed on alert, warships entered Glace Bay Harbour, and twelve hundred cavalrymen were dispatched to Cape Breton. The miners accepted a 20 per cent wage cut and went back to work.

The following year, the steelworkers struck. A mounted force of company police and militia, armed with baseball bats and whips, rode into a Sunday morning crowd in Sydney's Whitney Pier district, beating everyone they could reach. One trooper rode his horse to the second floor of the Atlantic Hotel, beating every lodger along the way. When labour leaders protested— like J.B. McLachlan, head of the United Mine Workers—they were charged with seditious libel. The attorney-general of Nova Scotia personally prosecuted McLachlan, and won. McLachlan appealed. The chief justice had been president of a BESCO subsidiary before going to the bench; three others of the six judges had important BESCO connections. *Mirabile dictu*, McLachlan's appeal failed. He spent four months in Dorchester Penitentiary.

Laws are made by those who have the power to enforce them.

In 1925, wages were cut again and miners' hours reduced still further. Families were dying of malnutrition. When negotiations failed, BESCO cut off credit at the pluck-me's. During the ensuing strike, the company tried to evict miners from their homes and cut off water and power to New Waterford. Mounted police again charged into unarmed crowds. On June 11—now a holiday known as Davis Day—a miner named Bill Davis was shot dead and others were wounded. Company stores were pillaged and burned in Sydney Mines, New Aberdeen, Reserve and Dominion. By then, the Royal Canadian Horse, the Royal Canadian Dragoons and the Van Doos were patrolling the streets of Cape Breton.

The company's actions were perfectly legal. They had the

complete support of the provincial government, which passed special legislation to assist BESCO. Small wonder that Glace Bay Mayor Dan Willie Morrison led the May Day parade down Commercial Street, carrying the red flag of socialism amid banners that read WORKERS OF THE WORLD UNITE! DOWN WITH CAPITALISM!

Laws are made by those who have the power to enforce them. The law which really matters in Cape Breton is an unwritten law, enforced by snarls and smiles in the workshop, the kitchen, the tavern. The code says: Help your neighbour. Support the union. Laugh when you can. Don't rat on your buddies. Survive. Screw the company. Don't fight fair: fight to win. Share what you have. Count on your family. It is more blessed to steal than to starve.

"B'y, them birds lives better than most Cape Bretoners."

On February 2, 1974, a squad of Mounties raided the Nova Scotia gamecock championships and arrested thirty-nine men and thirty-two roosters. The occasion had drawn competitors and spectators from Pictou, Guysborough and Springhill as well as Cape Breton. Johnny Rockett, a military pensioner, was fined $250 for maintaining a cockpit on his premises. The others were fined $25 and costs. The roosters suffered the death penalty. The Mounties tried to chop off their heads, but they botched the job. The cockfighters took over and wrung their own birds' necks.

It gave them great pain, for they prized their birds. In Scotchtown, a leathery little man named Wilson Cassidy showed me his fighting roosters in spacious cages out behind his crooked little house. He waved his cap inside a cage. The rooster immediately whirred into the air, wings outstretched, head back, slashing with the backs of his heels like a karate fighter.

"That's their nature," said Cassidy. "You can't *stop* 'em from fightin'. Look at that feller, now. Ain't he beautiful?"

Beautiful? A chicken? The cock was magnificent, and he knew it. Sleek, glossy rust-coloured mane. Deep green-black body feathers, iridescent as the sheen on a beetle. A tall, arrogant plume of tail feathers. Five pounds of speed and muscle.

Such a rooster would be a formidable opponent for an unarmed man. With his razor-sharp steel fighting spurs strapped on, he would be deadly. A year earlier, in Manila, a referee named Severino Redula picked up a cock which had turned away from his opponent. The rooster slashed up the man's arms and stomach so fast, and so badly, that Redula bled to death on the spot.

I have not talked to a cockfighter recently, but I imagine the fights continue. Like chess and the Christmas tree, cockfighting traces its origins back to antiquity — to ancient China, Persia and India, where the ancestors of all our modern chickens originated. It reached Europe via classical Greece. Themistocles, marching against the Persians, stopped his army to watch a cockfight so that his men might learn the meaning of courage. Cockfighting was a favourite pastime of the British aristocracy until its prohibition in 1849. In many parts of Europe and the United States, it remains legal. Abraham Lincoln declined to ban it.

"As long as the Almighty has permitted intelligent men, created in his image and likeness, to fight in public and kill each other while the world looks on approvingly," Lincoln said, "it is not for me to deprive the chickens of the same privilege."

Cockfighting is also popular in the mining areas of Pennsylvania and Northern Ontario. Like show dogs and racehorses, roosters are divided into many breeds: Clarets, Hulseys, Shufflers, Miner Blues, Whitehackes, Roundheads, Travelers. Cockfighting has its specialized lore, its fabled masters and even its own literature, from Gervase Markham's *Pleasures of Princes* (1614) to *Grit and Steel*, a monthly magazine published in Gaffney, South Carolina, since 1899.

When I knew him, Wilson Cassidy was seventy-six years old. His face was flecked with the blue-black scars which identify a coal miner — long-healed nicks and gashes with coal dust sealed inside them. He had spent fifty-four years underground, and he had seen the cave-ins, the explosions, the union battles, the deaths. He had knocked a cop off a horse the day Bill Davis was shot. He had the air and stature of a bantam rooster, and in fact he was once the bantamweight champion of Cape Breton. He was "terrible saucy," and still quick with his fists. When he looked at me pugnaciously, I almost expected him to whirr into the air and slash at me with his heels.

"I still don't take no shit off no one," he said.

He got his chicks and eggs from cockfighting centres in the States, looking to improve his own breeding stock. He cared for them carefully. His roosters would eat scratch feed, hamburger, raw egg, apples. They would be wormed, cleaned of fleas and mites, and given antibiotics if they fell ill. Cassidy would watch them and work them like a coach with a champion athlete.

"You got to condition 'em," he said. "You got to flip 'em, walk 'em, maybe spar 'em a couple of times every three weeks. Some of 'em needs it more than others. You treat 'em good. B'y, them birds lives better than most Cape Bretoners."

A cockpit is an open space, sometimes boarded in, with three parallel lines on the floor. The handlers buckle steel spurs over their birds' natural spurs, then bind their legs and take them to the centre line. The handlers hold the roosters while they taunt and peck one another, goading each other to fury. Spectators place their bets. The owner of the cockpit normally gets 10 per cent. The referee shouts, "Gentlemen, pit your cocks." When the handlers drop the birds, they fly straight into one another, fighting with wings and beaks as well as spurs. The fight continues until one of the birds quits, or is crippled or killed. A "battle royal" is a fight which pits a number of cocks all together; the winner is the last cock on his feet.

Cockfighting metaphors are buried in everyday language. In sport, in business, we "pit" opponents against one another. If they fight well, they are "game." When we are proud, we are "cocky." When we are utterly confident, we are "cocksure."

In Canada, rooster fighting is proscribed under the Criminal Code. It continues anyway; Wilson Cassidy had attended fights as far away as Vancouver. People everywhere love blood sports, it seems. Yet not all sporting folk are treated alike. Eight months after the Cape Breton bust, the Family Section of the *Toronto Star* ran a full-page feature on the Toronto and North York Hunt. Twenty-five miles from downtown Toronto, people with names like Sifton and Eaton rode horses in pursuit of foxes, which were occasionally caught and torn to pieces by hounds. The hunters were never arrested. Their sport was legal.

The manufacture of liquor is another upper-class amusement which is illegal if pursued by working-class entrepreneurs. Cape Breton is probably the moonshine capital of Canada. The centre of Cape Breton moonshining was always New Waterford. Red Angus MacGregor was once its leading moonshiner. He was my tutor.

"We had six stills running more or less around the clock, producing thirty or forty gallons a day," he said. "Mister Man, we had some great times. The winters was the best, after the first snowfall. The ploughs'd heap up the snow along the streets, and we'd hollow out the snowbanks and stick the shine in there. Shine won't freeze. Half the Mounties in Cape Breton looking for it, and there it was under their noses, right on the main street.

"We sold it in drums, and then we had other fellows that sold it to the public. We knew they were watchin' us, see? So Skinny'd get them watchin' him, acting suspicious and driving along in his station wagon, and then he'd high-tail it for Glace Bay with all the Mounties hot behind him. Soon's he got out of Waterford, why that's when we'd move the stuff out to our boys.

"I think there was only one half-gallon from our stills ever was seized, anywhere. They knew we were doing it, you know, but they couldn't catch us. But those Mounties were no better'n what we were. You remember that fire we had, Peggy?"

His wife laughed out loud.

"You tell him about that, now."

"Skinny's brother-in-law was a Mountie, see? And he had stashed all these blankets that he'd stolen from the force over at Skinny's place. Well, we were down in Skinny's basement with five stills going, 30 gallons of mash into each of them — and my old uncle had converted a bicycle pump so that it would pump naphtha into the Coleman stoves. That's what we used for to boil the mash, Coleman stoves. After a while Skinny looked down, and he said, 'Hey, the tube on that pump's on fire!' So I went over to stamp it out, and right then, Mister Man, is when lightning hit that basement. It had got into the naphtha, see, and the room was full of flames. The stoves were burning and the furniture was burning, and then we were burning, our pants and stuff. So we jumped right into the barrels of mash to put it out. Then we tried pouring water on it, and it went everywhere. Well, Skinny started calling out for his wife, the silly bastard— she was at work at Eaton's—and I said, 'Shut up, you fool, we're going to lose the house if we don't get moving.' I said, 'Grab them blankets of Pete's,' and after a while we smothered the fire.

"Course the blankets was pretty well ruined by it, so we took them over to my uncle's house and he let on that he'd had a fire in his chesterfield. So the insurance replaced the blankets—and them stolen from the Mounties in the first place."

"How hard is it to make shine?" I asked.

"Nothin' to it. All you need is—what did we use, Peggy? Three to one? Five to one?"

"Three to one."

"I thought it was five—no, by God, you're right, it was six gallons of molasses to eighteen gallons of water, and sixteen yeast cakes. You mix that up and let it brew for—oh, ten days is pretty good. Then you run it in the still, and that's it."

"Could I get to see a still?"

"Well, if a fellow lets you into a real commercial still, he's taking an awful chance. He could get six months and $500, and that's no joke for a coal miner in Waterford. Best way would be to run a few gallons yourself. Have a drink."

"I can't afford six months and $500 either."

Red Angus poured a tot of rum. I drank it, and the idea no longer seemed quite so bizarre.

"Maybe we wouldn't get caught," I said.

"No way we'd get caught," said Angus. "No way. Have a drink." He poured another.

"If we did get caught, I could always say I did it in the service of literature."

"Have a drink," said Angus. "I'll help you make the still. By the Jesus, it's a long time since I ran a batch of shine. Be like old times. Have a drink."

I mixed up four gallons of mash in a plastic bucket in my bathtub. Shine based on molasses produces a kind of rum; if you make it with sugar, it's whisky. When Red Angus was running shine, Peggy always kept a jug of molasses on the counter. If a stranger came in, she knocked over the jug—which explained the smell of molasses that always permeated their house.

Leaving my mash to brew, I went to see Angus in Waterford.

"This is good stuff," said Angus, licking his lips over a glass of shine. "You can drink it all night, and the next morning you won't even have a hangover. It's pure, eh? There's none of that crud you get in goverm't liquor. We call it Triple H, because you wake up in the morning healthy, hungry and horny. But don't drink water next morning; one glass of water then, b'y, and you'll be drunk all over again."

Alex the Dancer, Red Angus's father, was jailed for making shine in his renovated company house. "Great God A'mighty, yes, Donnie," Alex laughed. "And the joke was, when the Mounties were in my basement seizing me still, the fellow on the other side of the basement wall was running off a batch right then."

At sixty-six, Alex was a powerful man who shook my hand with a fist like a cottage roll. He was entirely self-educated, a great reader, full of intelligence and warmth. In thirty-three years underground, the coal mines had broken his feet and arms, smashed his back, squashed his head. One time Red Angus was called to the mine when Alex had an accident. Struck by a coal car and catapulted against the mine roof, Alex had a broken nose and a mouth torn wide apart. His shattered shin bone was sticking out through the flesh of his leg, and his foot was pointing behind him.

"You know what he did?" demanded Red Angus, who loves his father with ferocious devotion. "He sat up on the stretcher and started a conversation with the doctor about the best way to treat the leg, y'know, talking about each of the bones by its proper name." Alex was laid up for seventeen months that time.

Alex went to work in 1925, the year of the Great Strike. He was seventeen, and he earned $2.89 a day. The miners clothed their children in flour sacks and boiled soup from potato peelings. The strike lasted 155 days.

"It was a hard, hard time, Donnie," sighs Alex. "Lord sufferin' Moses, a hard, hard time. They cut off our power, so we had to steal that, and they cut off our coal, so we had to steal to keep warm."

Three thousand on relief in Waterford alone—"and the relief, Donnie, 'twas nothing but a codfish and a bun of bread a day for each family, families of twelve and fifteen. But we survived, what with robbing a few hens and raiding some gardens, making a little shine and buying fish from the fishermen—you could get a dozen mackerel for seven cents or so—ah, yes, b'y, we survived."

When you ask men like these why moonshining is illegal, their answers are crisp. "Excise tax," snaps Red Angus. "The government ain't makin' anything off of shine," grins another. "The way it is now, they got a monopoly," explains a third.

That's not what the government says; they claim that shine is dangerous. But in talking to half a dozen moonshiners and innumerable clients I found no evidence that it is any more dangerous than any other strong liquor. Moonshine can certainly kill you—but good whisky can kill you, too. Bad shine— shine which was distilled too fast, or made in a galvanized still, or bottled with impurities—bad shine will make you miserably ill, and you'll throw it up. But it won't blind you or kill you. Or so they say in Waterford.

The present monopoly generates huge profits for governments and distillers. At the local grocery store, a gallon of molasses costs $8.19, and yeast costs $2.45. I can make a 40-ounce bottle of moonshine for about $2.65, compared with a bottle of much weaker rum at the liquor store for $32.05. That legal bottle of rum includes $5.05 in excise tax, $1.91 GST and $2.91 provincial sales tax. The rest of the price is freight, markup and the actual price of the grog. The Nova Scotia Liquor Commission won't say what they pay for rum, but tourists buy it for $4 and $5 in the Caribbean. If a big distillery can't produce 40 ounces of liquor for less than I can, there's something wrong with them. If they produce at the same price they must be making a profit of 100 per cent or better—and the bandits at the Liquor Commission are making even more than that.

"With shine, you got to be careful, Donnie," said Alex. "When you come to run your shine, use hardwood to boil the brew. You want a nice steady heat, nothing too strong, and hardwood don't make any smoke. The Mounties today has planes and helicopters, and when they see a smoke, why they got you then."

How would I make a still?

"We used to make our stills out of 45-gallon drums," Alex recalled, "or two drums welded together, that made a nice still. Or if you could get hold of one of those big puncheons, yah, that molasses came in, 50 gallons I think they were."

Red Angus was ready to make a still. But in the meantime I visited another moonshiner, the Drummer. The Drummer poured glasses of clear alcohol smuggled in from St. Pierre, stuff that reams out your innards the way a blowtorch lifts paint. He gave me a flask to treat my friends, and he reminisced about the game.

He told me about the moonshiner in Reserve whose wife distributed the product from her baby carriage, a couple of gallons cunningly concealed under its floorboards. He remembered the Mounties who used to come and buy shine from him after hours, and the fellow who kept his private stock of shine in an old car battery, which the police dutifully shifted around as they searched the house. The Mounties once arrived at the Drummer's house when he had a pitcher of shine on the table; he handed it to his wife, who squirted in some detergent and washed the dishes in it. When I said I thought I'd run some shine myself, he beamed.

"You got a still?" he demanded.

No. I reckoned we'd have to make one.

"You just sit right here, b'y."

Twenty minutes later, soaked to the knees from wading in a swamp, he proudly held out a copper drum 16 inches in diameter, with two tubes at the top and a drain cock at the bottom.

"This here," he said, "is as nice a little still as you're ever going to see. It's a present from me to you. Too small for commercial use, but it's just the rig for you. I couldn't find the worm for it; that you'll have to make yourself."

Three nights later, Red Angus fitted the necessary reducers and wound a 25-foot coil of three-eighths-inch copper tubing inside a tin lubricant bucket. Alex the Dancer used to form the tubing around the outside of an electric motor, a technique which makes "the most beautiful helix you ever saw. When I done my last one it was that pretty it should have been photographed."

Nine of us went for a picnic on an island off D'Escousse. While we ate hamburgers on the beach a propane stove hissed behind us in the woods, under the Drummer's copper boiler. The tubing ran through the lubricant bucket to condense the steam, and out of the end ran a liquid clear as water: pure moonshine that burned in a spoon with a pale blue flame.

"Whooh!" said Red Angus, swallowing a bit and shaking his head vigorously. "Ah, this is good shine, Donald."

"The best," said Peggy. "See what you can do when you get good teachin'?"

It was stronger than brandy, with a rich flavor like rum. We ate and sang and told stories. In the evening, we wobbled back onto the boat. On the way home, we threw the still overboard, because none of us could afford six months and $500.

So there's no still, no moonshine, no evidence. I'm a law-abiding citizen who drinks government booze. But, as they say in Waterford, whether you believe that is entirely up to yourself.

HAND

OF

GOD

In the morning, the vanguard breezes of
Hurricane Bertha were lashing Glace Bay with heavy, warm
rains and sporadic blasts of wind, but the centre was still several
hundred miles away.

"Even after the storm passes, you want to wait a day or so for
the sea to go down," said Kenny Muise, adjusting his own
mooring lines. I called Cordell Wynne, the director of "Peggy".
Let's have our conference tomorrow, I said.

"Silver Donald!" cried Ray Goldman as I passed by the open
door. "Here's someone you should meet! This is Mr. Seward.
He's formerly from Port Hawkesbury. He lives in Ottawa now. I
told him that was your boat. He reads your work all the time."

"You wrote something about Creignish Rear," said Seward,

shaking hands. "Excellent. I had family connections back there."

"Thank you," I said. "It's going into a book I'm doing."

"I'll buy the book," said Seward.

"Isn't this fun?" grinned Ray Goldman, as Seward left. "You meet *everybody* here!"

"So I see," I said. "Ray, we could walk from here to the Miners' Museum, couldn't we?"

"Sure you could," said Ray. "But you aren't going to. I'll drive you over and you can walk back along the cliffs."

The Miners' Memorial Museum was built in 1967. The exhibits include antique tools, mine-rescue gear, a mock-up of the Carboniferous forests which became Cape Breton coal, and mementoes of Guglielmo Marconi, who sent the first transatlantic radio signals from Glace Bay to Poldhu, Cornwall, in 1902. But its most memorable feature is the Ocean Deeps Colliery—a real mine, albeit created for the museum. It was the first mine I ever went into, nearly twenty years earlier, and I wanted to share it with Lulu and Mark. As we donned rubber boots, rubber coats and hard hats, I remembered Archie McIntyre, my guide that first time.

"*Send us two hundred brogues,* that was the message, but they thought it said two hundred *rogues.* And that's how the McIntyres came to Cape Breton." In 1971, Archie was sixty-eight, bald and rotund and genial. He had worked over fifty years underground. When he started, miners used pit-ponies, mules, and caged canaries to warn of the presence of gas. They drilled into the coal face with hand augers, shattered it with explosives and shovelled it into carts. The height of a mine's working tunnels, or "roads," is the thickness of the seam of coal. Archie worked most of his life in a seam just three feet thick, bent double, loading coal with a pan shovel while black water trickled around his feet and rats scuttled just outside the range of his light. In winter, he never saw the sun: he went to work in the dark and went home in the dark. For the first twenty-eight years, he had no vacations at all.

Archie's grandfather was working in Caledonia pit when a man came along the shaft one day with a queer instrument in his hand. His name was Gardiner Hubbard. He was the father-in-law of Alexander Graham Bell, and the instrument was the world's first mine telephone. A miracle. Now the blackened, sweaty men at the coal face could talk directly to the men at the pit-head. If they had trouble, they could get help right away.

Today's guides are twenty years younger, and their memories do not quite reach back to the barbarism of BESCO. Twenty of us trooped through the mine, banging our hard hats on the overhead beams. The high point was a totally unexpected explosion of colour under a bank of fluorescent lights: a flower garden, blossoming defiantly in the black, wet bowels of the earth, a memorial to a Cape Bretoner who grew the first such underground garden in 1929.

Standing among the tourists, I felt the old labour battles grow faint and fabulous, as distant as a romance of knights and dragons. Over the summer, I tried to tell Mark about the viciousness of unchecked corporate greed and about the unions' stirring vision of a new world rising from the ashes of the old. Mark is a Cape Bretoner: he owns that history, too. He listened politely. But "Star Trek" and Madonna are more vivid and potent in his internal mythology than those heroic, dusty battles at home.

"Excuse me, sir, I have two questions—" began a little tyke, tugging on the guide's coat. Everyone laughed: such exquisite manners, such a tiny gentleman.

"Mommy," said his older brother, a man of six or seven, "Brian is making us the laughing-stock of this whole tour!"

We trudged back out of the colliery, hung up our mining togs, went into the museum theatre to see a National Film Board show about the heroic period. Old men and women—Red Angus's grandmother among them—trudging out to the overgrown foundations of the Waterford Lake powerhouse, where Bill Davis was shot. Blinding pain and fear like the taste of copper in the mouth, transmuted into the memories of the aged and destined for the dusty boxes and albums of an archive.

> It's a working man I am,
> And I've been down underground,
> And I swear to God, if I ever see the sun—
> Or for any length of time

I can hold it in my mind—
I never again will go down underground.

The dead are made real only by art—by Jeremy Akerman's novel *Black Around the Eyes*, or by Leon Dubinsky's unfinished rock opera about the miners. Any Cape Breton crowd will sing along with Rita MacNeil's "Working Man". She is often backed up by The Men of the Deeps, a chorus of miners who rehearse and perform at the Museum. When Rita and The Men of the Deeps really dig into "Working Man", people cry.

The Men of the Deeps touch hearts wherever they go, with their repertoire of work songs, their unaffected directness, their joy in the singing they do. In June 1976, they became the first Canadian cultural group to tour mainland China. Since they were not supposed to have any writers with them, I impersonated a miner and sang first tenor. We gave an impromptu concert one evening in the Peking Hotel for our own guides. The Peking Hotel overlooks Tiananmen Square and the Forbidden City, where Chairman Mao lay dying, although we did not know that at the time. We sang "The Ballad of Springhill":

> In the town of Springhill, Nova Scotia,
> Often the earth will tremble and roll;
> When the earth grows restless, miners die:
> Blood and bone is the price of coal;
> Blood and bone is the price of coal.

Our Chinese guides spoke good English, and they were well-briefed. They knew the song. But they were not prepared for the organ-like sound of thirty men who felt every word. Chou Rong-jin mentioned it later in Tangshan. He said it had been "terribly moving" to hear that fine poem sung *by miners*.

Our guides took us to the Great Wall, and the carpet factories; to the graves of the emperors, and the enormous open-pit coal mine at Fushun; to the marble boat of the Dowager Empress, and to tiny agricultural communes high in the barren mountains. None of us will ever forget the opulence of the ancient empire—nor the concerted effort to spread what little wealth there was, and to turn the class system on its head.

"Look, b'y, you don't know what it means to see a country

where a coal miner is a hero," said one of the miners. "It takes some gettin' used to. It's like a dream, b'y—a beautiful, beautiful dream."

In Tangshan, our guides took us down into a coal mine.

We packed ourselves into the cage, and someone said, "Rap 'er away," and everyone laughed. We started to sing, and the ones who stayed on the surface heard the music fading as the cage dropped straight down for half a mile.

> Down deep in a coal mine, underneath the ground,
> Where a ray of sunshine never can be found,
> Digging dusty diamonds, all the seasons round,
> Down deep in a coal mine, underneath the ground!

The mining equipment was old and obsolete. In today's mines, huge circular saws range back and forth across the face, slicing off the coal and dumping it onto conveyor belts. The Tangshan saws were single-cutters, which cut in only one direction; in Cape Breton, these had long been replaced by double-cutters, which cut a slice of coal both going and coming.

"But their gas detectors were away ahead of ours," said Tommy Tighe, who worked in mine safety. "It seemed like we cared most about getting the coal out, but they cared most about getting the men out."

The unforgettable feature of the visit was the welcome of the Chinese miners. They knew nothing about us except that we were singing miners from Canada, but wherever we went they emerged from behind pit props and railway cars, jet black but for their eyes and teeth, grinning and clapping us on the back and shaking our hands.

"That's what takes you back in the pit after an accident," Bobby Roper said later. Bobby is a little snack of bone and gristle from New Waterford, with a face and body which have been considerably rearranged by rock falls and cave-ins. "In the pit, you *got* to trust your buddies, and they got to trust you. Your life might depend on them. You get a brotherhood down in the pit that you don't get anywheres else, and if you're used to that you don't want to work any other way.

"Those Chinese miners are just the same. You can tell it by

the way they grab ahold of you and pump your hand. You don't have to talk their language. You *know* what they're like."

The men on the surface heard us coming back up, like a long slow crescendo:

> And many a miner has laid his head
> In death on the coal's black lap;
> So don't forget, he's a hero too:
> The man with the torch in his cap.

Murray Graham didn't go down the mine in Tangshan. When I asked him why, he told me about the accident that made him quit mining. With eight others, he climbed into the cage at the end of the shift. The operator was inexperienced and brought the cage up too fast. It swung from side to side, hooked under a ledge of rock, and tore apart. Murray grabbed the belt of another miner who was clinging to the ruins of the cage. They survived—but four men spilled out and fell to their deaths.

Five years later, Murray tried the pit again. But his nerves wouldn't take it. He finished his working life on the surface.

A month after our visit, China suffered a terrible earthquake. The Tangshan mines collapsed. Hundreds of miners died. Some of them were the men whose hands we shook.

We walked along the cliffs in a heavy, blowing mist. The air was humid and threatening, the sea grey and sullen. The forecast said Hurricane Bertha would pass 30 miles east of Sydney overnight—almost exactly where we were. Strong westerly winds would follow it. Kenny Muise came down to check his lines.

"Won't be too bad if she don't come northeast," he said. "A northeaster blows right into this harbour." Together we checked not only our own lines but also the lines of nearby boats. A neighbouring boat on a rampage could be just as bad as breaking loose ourselves.

Mark went to Sydney with his uncle Bernie. The wind was already howling from the southeast, the boat heeling over as the gale caught the bare mast and rigging. Lulu and I set an anchor watch: she would stay up till three o'clock; I would spell her then, and watch until morning.

When she woke me, the boat was strangely quiet.

"Funny," she said. "It blew really hard till one o'clock, and then it died out. But I think we're too close to the boat behind us."

I pulled on my clothes and went on deck. The night was humid but still, and the rising tide had given extra slack to the mooring lines. I drew *Silversark* forward and pulled the other vessel a little bit astern. When I came below, Lulu was sleeping.

The wind struck again at five, but this time from the southwest—howling and screeching, plucking at the rigging, making the boat pitch and heave. In the narrow waters of the harbour, it was still only a good strong gale. When I went on deck at six, I saw patches of blue sky. Bertha had kissed us gently and gone on her way to Newfoundland. After confounding our planning for three days, she had been an anticlimax. That suited me fine. I lay down on the settee and drifted off to sleep.

Cordell Wynne flew in, full of ideas about "Peggy"—and concerned about the onrushing shooting date, just ten days away. By the end of the day, when Cord drove off to the airport, we had agreed on a number of changes. I was also worrying about time: Mark had two weeks of summer camp coming up, I had commitments in Halifax, and we still had 90 miles of wild coastline to cover.

I would have liked to stay longer in the mining towns, listening to their blunt speech, enjoying their sense of humour. I remember Alex the Dancer describing the character of one of his fellow moonshiners. Jim, said Alex, was "the kind of a feller that if he saw a man drowning, he'd jump overboard, and as he pulled him ashore he'd take his watch."

There was once in Glace Bay a town councillor known as Angus Blue whose inspired riffs on the English language are still repeated with joy. When plans for a new school were under discussion, Angus Blue took exception to the urinals.

"We don't need urinals," he said. "Them is just a waste of money. I won't approve of them in any way, shape or form."

The other councillors eventually yielded. As he left the hall,

Angus whispered to another councillor, "Listen, buddy, what the hell are them urinals, anyways?"

"Jesus, Angus, them are piss troughs."

"Piss troughs!" cried Angus. "Oh, we got to have *them*!"

At the next meeting, he confessed that he had been mistaken.

"On second thoughts," he said, "I was wrong about them urinals. We got to have them—and while we're at it, we better put in some arsenals as well."

He also argued against the installation of a chandelier in the town hall on the grounds that "there's not one person in the whole of Glace Bay that knows how to play one." And he shrugged off an accusation by saying, "I have heard the allegation—and I know the allegators."

Bill Howell would call the mining towns "a language community." He and Bev arrived at the wharf with their daughter, Allison, and Morgan the Terrible Terrier, a visit that dissolved into dinner at Joe's Warehouse in Sydney. A maniac poet and broadcaster, Howell was executive producer of "What Ever Happened To Peggy?", the one-hour radio play which became the film.

"I don't know how you're going to ram all that story into half an hour," Bill said. "Less than half an hour. Twenty-four minutes or something, with time out for the commercials."

"It'll work. We can show a lot of things we had to describe on radio. Like the peggy game, for instance."

"Yeah, but even so—it's a big, brain-damaged story, man! Those two brothers are swimming to that island through their own blood! You need some space for echoes!"

"It's done. We're just cleaning it up now."

"I want to see it."

"You will. Promise."

As we left the restaurant, a well-dressed man jumped up behind a nearby table and called to Lulu.

"Excuse me. Where did you get that hat?"

"This is a genuine Tilley hat," said Lulu. "It's made in Toronto. It's a great sailing hat."

"It's a wonderful hat. I've been admiring it all through dinner."

Lulu took the hat off and rummaged inside the lining. Alex Tilley—who created the hat because he wanted the best sailing hat in the world for his own use—provides "Brag Tags" for such occasions. The tag explains how to measure yourself for a hat and gives Tilley's toll-free phone number. Lulu tore off a Brag Tag and handed it over. It said:

> Most Tilley Hat wearers, and *the person beside you is a prime example,* are interesting people of sterling character. It is well worth cultivating their acquaintance. To that end, you'll be pleased to learn, **it is customary to provide the giver of Tilley Hat procurement information with a warm hug, or stand him or her to a drink.**

"Very good of you," said the man.

"Not at all," said Lulu, tipping her hat.

In the morning, I told Lulu that I wanted to stay in Glace Bay another day and deal with the script.

"I know," she said.

"You do? How?"

"I know you. And it's a good idea."

Ray Goldman was on the board of the local museum. He knew everyone in town. Could he help me find an office for the day?

"Right upstairs!" he said. "No problem at all!"

"Upstairs?"

"We've got three offices upstairs, and we're only using one. There's a phone up there, copier, fax machine, whatever you need. Come on, I'll show you."

The office was perfect: eight feet square, with a big old wooden desk and a phone at my elbow. Ray bustled around happily, introducing me to his colleagues. One was named Ross Bennett.

"Ross Bennett?" I said. "Aren't you with Nova Aqua?"

"That's me."

"What are you doing here, then?"

"Oh, my partners and I bought into this business a few months ago. It's a good fit with Nova Aqua."

Ross Bennett once worked for Devco's marine farming operation. When Devco got out of that business, Bennett found some investors, bought some of the assets and formed a joint venture with Norsk Aqua, an innovative Norwegian aquaculture company. When the Glace Bay heavy-water plant was closed, Nova Aqua established a fish hatchery there, rearing up to a million trout and salmon annually before transferring them to sea cages.

Fish grow slowly in Cape Breton's cold water, but the Lingan power plant cools its turbines with ocean water. Its effluent is *warm* water, ideal for growing fish. In Norway, Norsk Aqua had learned how to raise a smolt to a 10-pound salmon in eighteen months. At Lingan, Nova Aqua did the same thing. Bennett and two partners then bought a majority share in Ray Goldman's business, which delivers fish to customers. How does Ray feel about being a minority shareholder in his own company?

"I love it," he says. "I have just as much fun as ever, and I let those fellows worry about the future."

I toted my laptop computer upstairs and immersed myself in "Peggy", leaving Lulu and Mark to entertain visitors. As Ray had remarked, a yacht in Glace Bay is rare enough that it draws a constant stream of observers, inquirers and dreamers. His office was a good place to work. I charged through the script, printed it out and faxed it to Halifax. I was finished by five o'clock.

Kenny Muise and George Brown were sitting in the cockpit. They were close friends, despite a difference of about thirty years in their ages, and they dropped by regularly, like a pair of improbable guardians, talking amiably about everything from warts to politics. George was the storyteller, Kenny the chorus.

George was a Newfoundlander from Harbour Le Cou, near Port-aux-Basques. He still spoke with a Newfoundland lilt, though he had lived in Glace Bay for more than forty years. There are men like him in every Nova Scotia port—men who drifted over to Canada with the fishing vessels and stayed because they met a girl and married her, or because their brothers were already living there, or simply because times were always harder in Newfoundland.

George was not surprised that Hurricane Bertha touched us so lightly. You can never tell about these storms, he said.

"One time we was out swordfishin', and I was on watch," he said. "S'posed to be a gale comin'. The skipper told me, 'Now

Jarge, see you listens to d'forecast.' And then he went below, see, and I forgot. By and by he comes back up: 'Well, what's forecast?' 'Don't know,' I said. 'Well,' he says, 'can you tell me why we're the only boat still out here? Looks to me like we're goin' to stay out here and take whatever we gets, b'y.'

"Oh, my dear! Well, we called on the radio, and all the other boats was in along shore, right into the storm, takin' a terrible beatin'. Seas breakin' over them, and some bein' driven ashore. But where we was, it was beautiful weather. We stayed there, waitin' for the gale to strike — and it never did. It went right in between us and the shore. And the best of it was, we got eighteen swordfish, too."

"Pretty fair trip," said Kenny. "You made a dollar there."

George especially loved swordfishing, which is somewhat like big-game hunting. Swordfish swim right along the surface, parallel with the waves, and fishermen are downright lyrical about the beauty of a swordfish in a wave crest, backlit by the sun, a living fish in a wedge of crystal water. Swordfish are common off Glace Bay in midsummer, attracting fishermen from as far away as Newfoundland and the southern tip of Nova Scotia. Ray Goldman had a photo of Glace Bay Harbour in the early twentieth century, with rank after rank of small schooners. He pointed at one row after another, reeling off their home ports.

"These here are from Newfoundland, and these are from Lunenburg. This bunch here are from your part of the country, Isle Madame. These ones are Acadians from Pubnico . . . Oh, they came from all over. They took a lot of swordfish out here."

When a skipper sees that big dorsal fin slicing through calm water, he manoeuvres the boat so that a man in a long pulpit at the bow can harpoon it. The "iron" is tied to a stout line with several wooden kegs on it. The kegs keep the fish from diving and tire it out. Eventually the crew can haul it aboard.

"Swordfish is full of tricks," said George. "One time I was out in a dory and I had one on, and then the line goes slack. Where'd he go, now? I knowed I hadn't lost him. Then I thought, by God, he's goin' for the dory! Hardly had the thought before BANG! — there's the sword, drove right up through the bottom of the dory. He hit that hard that he toppled me over, and I banged me neck on the trawl tub. Well, I went to signalling the skipper, *Come and get me, the dory is sinkin'!* I cut off the sword and away went Mr. Swordfish. But I got him back on—he was only a little feller, sixty or seventy pounds—and be damned if he didn't attack the boat again."

"He was determined," said Kenny.

" 'Nother time we took a big one," George said, "and we found he had no sword. Well, we never thought too much about it till we tied up, and then one of the fellers come stormin' up on deck wantin' to know who was playin' tricks with his suitcase. We told him, 'Nobody touched your foolish suitcase.' 'Well,' he said, 'how come I can't budge it?'

"We went down to have a look. He had jammed his suitcase right up in the bow, between the stem and the planks, and sure enough, wouldn't move. So then we come to find out what was holdin' it—the sword from that fish, that's what. He'd gone for the boat and drove his sword right through two and a half inches of plank, one-and-a-quarter-inch ceiling, then right through the suitcase and buried it in the stem. Pinned it right in, b'y, just like you'd drove a nail through."

"Lot of strength in a swordfish," nodded Kenny.

We left Glace Bay at 6:45 A.M. under our two-oarspower engine. It was another glorious morning, with the sunlight gilding the wharves and fish plants along the narrow harbour. The forecast called for southwest winds—a reaching wind for almost the whole leg across Morien Bay and Mira Bay, then down the Main-à-Dieu Passage and on to Louisbourg.

At the first seaward buoy we picked up a faint southwest breeze, the ambassador of a fair wind to come. We shipped the oars, made sail and idled along the coast towards Cape Percé, the east-pointing headland that defines the limit of Morien Bay.

The breeze died.

We dawdled for two hours, catching a vagrant puff here and there, slowly approaching the cape. Flint Island gradually took shape. A well-known seamark, it is little more than a lump of fractured sandstone with a bad reputation: rocky shoals, irregular tidal streams and rip tides.

The breeze returned—from the southeast. Dead on the nose. Under the tall white lighthouse of Flint Island, we tacked up into Morien Bay, with Port Morien far ahead off the starboard bow. The wind piped up, and we shot past Cape Morien and into Mira Bay. The bay drains the Mira River, a broad and placid stream on which the French established farms to supply the fortress. Across the southeastern horizon lay a long, ragged piece of land, almost lost in the mist: Scatarie Island, another famous fog-bound boneyard of shipping. Mira Bay has no harbours; the nearest refuge ahead was Main-à-Dieu, beyond Scatarie.

Main-à-Dieu: Hand of God. Where did the name come from? The natives, says one story: it is a corruption of *Mandoo*, a Micmac word for "devil"—an exact reversal of the French meaning. Wherever it comes from, it is a lovely name for a village.

Unfavourable though it was, the wind was firm and steady. *Silversark* loped across the bay while we lunched. A tall white sail appeared on the horizon astern, coming up fast. She overhauled us, half a mile to starboard and heading like an arrow for the notch in the land which marked the western end of Scatarie. She was *Glenda*, an American cutter bound from Baddeck nonstop to Maine: the only yacht we saw after Cape Percé.

In Mira Bay, the land changes from undulating, coal-seamed sandstone cliffs to low-lying basalt and slate covered with swamps, ponds, scrub spruce and moorland. As we drew closer, the shores of Scatarie emerged, brown rock against the green spruce trees, swept by small wandering clouds of fog. We tacked and tacked again, past the humps of Great Shag Rock and Little Shag Rock, and into Main-à-Dieu Passage. The village of Main-à-Dieu lay to starboard in a bay at the head of the passage. To port lay the fog-streaked waterway behind Scatarie, leading to the open sea. It was 5:15. Which way?

To seaward. But the Main-à-Dieu Passage had captured us: the fog teased us, opening before us and then closing again. Fog signals whooped intermittently around us, and we made miserably slow progress. The tide, it appeared, was against us.

Run through here in the fog, at night? The *Pilot* notes that "dense fogs are common, and the passage is dangerous in bad weather conditions. The holding ground is poor, and there is no shelter from the heavy seas which result during east and south winds." The Passage "is made intricate by several shoals" with such picturesque names as the Thoroughfare and Mad Dick Rock.

No, thanks. We dropped the jib and scooted into Main-à-Dieu, slipping between yet another set of rock breakwaters. Lulu steered for what seemed to be the government wharf. A hundred feet away, we dropped the sails. *Silversark* coasted gently up beside *April and Brothers*. In a trice, Mark and I were ashore with the lines, and *Silversark* was secured in Main-à-Dieu.

LORD OCHILTREE

AND THE

NAKED TRUTH

I had a friend in Main-à-Dieu, Syd Forg-
eron, who taught me the first tenor parts by singing them into
my ear throughout the first week in China. His brother Ted was
on the wharf, and after supper we made our way to Syd's house,
but it was locked and dark. We walked back to the boat under a
full moon, with the frogs peeping and the sea making a soft
whush over the pebbles.

At 5:30 we looked out to see—nothing. The world had vanished behind a grey miasma of fog. We couldn't see the shore
from the end of the wharf, and there was no wind at all.

At 7:30 the fog was breaking up, stirred by a vagrant zephyr.
Moderate southwest winds, said the forecast. That meant a beat
to Louisbourg, but it would probably clear the fog—and the

current should be with us in Main-à-Dieu Passage. We ate and readied the boat, chatting with a group of fishermen on the wharf. By 8:30 the fog was halfway down the passage, leaving a beautiful sunny day behind it.

We took a short tack across the little harbour and a long tack out, shaving the starboard breakwater, and chased the fog slowly seaward. We caught up with it just beyond Bar Reef, a nasty-looking tangle of rocks and ledges. In a few seconds, the world disappeared again, leaving us surrounded by fluffy grey murk. Well, the fog was clearing: no doubt it would depart again just as quickly.

Instead, the fog settled in around us—thick, heavy, clammy, darkening the sails, beading the lifelines with pendant droplets, playing tricks with our vision. What was that dim shape up ahead? Was it anything at all? Sailing in fog is profoundly disorienting. Left, right, east, west—it all looks the same. The boat sails on, but nothing falls behind. The log and compass are your only guides, but it is hard to trust them. Your instincts rebel. We *must* have reached that buoy by now. Don't I hear surf over there? You sail on and on, and nothing changes. You grow anxious, even panicky. You feel trapped, claustrophobic. It is like sailing inside a grey fur hat.

The wind picked up, blowing from just west of south. *Silversark* was clip-clopping right along.

Behind the murk to starboard lay Cape Breton—the actual cape, the southeastern extremity of Cape Breton Island. "Cape Breton" is one of the oldest European place names in North America, conferred during the Renaissance by venturesome French sailors. Running to seaward from the cape is a rocky spit a mile long, with Port Nova Islets on its tip. Midway between the islets and the cape is Chameau Rock, which "dries" two feet at low tide. In April 1834, a nameless passenger ship took 265 Irish immigrants to their deaths on the Port Nova Islets. The rock is named for a French pay ship named *Le Chameau*, which tore out her bottom here in 1725.

Nobody knows how many ships have been wrecked on the Nova Scotia coast, but Jack Zinck, author of two books on the subject, believes it may be as many as five thousand. A shocking number lie along the 25 miles of rocks and shoals in the approaches to Louisbourg, from Scatarie to Guyon Island, a stretch of the coast plagued by heavy winds and thick persistent fogs. The Louisbourg fog signal sometimes blows for days at a time; one year it sounded every day during the entire month of July. By leaving this leg of our voyage until early August, we had hoped to avoid the constant fogs of early summer. But no such luck.

Under these waters lie schooners like the *Valentine*, *R.R. Bennett* and *Susan*, the square-rigged ship *Columba*, and the Norwegian freighter *Ciss*. Somewhere nearby lie the bones of a mysterious vessel named *The Naked Truth*. The naval transport HMS *Faversham* crashed into Scatarie Island in 1711, in company with three other vessels. The Newfoundland ferry *Bruce* died there exactly two centuries later. The immigrant barque *William Ewing* struck Scatarie in 1835, but her 250 immigrant passengers were saved. They were lucky: a year earlier, the barque *Astraea* struck Little Lorraine Head, a few miles south, and 250 Irish drowned. That same night, the brig *Edward* sank nearby without loss of life.

Radar, lighthouses and buoys have reduced the danger, but not eliminated it. As recently as 1967, an eleven-year-old boy walking along the shore near Fourchu was thunderstruck to discover a ship sitting high on the beach. She proved to be the trawler *Iceland II*, and all ten men aboard her had been lost.

In the fog, your best friends are your ears. At the mouth of Main-à-Dieu Passage is Port Nova whistle buoy. Whistle buoys contain perforated metal pipes, open at the bottom. As the buoy rises and falls in the waves, air flows in and out of the perforations with a deep, mournful sound which has led fishermen to dub these buoys "groaners." If we came anywhere near the groaner, we should hear it.

Beyond Bar Reef and Helen Rocks, the shores of Cape Breton are bold, and we wanted to follow that shore. At 11:15 we tacked towards the land till we could hear the surf, then held our course till we could dimly see it, 50 yards ahead. That white lace of surf against low black rocks was all we ever saw of Cape Breton. At 11:30 we sailed out into the fog.

For half an hour we sailed in our grey cocoon. And then— *ohhhh-woe . . . ohhhh-woe . . .*

"Over there! Off the starboard bow!"

The buoy was to windward. We sailed until the sound seemed to be coming from abeam, and tacked. As we zig-zagged our way up to it, the buoy became louder and louder.

OHHHH-WOE . . . OHHHH-WOE . . .

"There it is! I see it!" cried Mark.

Faint as a pencil drawing on grey paper, the steel tower of the buoy heaved in the seas.

I turned to Mark. "You know how to save a waypoint on the Loran?"

"Yep."

"Lulu, steer as close as you can get to that buoy. Mark, when I say *Now*, you save it as Waypoint 27."

Loran signals can be distorted by hills and other landforms. Inexpensive Loran receivers thus have slight inaccuracies. If you tell them to go to a particular latitude and longitude, they may miss by several hundred yards. But when you "save" a position—just as one saves data in a computer—you tell the Loran to take note of its present position. When you want to come back to the same spot later on, it will bring you within a boat-length.

Lulu steered almost close enough to touch the buoy.

"*Now!*"

"Got it!" said Mark.

The bell buoy at the entrance to Louisbourg was 7.7 miles away. The direct course from the Port Nova groaner was 282 degrees magnetic, a little north of west. But the wind was blowing us onto the shore, and *Silversark* was bound to make leeway, slipping sideways even as she sailed forward. There might also be unknown tidal currents, as there were in Main-à-Dieu Passage. So we should steer a little further off the land, allowing some room for error.

"We'll tack and then steer 270," I said, coming on deck. "We should hear a groaner away off to port and the Louisbourg fog signal to the right—and a bell buoy almost dead ahead. The fog signal is at the lighthouse, right at the entrance, and the groaner is well out to sea."

"I can hear a fog signal now," said Mark. "Listen."

We fell silent. Then we heard a group of three blasts— *whoop, whoop, whoop!*—and a single blast a few seconds later.

"There's two of them," said Mark.

"Which is which?" Lulu asked.

I jumped below and looked at the pilot book.

"Three blasts is Scatarie—that should be behind us," I said. "One blast is Louisbourg. Should be off the starboard bow."

"That's right," said Lulu.

"I think I hear the groaner," said Mark.

"It's a long way off yet," I said suspiciously.

"It's very faint," said Mark. "Listen."

I listened, but I couldn't hear it. But the Louisbourg fog signal was wailing out at us every twenty seconds.

"We should be blowing our foghorn," said Lulu. "Mark, get it out. Three short blasts, not more than a minute apart."

Our foghorn is an actual chrome-plated horn, blown like a bugle. Mark fished it out of a cockpit locker.

"Wait a minute," I protested. "No motor vessel is ever going to hear that little tin horn."

"Doesn't matter," said Lulu. "That's the regulation. If we had a collision, at least we'd have been doing the right thing."

"Just because you took a hundred-ton masters' course—"

WAAK WAAK WAAK!

Drowned out by the horn.

"Look at these swells," said Lulu. "Wow."

Thousands of miles of open sea lay to port. The breeze was steady, as it can only be when no land breaks its flow. The southeasterly winds of recent days had created a big, smooth swell—undulant hills of water perhaps 15 feet high and 100 feet long, rolling in from Donegal or Senegal. *Silversark* sailed up the faces of these benign monsters and then down their backs.

Somewhere over there in the fog were three little rock-infested coves: Big Lorraine, Little Lorraine and Baleine (pop. 15), the site of the previous week's drug bust. Baleine was the first settlement established under the name "Nova Scotia," and its story explains why a small patch of ground in the precincts of Edinburgh Castle is still legally part of Nova Scotia.

In 1621, King James I granted all of the Maritimes, then called Acadia, to Sir William Alexander. Sir William named his fief New Scotland, or—in the Latin of the grant documents—Nova Scotia. Sir William, in turn, granted the rights to Prince Edward Island and Cape Breton Island to Sir Robert Gordon of

Lochinvar. To encourage settlement, Sir Robert sold baronet-cies—and in order that the new baronets of Nova Scotia might be properly created on Nova Scotian soil, a spot in Edinburgh Castle was declared to be part of Nova Scotia.

Sir James Stewart, Lord Ochiltree, paid 200 livres sterling to become a baronet of Nova Scotia. He landed in Baleine with sixty immigrants in July 1629, cleared some land for his Barony of New Galloway, and sent a party of men out to collect tribute from nearby French fishermen. This was a grave error. Laws should not be made by those who have no power to enforce them, and no European nation really controlled the region—certainly not Ochiltree and his Scots.

The French fishermen complained about Ochiltree's levies to Captain Charles Daniel of the Company of New France, who was building a fort at St. Ann's. Daniel attacked New Galloway, captured Ochiltree and his party, renamed the place Port aux Baleines—Whale Harbour—and carried off the Scots to work on his building projects.

WAAK WAAK WAAK!

"Mark!" I said. "Not in my ear!"

"Sorry, Dad."

I was edgy. Lulu and I had sailed into Louisbourg before, but not from this direction. I had navigated in fog before—but not often, not for long, and not in unfamiliar waters.

Navigation, like any genuine test, makes you humble. "Truth," says Belloc, "is the great gift of the sea." Yes, but not always a welcome gift. A navigator may fail, with disastrous consequences, and there is no concealing the failure. If the ship is on the rocks, the problem is not politics or a personality conflict. You can't blame an unsympathetic teacher or editor or jury. It's outright failure, it's real, and it's *yours*.

Whoop! The Louisbourg lighthouse, much closer now.

ohhhh-woe . . . ohhhh-woe . . .

"Can't you hear that groaner?" said Mark.

"Yep. Now I can. Where is it? Over there?"

"Well out to sea," said Lulu.

"It seems like we're heading much more towards the light-house," I said. "We should be heading almost between the two sounds. Anybody hear the bell buoy?"

Nobody did. I checked the Loran. A mile to go.

"I'm going to call the Coast Guard lifeboat in Louisbourg, let them know we're out here," I said.

"Good idea," said Lulu.

I called on the VHF, and a voice came back immediately. What was our situation? Did we need assistance?

No, I said. But we were preparing to enter the harbour in terrible visibility, and we wanted the Coast Guard aware of our presence in case we did run into trouble.

"Now just where are you at, do you know?"

"According to our Loran, we're .8 miles from the buoy."

"Good enough, we'll be standin' by. Over and out."

WHOOP! The Louisbourg lighthouse, closer—and drawing aft. We were passing it. And a distant sound of surf.

"We could probably get in just by steering around that light-house," I said. "Just make a big arc, keeping it the same distance off to starboard. But I'd rather hear that bell."

"Listen!" said Mark. "I hear it!"

Ting-ting! Pause. *Ting-ting!*

"That's it," said Lulu. "Off to port. Let's tack."

"Tack," I said, going forward to handle the jib. We beat up to it as we had beaten up to the Port Nova buoy.

"There it is!" Again, the grey pencil sketch of a steel tower on a metal disk, rocking slowly in the waves. Again we sailed right up to it while Mark saved it as Waypoint 28. We let the sails out for the reach into the harbour. I ducked below and looked at the courses I had drawn on the chart.

"Steer 315," I said. "Nothing to starboard. If you yaw, yaw to port."

"All right," said Lulu, fixing her gaze on the compass.

"Mark, we're looking first for a red spar buoy."

"Right over there," said Mark, pointing to port.

"*What?*" Sure enough, we were rapidly passing a red spar to the left of our track. But the rule is Red to Right when Return-ing. How could there be a spar on the wrong side—?

I jumped below and gazed at the chart. Whew!

"That one marks another channel," I said. "There's a rock between us and it, but there's 23 feet of water over it."

"Hold my course?"

"Rigidly."

The entrance is 500 yards wide.

Listen, now. The deep wounded bellow of the groaner, far astern. The fading TING-TING of the bell, falling behind. The overpowering WHOOP! of the lighthouse fog signal, high above us on the rocky cliffs. Everything where it's supposed to be. Now the sound of surf to port. Surf to starboard.

A rocky spit appeared to starboard, washed by breaking seas. We passed quickly by. I glanced at the chart.

"Nag's Head, likely," I said.

"Okay?" said Lulu, her eyes fixed on the compass.

"Fine."

"Red spar!" cried Mark.

"Steer for it," I said. We bore down on it fast. It was marked JU4.

"Steer 335," I said, glancing at the chart to confirm it.

"Look!" said Mark, almost immediately. For the third time, the pencil sketch of a steel light buoy took shape in the mist.

"That's it," I said. "We're inside the harbour."

"What do I steer?"

"023. Hey, the fog is lifting!"

Someone had drawn a curtain and let the light in. We could see right up the harbour. The National Sea plant to port. The little wharves and fishermen's houses in Havenside, off to starboard. The government wharf, half a mile dead ahead.

A band of fog flowed across the harbour, closing down the view. We sailed blind for few moments. The fog cleared again. A man in Coast Guard uniform was walking down the wharf.

"It's Harold Fudge!" I said, delighted. "Hello, Harold!"

"Hello, me son," said Harold with a grin. "I kind of t'ought it sounded like you on the radio, there. Hi, Lulu. Good to have yous back in Louisbourg."

THE ONCE
AND
FUTURE
FORTRESS

Lulu and I first sailed together on a three-day voyage to Louisbourg in my schooner, *Hirondelle*, illuminated by the dawning awareness that we were already linked, that we had commenced more than one voyage when we sailed from D'Escousse. It had been a very different entrance into Louisbourg, almost exactly ten years earlier, on a hot autumn day when the blustery northwest wind was heaving the afternoon sea into roiled aluminum. Running down from Fourchu, we could see the lighthouse all the way from Guyon Island — the second oldest in America, standing like a white pencil on the cliffs. To port, Gabarus Bay stretched back into the land, broad enough to hold an armada — as it did in 1745 and 1758, when the

British landed armies to capture the impregnable French fortress and destroy the French empire in the north.

I was coming to Louisbourg to do research at the most important historic site in Atlantic Canada, the fortress whose fall would affect the shape and future of France, England, the United States and Canada. For me, Louisbourg was the fortress; it was only later that I truly saw the town.

Approaching Louisbourg that day, we saw a ruddy block surmounted by a graceful spire capped with a fleur-de-lis: a French royal building, the most important in Bourbon Louisbourg. The Château St. Louis contains the governor's residence, the chapel and the barracks. The silvery slate and shingle rooftops around it mark the homes of officers, merchants, fishermen, innkeepers and judges. A whole town clusters on the low neck of land which almost seals the harbour mouth: an eighteenth-century French town, painstakingly reconstructed on its original foundations.

We rounded Battery Island, which was fortified by the engineers of Louis xv, and was protected by another battery of guns dead ahead of us, on the inner shore of the harbour. As we turned inside Lighthouse Point, we passed the cove where the French once careened their men-of-war to scrub and paint their bottoms. Astern lay the quay along the town's front, with the king's vast storehouse, the tavern, the flophouse, the armoury, the home of Judge Lartique and the spacious home of the civil administrator—none other than François Bigot, the corrupt official whose name has entered the English language. Beyond the wooden quay wall, outside the faintly Oriental Porte Frederick, a small brick-red boat lay at anchor: an open *chaloupe*, a faithful reproduction of an eighteenth-century fishing boat.

Ahead lay fish plants, trawlers, and a town of 1,500 souls. At the tip of the concrete government wharf, a chunky figure stood resplendent in big black sunglasses, a once-white sweater, ruined slacks and tennis shoes without laces. It was Kippy Shaw, the wharfinger, and he was beckoning us to a berth.

French or English, old or new, Louisbourg has always been a

fishing and shipping town. In 1713, when the Treaty of Utrecht rousted the French out of the south coast of Newfoundland and left them with the islands in the Gulf of St. Lawrence, the French fishermen unhesitatingly adopted the convenient ice-free inlet of *l'havre à l'Anglois*, English Harbour. In an age when famine still stalked Europe, codfish was as vital as oil is today. The government followed the fishermen and renamed the harbour in honour of Louis XIV.

For thirty eventful years, the town flourished, becoming the fourth-busiest port in America, after New York, Boston and Philadelphia. Louisbourg merchants traded salt cod to the West Indies for rum, sugar and molasses, traded it to France for luxury goods and manufactures, and traded it illegally—along with French wines and lace—with New England for foodstuffs and building materials. A standard finish in a Louisbourg home was *planches bostonnais*—Boston boards.

For New England, however, Louisbourg was a haven for privateers and raiding Indians, a den of papists, a stronghold of the enemy. In 1745, with Europe again in arms, the New Englanders ventured an expedition daring to the point of madness: an attack by what Francis Parkman calls "staring rustics" on a fortified town defended by European regular troops. Through a combination of good luck and good leadership, they succeeded.

Louisbourg was occupied by the *Bostonnais* for three years, until Britain gave the town back to France in the Treaty of Aix-la-Chapelle. Having manned, planned and paid for the assault, the New Englanders were furious. Their resentment helped to fuel the American Revolution, and their success at Louisbourg prepared many of the same men to confront British regulars at Bunker Hill.

The following years were not really peaceful; an undeclared war went on continuously in the colonies, and by 1756 the Seven Years' War had broken out. Wolfe and Amherst recaptured the impregnable fortress in 1758, and two years later British sappers under "Foul Weather Jack" Byron—grandfather of the poet—blew the walls apart, stone by stone: an American Carthage.

For two centuries the ruins lay undisturbed. Then, in 1961, the federal government declared that it would employ redundant miners in a partial reconstruction of the fortress. The result is an astonishing re-creation of "a moment in time" — Louisbourg as it was in the summer of 1744, just before the first siege. It is a national treasure unknown to most Canadians.

Visitors arrive first at the DesRoches house, outside the walls. George DesRoches was a Basque fisherman, with a house typical of the modest dwellings along the shores, built of vertical logs and massive timbers held by mortise-and-tenon joints and wooden pegs. But the roof, green and growing, ripples in the wind: it is the only sod roof in the reconstruction.

You walk a couple of hundred yards to the Dauphin Gate, and there a scruffy-looking soldier in the blue coat and white breeches of the Compagnies Franches de la Marine demands the passports issued at the reception centre. The sentry explains the rules: keep off the ramparts, no attempts to communicate with the English prisoners, off the streets at dusk. Louisbourg is at war, and discipline is strict.

Once inside, you plunge directly into an eighteenth-century French colonial town. Bakers slide long wooden paddles into brick ovens and extract round loaves of brown bread. House-maids and children weed the gardens. Buff-coloured Jersey cattle browse while a young soldier feeds the governor's chickens. Sentry parties file down the streets. A young girl drops to her knee and crosses herself as she passes through the white-and-gold chapel. Soldiers and fishermen stop in at Pierre Lorant's tavern.

Follow them in, and enjoy. Pierre Lorant's L'Hotel de la Marine is for working people; next door at Jean Seigneur's L'Epée Royale, sea captains and officers demand finer fare and fancier service. Pierre Lorant offers potages and chowders, meat and fish pies, cabbage and sausage, heavy brown bread. The beer comes in pewter mugs, and the client provides his own knife. L'Epée Royale offers stemware and silver on pressed and fringed linen. The beef is done in a savoury mustard sauce, and the fish is a delicately sautéed fillet of trout.

But life in Louisbourg was hard. Even the spring, said one eighteenth-century inhabitant, "everywhere else so pleasant, there is frightful." The winds are "unrestrained in those dreadful seas in the months of March, April and May," with fogs "so thick and frequent in these months that ships are in danger of running upon the land without seeing it." The town suffered an epidemic of smallpox in 1732, and the outdoor latrines of three thousand people on a few acres of bedrock mean that everyone, in effect, drank the neighbours' sewage. The buildings are plagued with rising damp, the woodwork rots almost visibly, and every single skeleton ever exhumed on the site shows at least traces of arthritis.

Governor Jean Baptiste Louis Le Prévost, Seigneur du Quesnel, was buried under the chapel. Researchers found that one of his legs had been amputated below the knee, and the other tibia, ankle and foot were distorted by infection following a compound fracture. He was suffering from arteriosclerosis, and widespread arthritis had virtually fused his spinal column. Some teeth were missing, others were decayed, and a dental abscess was draining into his sinus cavities. In 1744 he was surly and abusive and given to excessive drinking. Small wonder: he was in agony, and he died on October 9.

The fortress's restoration is both meticulous and specific. It shows not "a typical officer's house" but the home of Captain Michel de Gannes de Falaise, built from the original plans and building contract. De Gannes himself is not at home, though his family is; in 1744 he was on a successful expedition to capture Canso and an unsuccessful attempt on Annapolis Royal. The soldiers are ill clothed, ill fed, ill paid and discontented. They will have mutinied by Christmas.

We know these details because the French bureaucrats sent reports home in triplicate, on three separate ships, to the French Ministry of Marine, which filed them in well-protected archives. We have the court records, military documents, building plans, parish records and shipping records. We have inventories of personal property taken when people died, we know what passed through customs (and something about what didn't), we have letters and diaries from both sides of both sieges. In many ways, we know more about eighteenth-century Louisbourg than we do about the modern town: we have the French confidential records, but Louisbourg today jealously guards its scandals and secrets.

Louisbourg is not merely an intellectual delight; it is a tactile, sensuous experience. The grey stones, the brown half-timber-ing, the cobbled streets—with the original French cobbles, in most places—the sweeping views and the clammy fog, the reek of fish coming across the harbour, the liquid French voices, the taste of brown ale, the salt smack of water on the quay, the blowing fields of angelica—it all adds up to a unique experience of a critical passage in Canada's past.

The angelica itself is a story. A wild plant with blooms which resemble an umbrella's ribbing, angelica was used by the French as a medicine against colds, bronchitis, pleurisy and rheumatism; its roots were candied and eaten as sweetmeats, its leaves were eaten like spinach and its stalks like blanched celery; it was made into jams, jellies and even perfume. Its seeds flavoured gin, and in desserts it was used as a vanilla substitute. The roots also provided a clear yellow dye. During the years of neglect, the angelica was kept down by the sheep who grazed over the broken casemates and fallen walls, but once the reconstruction banished the sheep, the angelica escaped into the countryside and spread for miles along the coast.

Louisbourg is full of such details, and fortress staff are almost painfully eager to share their incredible project. The fortress also sells reproduction pieces which are good enough to pass for originals. Not all such items can be made in Cape Breton—eighteenth-century Louisbourg itself imported crystal, china, faïence, linen and the like—but local people do produce everything from pewter spoons and toy boats to birch dining sets, luxurious sedan chairs and 18-pound cannon.

So many differences, and so many similarities. Louisbourg's settlers came from Newfoundland; the modern town is full of Newfoundlanders. In 1749, many Louisbourgeois who had been banished to France returned to Louisbourg, just as many a Maritimer today returns from Ontario when a job opens up down home. What issues concern us now? French versus English. Smuggling and drugs—alcohol then, other drugs now. Control of the fishery. Relations with the Americans. Bureaucracy, and the fiats of distant governments.

Welcome to the eighteenth century. Or the twentieth.

The fortress provides a powerful, tactile experience—but it *is* mostly reconstruction. The untouched relics are under water.

On a rare Indian summer day, years ago, Jim Wilson and Dave Bateman took me diving in Louisbourg Harbour. Dave, a fortress draftsman, also ran the dive shop. Jim, an instructor in chemical technology at UCCB, was an authorized guide to a national park component unique in Canada: an historic territory entirely under ocean water. Aboard his 38-foot *Wreckhunter*, Jim explained why the harbour was placed off-limits to unauthorized divers.

"The night in 1758 when the British destroyed the French fleet here," he said, "two of the French ships were driven ashore in about ten feet of water. The British salvaged a good deal of their gear after they recaptured the fortress, and everyone else has been salvaging them ever since. There's virtually nothing left in the water. So the other wrecks had to be protected, if we were going to have anything left to show our grandchildren."

We moored the boat, and Jim unrolled a drawing. "We believe this is the wreck of the *Célèbre*," he said, crouching over a six-foot-long plan of the bottom, "but it's hard to be absolutely positive. That buoy is fastened to this big cannon here, and the ruins stretch out about sixty feet on each side of it."

Splash. Tumble. The cool green light, the trickle of water into the wet-suit. Trailing silver bubbles, we fly slowly over the wreckage, like a silent, finny ballet: Jim in his red and black suit, Dave in black and yellow, me in black except for my blue fibreglass backpack.

Jim glides down to a shapeless hump on the bottom, perhaps two and a half feet across, and signals that this is the base of the mizzenmast. From above you can see that it was round, all right, but the shipworms who have been chewing on it for two centuries have distorted its profile almost beyond recognition. Reaching to the base of the mast, Jim picks up a small, arc-shaped piece of wood, part of a barrel hoop, and points at three staves protruding from the sand. He picks up the bottom of a broken wine bottle. We pass it from hand to hand and replace it.

Jim points at a brass sheave like a massive clothesline pulley. We find discs of lignum vitae, a tropical wood heavy enough to sink, and impervious to shipworm: the surviving sheaves of wooden blocks which have otherwise vanished. Jim points to an anchor whose wooden stock has been entirely consumed by the worms. Its shank is the size of a man's body. We flutter-kick onward through the kelp, raising milky beige clouds of silt.

Two brass tubes, a yard long and six inches in diameter, are the remains of the bilge pumps. A scattering of bricks near the stern may have been part of the galley. Piles of metal, encrusted with Cape Breton's thin purple coral, prove to be bar shot and cannon balls. A massive timber, two feet square, lies embedded in the sand, with slightly less massive timbers reaching away from it at right angles. Jim's mittened hand tells us that these are the remnants of the ship's backbone.

Near the bow lie several triangular wooden structures, like small roof trusses. Jim hitches himself up on a section of the stem which protrudes from the seafloor like a bowsprit and waves his hand, setting us free to explore the wreck for ourselves. And away we go, porpoising and doing somersaults, capering over the ruined hopes of France in America.

Louisbourg's brief history ended in a hailstorm of fire and iron. In the summer of 1758, when this ship last floated, women and children huddled in casemates under the fortress walls. Mortar shells and cannon balls screamed through the smoky air, bursting in the streets, shattering shops and warehouses. Outside the walls, 14,000 British troops methodically extended their trenches closer and closer to the doomed town.

"Not a house in the whole place but has felt the force of their cannonade," despaired a French diarist. "Between yesterday morning and seven o'clock tonight from a thousand to twelve hundred shells have fallen inside the town, while at least forty cannon have been firing incessantly as well. The hospital and the houses around it, which also serve as hospitals, are attacked with cannon and mortar. The surgeon trembles as he amputates a limb amid cries of *Gare la bombe!* and leaves his patient in the midst of the operation, lest he should share his fate."

To encourage the troops, the wife of the Chevalier Augustin de Drucour, Louisbourg's governor, had fired three cannon every day; the English had dubbed her "Madame la Bombardière." But after weeks of warfare, the slow, weary reports of his own cannon sounded to Drucour like a funeral salute.

Drucour was no great soldier, but he had done his best. He had gathered his best fighting forces into the town, he had destroyed outlying buildings which blocked the fortress's field of fire, and he had scuttled half a dozen ships to block the harbour mouth. But the essence of his strategy was to strengthen the beach defences to prevent the British from landing, and that strategy had already failed.

And DesGouttes, the naval commodore, would not fight. DesGouttes commanded five men-of-war mounting a total of 330 guns, but they lay against the quay wall like terrified waterhens. Drucour wanted them to cannonade the British forces and disrupt their steady advance. DesGouttes wanted chiefly to save his ships. He stripped them of their powder and their crews, leaving only a handful of watchmen aboard. And Drucour had no authority to countermand the commodore.

Captain Jean Vauquelin, by contrast, commanded only a little 36-gun frigate, *Aréthuse*, but he had harried the British so effectively that Brigadier James Wolfe had built an entire set of entrenchments just to drive him off. Vauqelin then offered to run the British blockade with despatches for France. Des-Gouttes disagreed: Vauquelin might still be useful at Louisbourg.

"Yes, by God!" declared Vauquelin. "If you will give me one of your ships of the line that are laid up doing nothing, you will see that I will do much more yet than I have done hitherto with the frigate!" On July 15, Vauquelin left Louisbourg with only sixty men fit for service—not even enough to man his guns. Dodging the British fleet, he reached France in eighteen days. Two years later, at Quebec, he fought till his ship was a ruined hulk, and even then refused to surrender. When the English captured him, they sent him home with every honour.

In the eighteenth century, wars could be genteel affairs. General Jeffrey Amherst sent two pineapples to Madame Drucour—though his messenger took a route which showed him the town's defences. The Drucours sent Amherst champagne. An English woman called on a French captain whom she believed was her cousin; they had refreshments, and she picked a salad. A diarist remarked that war had never been carried on with more courtesy.

In the end, DesGouttes did not even save his precious ships. A week after Vauquelin left, a British shell struck the after-deck of the 64-gun *Célèbre*, and set her afire. Sparks jumped to *Entreprenant* and *Entreprenant* set fire to *Capricieux*. The three burning ships drifted towards the shallows. Their crews worked frantically to put the fires out—but, said Wolfe's subordinate, Captain Samuel Strache, when he saw the first ship burning "I Immediately fir'd on her very briskly to prevent the boats that came to her assistance from putting it hout, it Communicated to the next and to the third Ship, I still kept on my Canonading till it was impossible to put the fire out so that three of the line was Intirely Consumed." Amherst noted with satisfaction that "they burned very faft."

DesGouttes had two ships left: *Bienfaisant* and his flagship *Prudent*. Four days later, Admiral Boscawen sent in five hundred seamen in small boats with muffled oars, while Amherst's gunners bombarded the French from the land. Cheering British sailors boarded the ships, armed with muskets, pole-axes and cutlasses, and, says an anonymous eye-witness, "foon found themfelves in poffeffion of two fine fhips of the enemy, one of 74 and one of 64 guns, with the lofs of very few of the feamen, and but one mate."

The French launched "a moft furious fire of cannon, mortars and mufkets from all parts," and the British found that *Prudent* was aground. They set her afire and towed *Bienfaisant* neatly out of range of the French guns. Stripped of its ships, low on supplies, with its walls crumbling, its buildings in ruins and its people demoralized, Louisbourg surrendered the next day.

I tapped Dave Bateman's rubber-clad shoulder, pointed at my mouthpiece and drew a finger across my throat. My tank was almost empty. Dave nodded, and we rose slowly to the silver surface, following our own bubbles.

Harold Fudge is a Newfoundlander who drifted across Cabot Strait around 1950. His whole family followed; only two cousins remain in François, the tea-cup harbour where they all grew up.

"Me father's next door, living with me brother," Harold said. "We all made a good livin'—nothing extra special, but we all own our own houses and cars, and we eat well. What do you want out of life?"

We were sitting in Harold's house in Havenside, eating well. Once we were properly moored, Harold had gone home; it was the end of his shift. An hour later he was back, standing on the wharf looking down into *Silversark*'s cockpit.

"How ignorant can I be?" he said. "I got home and I thought, those people wanted a shower and I could have had them over for a bath, and for supper—come on now, hop in the car." We had been heading for The Grubstake, Louisbourg's improbable Wild West restaurant. Instead, Rita Fudge gave us steak and vegetables, accompanied with homemade rolls and capped with a rhubarb pie in a breadlike crust, with tinned milk poured over it—a Newfoundland favourite, developed when fresh milk was an impossible luxury in the outports.

"I'm a fan of the good old food," smiled Harold. "Lots of fish, plain vegetables, and a nice pie like that, what?"

"We're fans of it, too," said Lulu.

Harold fished out of Louisbourg for more than twenty years. He joined the Coast Guard in 1974, when the Louisbourg lifeboat station was established. Eleven such stations are sprinkled along the Atlantic Coast, with crews on standby round the clock. Each is crewed by experienced local seamen who know the nearby waters well. Of all the services government provides to the fishery, the lifeboats are among the most valued.

The Type 300 Waveney-class lifeboats are incredibly tough little boats—44 feet long, with twin engines, shafts, propellers, battery banks, filters, pumps. The wheelhouse bristles with aerials: radar, VHF and SSB radios, Loran, satellite navigation system. With nearly 600 horsepower, they do 14 knots. Their steel hulls and aluminum superstructures allow them to recover from a complete capsize in seven seconds. Their crews wear harnesses at sea to hold them in their seats, and headsets to protect their ears from the noise. They are "about as comfortable as goin' to sea in a 45-gallon drum," said one of their skippers, "but they're powerful little boats, and they'll take an awful beatin'."

They have a 50-mile range, but the crews often go further in emergencies, sometimes running out of fuel on the way back in. The Waveneys are being replaced by new $3-million Arun-class vessels, one of which is in service at Port Bickerton, N.S. Bigger, heavier and more sophisticated, the Aruns have a 150-mile range, which will allow the Louisbourg station to cover the whole eastern coast of Cape Breton.

The lifeboat office is a sociable place; when I lived in Louisbourg, I used to drop in and visit with the crewman on duty, or with visiting fishermen. I learned a lot from those leisurely chats with Wayne Dowling, Vic Anderson, Bill Banfield, Warren Bagnell. The crewmen are good company, and they welcome a break in what is largely a career of waiting. One of them once remarked that "it's a queer old job, like a fireman: a good day is a day when nobody needs you."

Most of the lifeboats' work is routine: keeping buoy lights operating, taking injured seamen ashore, towing yachts off reefs, towing disabled fishing boats to harbour. Though the Canadian Coast Guard, unlike its U.S. counterpart, is not a law-enforcement agency, it sometimes provides transport for the RCMP, and the lifeboats occasionally make spectacular rescues—like the July day in 1979 when George LeMoine's *Lady Marilyn* called in distress near Little Lorraine. The wind was blowing between 60 and 70 knots, the seas were mountainous, and the motion had rolled dirt from the gas tank into LeMoine's fuel line. When he tried to clean it out, he broke the fuel line.

LeMoine and his crewmen put out every anchor they had aboard—five or six in all, including the trawl anchors, which hold fishing gear on the bottom—but *Lady Marilyn* dragged them all. LeMoine's father tried to go out for them, but the seas were too much for him. When the lifeboat reached them, *Lady Marilyn* was just 300 to 400 yards from the tumultuous surf on the rocky shore. The lifeboat circled behind her, almost in the breakers. She put a line aboard and towed the fishing boat home.

"I was glad to know you were there today," I told Harold Fudge over the kitchen table. "I don't like blundering around in the fog."

"Nobody does, b'y," said Harold. "Don't matter how long you been sailing. It always puts a kind of dread on you, like somebody bandaged your eyes, and you never know exactly where you're to." He looked over with a smile. "You people must be some smart, though. There's lots of fishermen couldn't

do what the three of you done today. We had to guide a whole
fleet of New Brunswick shrimpers in here this summer. They
got outside the harbour in the fog—had radar and everything,
but they didn't trust themselves to come in."

Harold came back in the morning with his grandson, Chris
Lunn, and took Mark away for the day. They spent the day
carving, and continued in the evening, when Harold brought
them back. Meanwhile they talked constantly, as twelve-year-
olds do—and sometimes surprisingly. Working down below, I
suddenly tuned into the conversation to hear Chris saying,
"You don't really identify your intellectual interests till you're
in university."
     Oh.
     Lulu and I went to the Atlantic Statiquarium, a museum of
models, fish and sunken treasure, about which the owner knows
a great deal. Alex Storm is the Dutch-born fortress draftsman
who found the treasure of the French pay ship *Le Chameau*.
Wreck-hunting, says Storm, "is just logic and common sense.
There are lots of ships out there, and there's a wealth of information in the archives, provided you know what you're looking
for."
     For treasure-hunters, the major problem is the federal gov-
ernment, which claims everything found on the bottom. Alex
Storm was among the first east-coast scuba divers, and he
obtained a "dispensation from delivery" from the Department
of Transport. The officials considered him a kook, so they gave
it to him. After he found the treasure, they changed the rules.
Today, divers who find treasure often don't report it; they
quietly sell it abroad. Canada is the loser, for such finds are
"little time capsules," says underwater archaeologist Andy
Lockery of the University of Winnipeg. It is our history which is
sold abroad.
     For recreational divers, however, Louisbourg's wrecks are a
joy. Some modern wrecks are largely intact; local dive clubs
often visit the *Montara*, for instance, a coastal steamer which
sank in Gooseberry Cove in 1920. An anchor, some cannon and
a pile of shot lie near a pinnacle of rock in about 100 feet of water

at the entrance to Louisbourg Harbour; they were dumped by a French merchantman, which ran aground on the pinnacle. Scattered bits of a tea clipper lie nearby, along with the wreckage of a World War II minesweeper. There are seafloor caves at the harbour mouth, too, but any diving in the harbour requires Park supervision. Jim Wilson found all kinds of things on the harbour bottom—old anchors, new anchors, oil drums and boots. His most alarming experience was the discovery, right inside the harbour, of an unexploded depth charge.

I needed to charge our big battery. I went sniffing around the wharves, looking for an electrical outlet.

"Holy Jesus, look what come in on the tide!" cried a big, curly-haired fisherman at the next wharf. "Come on aboard, b'y, how the hell are you?"

"Con Mills!" I said. "How the hell are *you*?"

Con Mills was a leader in the labour battle which brought me to Cape Breton in the first place. In 1970-71, 235 fishermen in Canso Strait tried to force the fishing companies to recognize the Vancouver-based United Fishermen and Allied Workers' Union as their bargaining agent. The battle went on, in various ways, for a year and a half; it galvanized the whole labour movement and nearly caused a province-wide general strike. The UFAWU was defeated—but the companies recognized a rival union, and the offshore draggers have been unionized ever since.

I wrote a book about all this, and Con Mills is in it. When the strike ended, he moved to Prince Rupert, B.C., to work full-time for the UFAWU. A few years later he came home to Louisbourg, bought a boat and went fishing. Strong, energetic and smart, he knows exactly where he stands in a highly politicized, regulated industry. He is not happy.

"I've been allocated 15,000 pounds of cod for next year under this boat allocation system," he said. "What good is 15,000 to me? That won't even pay my gas bill. Yet the other fellow across the wharf there, he's got 500,000 or 600,000. And why? Because he needs it, he's going to go broke without it. Well, it's not my fault he followed their advice and got himself a quarter million dollars in debt. Why should I pay for that?

"You want a cup of coffee? Sure you do, I'll make it. This here is my brother Sam—'scuse me—"

He went out on the afterdeck to give some instructions to his crew, who were hosing down fish boxes and pen boards. He came back in with a plastic bag in his hand.

"Here's a couple of mackerel for your dinner. We've been out jigging for bait all morning. Where's your schooner?"

"I'm in the little black cutter over there," I said.

"Jesus, she's a pretty little thing. Where'd you get her?"

"Built her."

"G'wan, did you? I got to have a look at that. We'll have a cup of coffee first, anyways. You know somethin' you should write about? This by-catch racket. Now b'y, that's a scandal, that is."

A by-catch consists of fish beyond your allocation from the Department of Fisheries and Oceans. If DFO has given you a quota of 15,000 pounds of redfish, everything else—even more redfish—is by-catch, and you can land only a small percentage of it. The rest is thrown back.

"They shouldn't be *allowed* to dump it," Con said. "If a fellow catches 30,000 and he's only got a quota for 15,000 he should bring the 30,000 in and not go out the next trip. But they're wasting fish continuously. Sometimes a boat dumps more fish than it lands.

"Now I been at all kinds of meetings about this, and DFO says, 'Oh, that's not *dumping*, that's *discarding*.' Well, you tell me the difference. They say, 'Well, you take the big ones and release the little ones.' The hell I do. I get just as much for the little ones as I do for the big ones. There's all kinds of different grades of cod now—scrod cod, market cod, jumbo . . . And the fish you dump are dead anyway. You can imagine the pressure on them in the bottom of the drag. So why not land 'em? Jesus, and they call this 'management'!"

After coffee, Con and I went over to *Silversark*. A grinning figure in dark glasses was standing beside the boat.

"Remember me?" it asked.

"Kippy Shaw," I said. "Lulu! Here's Kippy! How are you?"

"Great!" said Kippy, shaking hands vigorously. "And you remember this fellow?"

"Bill Banfield!" I was momentarily unsettled to see him alive because, imaginatively, I had killed him. I once wrote a series of radio plays based on the work of the Coast Guard lifeboats, and Bill had been the inspiration for one of the characters. But that character had drowned, and here was Bill, indubitably alive, a gentle, wise old Newfoundlander whose pink, childlike complexion is curiously at odds with his white hair. Reality and fiction in collision. It was a special treat to see him.

The three big men filled *Silversark*'s small cabin.

I glanced at Lulu, my mind going back to that first trip, when Kippy and his first wife fed us, let us use their shower and plumbed a bottle of rum with us. We went on to the tavern, where a new rock ensemble called the North River Band (since disbanded, alas) was blowing its head off to a packed house. The tavern turned away at least fifty couples before midnight. The dance floor was jammed, the music was hot, and when the band quit at one in the morning the crowd hooted and howled and banged on the tables till they came back not once, but three times.

We wobbled back down the wharf at two in the morning with three young people. We had reluctantly refused several invitations to "an all-nighter at Loretta's", thanks, but would they like to come aboard for a beer? They would. The stories and yarns rolled on till four, when we toppled exhausted into our berths. The three of them shook their heads at such dull folks and rolled away into the night.

Louis xv's governors passed ordinance after ordinance in a vain attempt to control Louisbourg's drinking: drunkenness, they complained, caused lost work time, sickness, disorder and crime. But Louisbourg's labourers and fishermen kept right on belting it back. *Plus ça change, plus c'est la même chose.*

Romantic memories. Our first dance together, and it all started with Kippy.

"Now you got to come and see my new boat," said Kippy, waking me from my reverie. "You want to charge your battery?"

"Right."

"You got a charger? Extension cord? I got all that stuff."

"No, we just need power."

"Right on the wharf," said Kippy cheerfully. "We'll just pull your boat forward a bit and plug it in. Anything you want, you just ask for it, ol' buddy. And then we'll go see my boat."

Kippy's boat once belonged to Con: a voluminous fibreglass hull which had been totally gutted by fire. He and his new wife, Olive, had worked together on it, rebuilding it from the engine stringers up. Now it had a wide, comfortable cabin, private stateroom, a huge open deck in the stern and a virtual dance floor behind the flying bridge. *Silversark* is a mini-van of the sea; Kippy's boat is a Winnebago.

"She does 14 knots," Kippy said proudly. "Baddeck in nine hours, either by St. Peter's or the Great Bras d'Or. Olive has a farm in Margaree, and I'm retired since two years, so we spend a lot of time over there. I'm going over there tomorrow. How long you going to stick around?"

"We'll probably go tomorrow, too. I'd like to spend more time here, though."

"Then come back," said Kippy. "Don't stay away so long."

THE HORNED MOON

From Louisbourg to St. Peter's is 50 miles of foggy, rockbound coastline, with scarcely a notch in it by way of a harbour. On our first voyage, Lulu and I had stopped overnight in an open roadstead at Michaud Cove and in Fourchu, a slot in the rocks with a tortuous approach. But *Hirondelle* had an engine. With a good breeze *Silversark* could cover those 50 miles in one long hop of ten or twelve hours; if we sailed at four A.M. we had a fair chance of arriving in daylight. The forecast was tolerable: three solid days of moderate southeasterly winds.

At three the air was calm. We went back to sleep. At four we felt a light southwest wind—exactly wrong for us.

"Maybe it'll be southeast when we get outside," said Lulu. "There wasn't anything else in the forecast at all."

At five we sailed across the harbour to Havenside and tacked directly in front of Harold Fudge's house. The fortress lay ahead, silver and black in the moonlight. Fishing boats murmured forth from little wharves, converging on the entrance like filings drawn to a magnet, their red and green running lights burning.

The sun rose like a huge burning orange behind the lighthouse. Outside the harbour, pilot whales plunged and blew, browsing among schools of mackerel. Half a dozen fishing boats bobbed and rolled among the rocks and islands, each with a row of men along the rail, each man with a line in the water. It is strange that mackerel—that sweet, fine fish—has so little value that the fishermen use it to bait their crab traps.

We waved, and they waved, and we sailed on—

—right into the fog. In an eyeblink. With the wind still southwesterly.

Oh, damn. Damn!

"I hate to go back," said Lulu.

"Okay, we'll go on," I said. "At least for now."

"What about Fourchu?"

"Not in the fog."

Now began a process of nonstop navigation. Sailing in the fog, to windward, on a rocky coast known for its currents, far from any easy refuge—in such circumstances you want to *know* where you are. If I had been asked the kind of sailing I did not want to do, this combination would have ranked high on my list.

An hour went by. A sleepy Mark stuck his head out the hatch.

"Where are we?"

"In the fog."

"I can see *that*!"

I swung below and put my finger on the chart.

"We're right about here."

"How do you know?"

I tried to explain. In navigation, you start with observed facts. *We were at the bell buoy at 6:15, and there we streamed the log. We're doing about four knots, steering 220. From these facts, you draw inferences. By 8:15 we should be about eight miles along our course, which is about here.* Check the facts. The log says 7.7 miles. So that's probably where we are—provided that the log is correct and that there's no current, no compass error, no steering error and so on.

You seize every pertinent fact to confirm your position—the depth of the water, the bearing of a lighthouse, a glimpse of a headland through the mist. To the navigator, a buoy isn't just a buoy: it's a confirmation of your position. Unless, of course, the buoy is out of place . . .

The possibilities of error are endless, and every navigator recalls with a hot flush of embarrassment at least one egregious, unforgivable mistake, based on a whole structure of faulty reasoning—assumptions balanced carefully on one another, buttressed by guesswork and mortared with wishful thinking. Then some terrible, undeniable fact knocks the whole house of cards flying. When you reach the buoy which should say Beak Point, it says Grand River. The apparent range lights turn out to be streetlights; on your present course you will sail straight up the yellow line. When you realize how wrong you were, how lucky you are that the boat is still afloat, the sweat pops out on your brow and an iron vise clamps your stomach.

Sailing home from Louisbourg, our course lay along the coast and almost against the wind. So we would sail a couple of miles down the coast, gradually converging with the shore. Then we would jog out to sea for half a mile before tacking again, making a saw-toothed course which followed the tendency of the shore. In the fog, I would plot those course changes scrupulously. I would study the Loran, which should give me bearings astern to Louisbourg and forward to the Guyon Island buoy.

"Oh," said Mark. "So that's how it works."

"That's some of it, anyway."

"I'm going to blow the horn."

"Good idea."

We sailed on in wet, grey limbo, moving smartly through the water without ever passing anything, like a child walking up the down escalator.

Two hours had passed since the fog rolled in.

Three hours.

"I see something over there," said Lulu.

"It's clearing," Mark said.

A hint of land, away off to starboard. Cape Gabarus, maybe? The fog blew away, blew back in, came and went in wraiths and tatters. At ten it cleared completely, revealing our position: well to seaward of Guyon Island and heading for the Guyon offshore buoy, a couple of miles ahead. Just about where we wanted to be.

"Nice fresh breeze," said Lulu.

"But it's still dead on the nose," I said. "I haven't given up the idea of going back to Louisbourg."

"*What?*"

"It's nearly eleven," I said. "We've been sailing for six hours, and we've only gained about ten or twelve miles. The wind is against us. We'll be groping into St. Peter's in the dark. Maybe in the fog. Dog-tired, after sailing to windward for twenty hours."

"Well, what about Fourchu? This wouldn't be a bad wind to go in there. And the weather's clear now."

"True."

"Let's sail over to Fourchu Head. If the wind is good, we'll go in," said Lulu. "Otherwise, we can go back."

"Why don't we go on?" asked Mark.

We crossed Fourchu Bay, with its tumult of rocks and shoals dominated by Gabarus Round Rock. I almost expected to see a sleek, powerful motor yacht come flying along, with *Dragon Lady* emblazoned on her stern. The boat played a role in my thriller of the same name, and the finale of the book took place here, on this sparsely inhabited stretch of coast.

As we approached the blocky lighthouse on Fourchu Head, a bank of fog blotted it out. Swiftly, inexorably, the legions of fog advanced on the sea. By 2:20 we had picked up Pot Rock buoy, off Fourchu, and we were back in the fog again, sailing onward.

"Bloody fog," I said.

"So much for Fourchu," said Lulu.

"Shark!" cried Mark, pointing.

A thick black dorsal fin knifed through the water a few feet away. Whales arc through the seas, rising and falling. This big fin stayed at the surface, nosing restlessly this way and that. A shark, all right—and a big one. There is something primeval about sharks, pitiless, hypnotic. We watched intently till the fin faded into the mist.

"I won't go swimming around *here*." Mark shivered.

Nor will I. I share the opinion of Ronnie LeJeune, a veteran diver from West Arichat who stayed out of the water when Chedabucto Bay was full of sharks one spring.

"The book says they're harmless," Ronnie explained. "Well, I know that, and *you* know that, and prob'ly most of *them* knows that. But who's to say there ain't *one* retarded son of a whore out there that didn't read the book yet?"

At three o'clock, as quickly as it had come, the fog moved on, chasing down the coast towards Louisbourg. Fourchu Head lighthouse emerged, far behind us. I was looking for another lighthouse ahead, where St. Esprit Island thrust outward into the sea. But all we could see down there was a single barren tree trunk, stark against the sky. So was that St. Esprit Island, or was it something else? Eventually it dawned on us: the tree trunk was a skeleton tower, and we were looking at its edge. To seaward, we could just see the groaner at Bad Neighbour Shoal.

Now we had a warm, clear, sunny afternoon—a perfect summer day, without a hint of fog. But the wind was almost gone. We were going to be out here overnight; becalmed, we would be the plaything of the currents. We put *Silversark* on the offshore tack, giving ourselves some sea-room. But we would get a breeze, surely, after the sun went down and the land cooled.

By six Lulu was jilling about in light airs, coaxing a few yards out of each vagrant puff. I went below and made sandwiches. We set things up for the night—flashlights handy, binoculars in the cockpit, wool socks and heavy sweaters under our robust, lined Helly Hansen sailing suits.

In a blaze of red, the sun dropped behind St. Esprit Island.

We ghosted on, trying to shape a course to seaward of the groaner. A bird splashed and fluttered on the water close under the bow, squawking indignantly: she must have been dozing on the surface, and we nearly ran her down.

Lulu curled up on the deck and took a nap in her oilskins.

"I'm going to stay up all night," Mark declared. He talked and read, and was sound asleep by midnight.

We were becalmed all night.

My first reaction to a calm is always surprise. No wind? How can this be? It always blows in Nova Scotia—and especially in places like St. Esprit. A calm throws me off balance. It is like reaching absent-mindedly for a cigarette, momentarily forgetting that you quit smoking. No cigarettes? No wind? What?

Surprise gives way first to pleasure. The calm is an unexpected holiday, a chance to do little things that are never important enough to worry about and so never get done. File off the sharp edge on the stainless fitting, scrub the deck, put a whipping on the fraying end of the main halyard.

By now, normally, a bit of wind begins to ruffle the sea. If it doesn't, you're puzzled. Maybe this is more serious than it seemed. Maybe a major shift in the weather is brewing. Maybe you're going to be here for a while. Well . . . Get into a good book, or haul out the guitar and practise. Do some writing.

Or even just look at the sea and the sky. At midnight the sky was absolutely clear, with a high cold moon. The dew lay puddled on the deck. It hung from the sheets and lifelines and beaded the surfaces of the sails. Every now and again a sea would roll the boat abruptly back and forth, shaking a heavy shower of dew from the sails. I remembered Coleridge's Ancient Mariner:

> From the sails the dew did drip—
> Till clomb above the eastern bar
> The hornéd Moon, with one bright star
> Within the nether tip.

"Hullo," said Lulu, waking up. "What's happening?"

"Frig-all. I try this and that, but the boat just bobs around in circles."

"Well, with no wind—" Lulu shrugged. "Why don't we row for a while?"

"Row? Are you serious?"

"Why not?"

"Why so?"

"We'd make a little progress, anyway," said Lulu. "It'd be better than just sitting here."

"We'd just wear ourselves out for nothing!"

"Don't be so grumpy!"

"I am *not* grumpy! Look, if you want to row, we'll row!"

"Get the oars, then!"

We rowed. Suddenly, without warning, completely spontaneously, I was *furious*. What in the name of God were we doing rowing this clumsy goddam boat around the goddam North Atlantic in the middle of the goddam night? Why were we *here*, anyway? What fool decided not to put an engine in this stupid sailboat? How could such a sensible, sane companion as Lulu come up with such a harebrained idea as rowing?

God knows whether we got anywhere—although, when I checked the Loran in the morning, I found we had moved half a mile along our course during the night. But after half an hour I was sweating and tired—and much more reasonable.

"Look, there really isn't any point to this," I said. "Let's ship the oars, and you get some sleep. I'll stay on watch—not that I think there's anything much to watch for."

"All right," said Lulu.

"I'm sorry I was so grumpy," I said. "I think I'm over it."

"Why did you think I wanted you to row?" Lulu grinned. She kissed me quickly and went below.

Hmm. Managed again.

Where had that fury come from? It occurred to me that I was responding to the loss of the wind as a person responds to the death of a loved one, and in the same stages: surprise, denial, fear, rage—and now, perhaps, resignation. All of it compounded by twenty-two strenuous hours on watch. Coleridge, with his usual brilliance, seized upon a becalmed ship—"as idle as a painted ship, upon a painted ocean"—to evoke the most vivid image of purgatory ever written:

> I looked upon the rotting sea,
> And drew my eyes away;
> I looked upon the rotting deck,
> And there the dead men lay.
>
> I closed my lids, and kept them close,
> And the balls like pulses beat;
> For the sky and the sea, and the sea and the sky

Lay like a load on my weary eye,
And the dead were at my feet.

Unlike the Ancient Mariner, The Skipper would have been philosophical. *What can you do?* he would have said. *When you're caught, you're caught. No point gettin' upset, you'll only discourage the crew.*

With no wind, there was no point letting the dew-laden sails drench me whenever the boat rolled. I lowered them and sank into a corner of the cockpit. August or no, it was *cold*—cold enough for winter clothing, especially sitting still in the cockpit.

It was also very beautiful, in a chill and lonely way, hanging between the fixed white light of Fourchu Head far to the northeast and the flashing light of St. Esprit to the west. The brightness of the moon subdued the stars, especially near the zenith. The masthead traced circles on the sooty sky. The shore was a dark smudge on the horizon, without yellow house windows or moving headlights and red taillights: the whole shore between Fourchu and St. Esprit is probably inhabited by fewer than a hundred people. Windless though it was, the ocean was never entirely calm; small seas rolled in like smooth, low extrusions of glossy marble, capped with quicksilver, impenetrably dark in their troughs. A black and white photograph by some old master: Cartier-Bresson, perhaps, or Ansel Adams.

And the darkness was full of life. Birds zoomed through the rigging and close overhead; they must have been petrels, which breed along this coast, feed at night, and fly with that breathtaking verve and assurance. I heard whales blowing; although I turned quickly to see them, I never caught sight of one—but once, while I was dozing, I heard the great sigh of a cetacean just a few feet away, and found myself enveloped in a foul cloud of fishy-smelling vapour: an exhalation right beside the cockpit.

The stark black-and-silver dissolved as the red blush of dawn suffused the seaward sky. The sun jumped up, hot and red, painting colours back onto the boat, the land, the sea.

I looked down at the water and saw a faint ruffling on its surface. Could it be—might it be—wind?

It was indeed: weak, tentative, but unquestionably a wind.

I scrambled up, creaking in all my joints, casting off sail ties, hoisting the main and jib. Lulu's sleepy face appeared in the main hatch.

"Wind?"

"Just a hint."

Pulling on her oilskins, she came on deck. I was looking aloft, swigging on the halyards, making sure the sails were hauled right to the masthead.

"When did the fog come back in?" asked Lulu.

"Fog?" I said, looking around.

We were completely surrounded by heavy grey fog.

"There was no fog when I came forward," I said. "There wasn't even any in sight. I can't imagine where it came from."

"My God," said Lulu, settling herself at the helm. "What's the course?"

"Three two oh. Don't overshoot the groaner; we're coming at it from seaward, and there's a four-foot rock just beyond it."

"You go below and take a nap," said Lulu. "You look absolutely wasted."

Did ever a pillow and bedclothes feel so good? I burrowed into a quarter-berth and fell deep asleep. I dimly heard Mark wake up and go on deck, faintly heard him get the foghorn out and blow it.

Waaaak! Waak waak! But it was all far away.

"Look! Look!"

Mark's urgent voice sliced through my sleep. I rushed on deck. A big pilot whale was disporting himself off the port beam, at the limit of visibility. It was 8:45, and Lulu was frustrated. She had just enough wind to keep the sails full, but not enough to manoeuvre. I listened: the groaner was off to starboard.

"Do we have to go right to that groaner?" Lulu demanded.

"Well . . . no. It'd be nice to save it, though."

"It's going to take forever. Look at us! I can hardly even keep the boat pointed in the right direction."

I knew exactly how she felt. *Silversark* is a sturdy little vessel, not a lightweight flyer. She disregards really light airs and slowly chases her own tail.

"Look! Look!"

Off the port bow was a pod of dolphins, rhythmically rising and plunging towards us. We watched with fascination as they approached — six or eight of them, fast, smooth, purposeful, like a herd of cantering horses.

"I hope they come over to us," breathed Mark.

"Me, too."

But though dolphins are famous for their interest in boats, these had business elsewhere. They came towards us on a converging path, passed 30 feet from our stern, and moved straight on into the fog.

"Dolphins!" breathed Mark. "Dolphins! Awesome!"

I went to the Loran to find the course and distance to the light buoy off Point Michaud, the next major headland.

"The fog is clearing," called Lulu.

Once again, the fog was pulled away like a veil, revealing the groaner half a mile behind us and the tiny fishing harbour of L'Archevêque off to starboard. The weather turned clear and warm, and the southwesterly breeze strengthened enough to send *Silversark* chuckling along her course.

Beyond L'Archevêque we could make out the entrance to Grand River — a lovely waterway, but too shallow to enter, too shoal-encumbered to navigate, though it sustained a considerable trade in the days of sail. Beyond Grand River were the seafront cottages of Point Michaud and the sweeping arc of Point Michaud Beach. The loneliest shores were behind us; we were back among the Acadian villages of our own county, and when we rounded Point Michaud we would see Isle Madame.

"I don't feel so good," said Mark. "But I'm hungry."

"I feel the same way," said Lulu.

The two of them looked at me with cocker spaniel eyes.

"Okay, okay," I said. "I'll make some scrambled eggs."

Silversark steered herself as we ate on deck, and I napped in the sunlight as the rocky, wooded tip of Point Michaud grew closer. We rounded the point at two o'clock, still in sunlight but with banks of fog offshore. Far off the port beam, coming and going in the greyness, were the islands off Canso, the most easterly point in mainland North America. Ahead of us, filling the horizon, was a green and welcome coastline: Isle Madame.

Home — but we were not going there yet. Cape Breton has two coastlines, one outside the island and one inside. The best sailing of all is in the Bras d'Or Lakes, beyond the St. Peter's Canal. We would not end our summer without sailing the Lakes.

The wind backed into the southeast, where it had been forecast so long ago in Louisbourg, and strengthened quickly, driving us fast up toward St. Peter's Bay and the eastern approaches to Lennox Passage. The Acadian villages flew by to starboard: Little Harbour, Lower L'Ardoise, L'Ardoise. And now the fog began playing tag with us again, blotting out L'Ardoise and then revealing it, blotting out Isle Madame. I looked astern, and another fogbank met my eye, rolling up behind us. Dear God, would we have to grope our way into St. Peter's?

Silversark boiled along, following one fogbank into Lennox Passage and chased by another. We passed Cape La Ronde, the entrance point for Lennox Passage and St. Peter's Bay, and turned for the St. Peter's fairway buoy. On the bay's western shore, a white farmhouse and a grey barn stood alone on a hillside, looking out to sea, the home of Farley and Claire Mowat.

"I wonder if Farley and Claire are looking," said Lulu. "Let's wave our hats, just in case."

We waved—and as we waved, the fog dropped over us again.

Damn. After the bell buoy, the buoys are mostly spar buoys—silent sentinels, hard to find in the murk. The bay's level waters conceal a few nasty shoals, and the brisk southeast wind was hurrying us into narrow waters. We found the first three spar buoys uneventfully but missed the fourth. I decided to jog to the eastward and then turn north again. That was a mistake: I should have held further to the east.

We peered into the fog. For half an hour we saw nothing at all. Then Mark gave a cry.

"There's a green buoy!" he said. "Over there!"

But the buoy should have been on the other side . . . So let's see, we must be—

—heading for Round Shoal! Which has no water on it at low tide!

"*Tack!*"

Lulu put the helm down, and *Silversark* spun on her heel. In an instant, we sailed right out of the fog. The canal was just a quarter of a mile away. We dropped everything but the jumbo and idled into the canal.

ARMS

OF

GOLD

Holding our dock lines, Mark and I walked along the canal towpath, "warping" our little vessel along. This was once the normal way to transit a canal, even for big ships; in the nineteenth century, many canals provided horses and mules, or even little railways. Remember the song?

> I got a mule and her name is Sal:
> Fifteen miles on the Erie Canal.

St. Peter's Canal pierces a narrow neck of land where the Bras d'Or Lakes almost touch the sea. The Micmacs portaged their canoes at this spot, and Europeans quickly saw its advantages. The Portuguese, who came here first, called the place San Pedro. Our old friend Nicolas Denys established a settlement here in 1650 and called it St. Pierre. During the French regime it was known as Port Toulouse; then it reverted to St. Peter's.

About 1669, Denys built the first passage for boats across the half-mile-wide isthmus—a skidway over which vessels were hauled by oxen. By 1820, when Cape Breton was annexed to Nova Scotia, the spot had become known as Haulover Isthmus, a name it retains on some charts. In those days, everything moved by sea; in 1800, Cape Breton boasted only six miles of roads. The interior of Cape Breton had gypsum, limestone, lumber and farm produce, all of which were bottled up in the Lakes. If there were a canal at St. Peter's, ships could also avoid the pitiless Atlantic coast and cut 50 miles off the passage from the coalfields of Sydney to the Strait of Canso.

The colonial government generated studies, committee reports, engineering analyses, surveys and reviews. The canal opened in 1869, after fifty years of discussion. It was enlarged between 1876 and 1880, and again during World War I. As many as 1,600 ships used it every year: schooners, brigs, colliers, paddlewheel steamers. But in 1963 only 353 vessels went through, and ten years later the transport department conveyed it to Parks Canada as a National Historic Site. With the rise of pleasure boating, the canal has become important again. About eight hundred vessels now use it each season, and 90 per cent are pleasure boats.

Mark and I warped *Silversark* into the canal's one lock. The tide rises and falls several feet on the Atlantic side but only a few inches on the Bras d'Or side. St. Peter's is the most important village on the south side of the Lakes and, with Baddeck, really the only settlement which offers full services to cruising sailors—marina, bank, bus service, supermarket, liquor store. But we were provisioned, and we were exhausted. We toppled into our berths, and slept.

We woke to another glorious morning, and a gentle southerly breeze. Eating breakfast as we sailed, we ran down St. Peter's Inlet, the sinuous 10-mile waterway to the main lake system, flanked by a dozen coves and twice as many islands, with Acadian villages on one side and Micmac settlements on the other.

The Lakes belong to two groups of people: vacationers and

Indians. (One reserve belongs to *vacationing* Indians.) The vacationers arrive every summer. The Micmacs are there all the time. In ancient times, Cape Breton was the most sacred of the Micmac domains; it is still the capital, the focus of Micmac society and spiritual observance.

The Micmacs have six reserves in Cape Breton—one in Sydney and five on the Lakes. Three of these are on the big lake: Chapel Island, Malagawatch and Eskasoni, the two latter on the opposite shore. You rarely meet Micmacs on the coast, but they are everywhere in the Lakes.

Holding our good south wind behind us, we wove our way through narrow guts and wide reaches. St. Peter's Inlet feels like a river, the channel twisting among the points and sandbars. The spruce trees grow right down to the water; sheep graze on some of the islands. Near the main lake, the inlet broadens into a generous basin, flecked with islands and notched with coves. We steered for the church at the end of the basin.

The church, and the gaily painted cottages around it, are on Chapel Island, where five thousand Micmacs gather on the last weekend of July for the St. Anne's Mission. The mission is primarily a religious occasion, but it also includes music, sport and dancing. Non-Micmacs are welcome, but the mission was over by the time we arrived. *Silversark* swept on through another narrow channel by Doctor's Island into "the big lake"—a part of the Bras d'Or system 50 miles long and 15 miles broad.

From a sailor's perspective, Cape Breton's greatest glory is this astonishing inland sea, 450 square miles of salt water ringed by 600 miles of ragged mountainous shoreline. The origin of the name Bras d'Or is uncertain; in French it means "Arms of Gold," but it may have been named for a Portuguese explorer, Joao Fernandez, who was a *llabrador*, a small squire. The Lakes are actually an inlet of the ocean which occupies the whole centre of the island, making Cape Breton a ring of land which both encircles the sea and is encircled by it. Fog-free, dotted with islands, inhabited by oysters and ospreys and otters, the Lakes attract cruising people from all over the world.

After twenty years, I still have plenty of new places to find in the Lakes—tiny coves where the salt water is as warm as the waters of Florida, rocky islands where the eagles nest. If the idea of cruising is escape, then the Lakes are the place to go. The labour and commerce of Cape Breton take place on the coasts, where almost every harbour is devoted to fishing and industry; in the Lakes, dozens of harbours are utterly unsettled. Many are not even accessible by road.

We settled in for a quiet sail across the big lake and down the far shore, steering for the Crammond Islands, well up in West Bay, and then for the new marina in Dundee. I had never been to the Crammonds, but *Cruise Cape Breton*, the sailing directions for the Lakes, made them sound enchanting: tropic islands, except for the palm trees.

"Remember Malagawatch?" said Lulu, as the outlines of the far shore took shape.

"Who could forget?"

We came into Malagawatch Big Harbour late one August afternoon in 1986, with Jerry Jones and Carmelline MacKinnon, who are now married. The wide basin of Big Harbour seems almost uninhabited, with only one trim farmhouse along its heavily wooded shores. We ran down into a cove, dropped the anchor, and then reconsidered. Jerry and Carmelline had to get home, and we saw no sign of a road. So we raised the anchor and moved to another cove where two small summer cottages stood by the shore.

A mini-van drove up to the larger cottage. A flock of children and two women emerged. We pumped up the inflatable canoe, and Mark—then eight—took the guests ashore, anxious to meet the children. Soon he was heading back, paddling hard against the wind, veering first to the left and then to the right while the women shouted messages we couldn't hear.

"That wind must be really strong," I said as I took his painter. "You usually steer a lot straighter than that."

"I was tacking," he explained.

"Oh." I chuckled. "How come you came back so soon?"

"Four girls."

We gave him a homily on sexism, a good supper and a chapter from Arthur Ransome's *We Didn't Mean to Go to Sea*, which we were reading together. Then we prepared to visit the family ashore.

"Can I climb the mast?" Mark asked.

"Sure," I said, going below. Daddy's principle: never say No when you don't have to. Let him try the impossible.

"Donald," said Lulu in a small voice, "he's on the crosstrees."

I vaulted on deck. Sure enough, he had grasped the halyards and shinnied right up. As we watched, he came down and went up again, just to show us how easy it was. So there, Daddy.

We paddled ashore. The two women and their children came down to greet us. They were a Micmac family. Willing hands took our painter and tugged the canoe across the matted eelgrass.

"Hi," said one of the women, shaking hands. "I'm Joan Denny, and this is my friend Mary Marshall."

"I like your boat," said Nicole, an eleven-year-old with liquid brown eyes, peering shyly out of the cabin's doorway.

"Thank you," I said. "We built it ourselves."

"Is it a pirate ship?" asked a young boy.

"Only when we're pirates," Lulu answered.

"Come in, come in," said Joan, laughing.

It was a proper summer cabin: two-by-four, plywood, used windows, a big wood cookstove, a kitchen table, well-used living room furniture, a couple of small bedrooms off the main room, and an infinite number of children. Joan had six of her own, including a serene baby who was soon produced from one of the bedrooms. There were nieces and cousins and nephews like four-year-old Dale, who broke into laughter whenever he looked at my briar pipe. Mark found a friend named Gary, and the two of them headed off to paddle in the canoe. Joan lit a kerosene lamp.

"I'm a little tired," Joan said, sinking into a chair. "We cooked today for two hundred people."

"Two *hundred*?"

"Two hundred. Once a year there's a mass here, and it was today. The bishop was here, and Father John Angus Rankin, and Jean Vanier—and two hundred people. We fed them all."

"Can we have a bonfire now?" demanded Nicole.

"Did you gather up wood like I told you?"

"Yes."

"Then go start it."

They had gathered only enough to get started, and Joan later added some split stovewood from her own woodpile. The children whooped and giggled, roasting wieners and piling brush on the fire. Nicole quizzed Lulu about the boat: where we slept, how she cooked, how she kept pots on the stove. Kids charged into the woods, making noises like bears. Mark and Gary climbed a tree.

The adults sat around the fire on stumps, each with a small child on our lap. By now Dale was smoking my pipe and roaring with laughter. On Lulu's lap sat Claire Mary, who preferred to be known as Claire-Bear, the name she had been given at daycare. "That's my little adopted one," Joan explained. Claire-Bear was the child of an unhappy marriage between a white man and a Micmac woman. Joan is a welfare officer at Membertou Reserve in Sydney, and when Claire's case came across her desk she solved the problem briskly by adopting the little girl herself.

Malagawatch, Joan said, is jointly owned by all five bands, and people from all the reserves have summer homes there.

"Our people were friends with the French," Joan said. "We got our religion from the French, and when the English took over they wanted us to take their religion, but we said No, we wouldn't—and we never did. Hello, Biege."

"Hello," said a young man, sitting down at the fire.

"This is my brother," Joan said. "He built the altar and the cross where we had the mass today. You tell about it, Biege."

The wind had died, and a full moon had arisen over the water, catching *Silversark* in a long path of silver leading to the campfire. People came and went: children went to bed, Joan's sister Melinda came to take her children home. A cloud shaped like South America drifted over the moon.

"My father was a mason," said Biege, whose English name is Joe Denny, "and he had a dream. He dreamed there would be a big stone cross at Malagawatch, in the cemetery where we know many of our people are buried. And there would be an altar where the priest could say mass, and a shelter at the altar. So he started to build the cross and the altar in 1981, but he only got it started and then he died.

"I had one brother, just one, and ten sisters, and my brother died a couple of months before my father. And I wondered why

God would do this to me, that these two men that I loved so much would both die in my arms, just a short time apart. When my father died, I went almost crazy. I couldn't understand why this thing should come to me. And my father wouldn't leave me alone. He kept coming to me in my dreams."

"We believe that a spirit won't rest if its work is not done," said Joan. "And his work was not done yet."

"I got into a fight," Biege said. "Two people ended up beating on me with guitars. I still got pieces of guitar stuck in my scalp. When they left me, I was nearly dead. Someone took me to a hospital, and the pain was almost more than I could bear. Terrible, terrible pain. Then they operated on me for hours, and they asked me if I wanted to be put out. I said no, just a local, I want to know what is this thing I am experiencing.

"Then the pain went away, and I saw a bright white light. I went to that light, and I found my father and my brother. They said, 'What are you doing here? You don't belong here yet, go back.' And I went back, back to that pain — but afterwards I knew what I had to do: I had to finish my father's dream."

Cruising brings more than its share of remarkable occasions, moments you know will remain luminous in memory. How many of us can ever sit by a campfire with a circle of Indians, hearing such stories of love and faith? The firelight played over Biege's strong, dark features, the children listened quietly, the moon sailed over us, high and small in the cool evening.

"Before that, you see, it was *my father's* dream to make that cross and that altar," Biege said. "I helped him, but it was his dream. But my dream was to finish my father's work, and once I had that dream I knew what I had to do. I came here in the winter, all by myself, and I worked five months in Malagawatch to build that shelter and that altar and that cross. The cross is ten feet high, for the Ten Commandments, and four feet wide, so the two together make the fourteen Stations of the Cross.

"When I finished it, I walked to the edge of the cemetery, and I looked back at the cross and the altar in its shelter. I said to the people lying there, 'There. There, it is done.'

"And today was the first time that a priest said mass at that altar, with all the people here, just the way my father wanted it."

"You must be very proud," I said.

"Yes," Biege said. "It was a very happy day for me."

I thought: I'd like to see that cross and altar. I glanced at Lulu and knew she was wishing that, too.

"Would you like to see it?" Biege asked.

"We'd love to."

"Then let's go there," said Biege.

Although it was 11:30, most of the kids were still up. We all piled into the mini-van and drove slowly over the brown dirt roads past little cabins tucked into the trees, most of them with kerosene lamps still burning. We emerged on the opposite side of Big Harbour Island, looking across the water at the lights of Johnstown and Barra Strait. Around us, the trees had been thinned and the grass allowed to grow. Biege slipped through a rail fence, and we all followed.

The cemetery is a shallow depression ringed on three sides by birch and maple, with the fourth side open to the water. In the open side, outlined against sea and sky, stands Biege's cross, a monumental sculpture in rough-cut stone. The ends of the arms have a small upward sweep—for joy, Biege said, for aspiration, to relieve the looming solemnity of the masonry.

Flanking the cross are two flagpoles. On the pole to the left is a plaque. Biege shone his flashlight on the plaque: it is sacred to the memory of Noel Denny.

"My father," said Biege.

At one side of the cemetery is a small circular building with a side cut away, topped by a shingled roof in the shape of a wigwam. Inside the shelter is the altar. Like the walls, the altar is made of cut stone.

"It's an awful job to cut that stone," Biege said. "Every piece has to be cut just exactly right to fit."

"And you did all that yourself?"

"My father did the first two courses," Biege said. "I did the rest. My uncle from Whycocomagh, he helped me."

"Has your father visited you since you finished it?"

"Yes," said Biege, quietly.

"He must be very pleased."

"Yes," said Biege. "He did something special for me."

"What did he do?"

"He brought my brother to see me."

Now, three years later, it was a scorching afternoon, and the wind was slowly dying.

"Can I go overboard and get towed along behind?" asked Mark.

Hmm. Never say No when you don't have to.

We lowered the boarding ladder, tied a loop in the end of a floating yellow polypropylene line and let it stream astern. Mark donned his lifejacket and jumped overboard. As *Silversark* slowly forged ahead, he splashed over to the line and held on, laughing and spluttering, making a little bow wave with his chest. Then he let go and swam forward to the ladder and clambered back aboard.

"Is that ever cool! Awesome!"

On an impulse, I stripped off my clothes and jumped overboard.

"*Dad!*"

Nothing shocks a child more than unseemly behaviour in a parent. But it *was* cool. I swam along beside the boat, pulling a little ahead, dropping a little behind.

Awesome.

We sailed on past the scarred white cliffs and the island-dotted bay of Marble Mountain, where limestone and marble were quarried a century ago. The late Harry Livingston, who lived there, believed it was favoured by the Vikings, too. After scrutinizing the Norse sagas, Livingston concluded that the Bras d'Or basin is the famous Vinland of Leif the Lucky. The evidence includes the strong tidal fjord with an island of birds at its mouth, which corresponds to the Great Bras d'Or; Thorvald, Leif's brother, explored to the westward and found many shoals and islands and a white sand beach below the mountains in a place beautiful to behold. Marble Mountain, said Harry Livingston, and it's still beautiful to behold.

Ahead of us, around the Crammonds, West Bay was speckled with sails—a race, it appeared. The wind picked up again, and we tacked up into the narrow channel between the two islands. Inside the channel is a sheltered basin. A couple of sloops had nosed right up to the beach, tied to a line ashore. The Lakes are like that: the shores often drop off so abruptly that a boat can put her bow aground while her keel is in deep water.

"Hi! Good to see you again!"

A sloop named *Water Witch* had cast off and was getting under way. I looked again at the skipper: it was Barry MacNeil, a sailor we had met at the Canso Causeway.

"Do we want to stop in here?" asked Lulu.

I looked around. The afternoon was ending, and the Crammonds seemed no more tropical than scores of other Bras d'Or islands.

"No," I said. "Hey, Barry! Can we sail right on through?"

"Follow me!"

We tacked out through the slot between the islands and back into the bay. Fibreglass sloops were everywhere, milling around, beating up towards the marina—more yachts than we had seen in the whole long summer. Some were indeed in a race, but many were just daysailing on this perfect August afternoon.

Up ahead, the face of the mountain was carpeted in light green: the Dundee golf course, eighteen difficult holes with a spectacular view of the Lakes. The resort at Dundee was built by Devco to provide some economic activity at this forgotten end of the Lake, and it now includes cottages, a lodge, windsurfing, tennis, a heated pool and a swish set of executive chalets.

One after another, the yachts entered the cove outside the marina and lowered their sails. We sailed on down the narrow channel to the marina proper. An outboard runabout roared up beside us: the marina's tender.

"Looking for a berth for the night?" called the young man.

"Yep!"

"Do you need fuel or water or anything?"

"No fuel—we've got no engine."

He looked at us with sheer horror: we might as well have said we were vampires. Then he roared on ahead.

Tying on our fenders, we slipped around the last turn, scanning the marina till we saw a berth open on the outer face of the floats. People were running around on the shore. We could hear their voices: *No engine! She's got no engine!*

We looked at one another and grinned. Let's not blow it. We were down to the jumbo now, just sliding in towards the wharf. Lulu gauged it perfectly.

"Drop the jumbo," she said.

Mark dropped it. People on the wharf were shouting instructions. I jumped on the wharf with the bow line. Lulu threw the stern line. *Silversark* came smoothly to a halt. While I chatted with Barry and some others, Lulu pinned our wet towels to the lifelines.

"Can I jump off the spreaders?" asked Mark, who had recently learned to do this.

Lulu and I looked at one another. Never say No when you don't have to. We stood on the port rail, tipping the mast out over the water. Mark shinnied up, stood for a moment at the spreader tip, and then cannon-balled into the water.

Later, up at the marina office, we saw The Sign. Boaters must not sail in the marina. Engines must be run Dead Slow. No children without parents, no dogs without leashes. No laundry on the vessel or the dock. No swimming. No diving.

Oh, dear.

At seven the next morning we pushed ourselves off the wharf with the boathook, rowed out to open water and hoisted the sails. *Silversark* caught the easy breeze and chuckled out of the marina. It had been pleasant: showers, a restaurant meal served by our neighbour Ann Delorey, and a drink with Steve and Carole Rankin, Devco's former president and his wife. But we are not marina people.

We had a fast ride down and across the bay to Barra Strait, where the Lakes are pinched tight between the red cliffs of Grand Narrows and the white gypsum outcroppings of Iona. Barra Strait is crossed by a steel railway bridge which always makes our hearts thump. The bridge has a swing span over a gap just 100 feet wide. The tides are strong, and the water is deep.

The Skipper came here once with a following wind and a fair tide, doing 16 knots over the ground in an engineless schooner — and the bridge failed to open. It was impossible to anchor and, said The Skipper, there was "no reverse into them vessels."

What did he do?

"I went below and got my wallet."

But the bridge did open, and The Skipper scraped through. When we arrived, the swing span was open and the wind was fair. *Silversark* raced through the narrow opening, driven by the wind and carried by the racing tide.

"*What's this?*" cried Lulu. Just beyond the railway bridge, a huge concrete abutment had grown out of the water, surrounded by barges and gear. In several elections, the provincial government had promised to build a highway bridge here. Now they were doing it. Barra Strait would be twice as difficult in the future.

But we were through. On we flew, the tiller pulling mightily, the water roaring under our bow. St. Andrews Channel opened to starboard, leading down towards the Little Bras d'Or and the open sea—although a highway bridge blocks that route for sailboats. Maskell's Harbour to port, with its square lighthouse high on a bluff. The tip of Boularderie Island and the Great Bras d'Or to starboard now, the broad highway to the sea.

Ahead of us lay Kidston Island, with lighthouses at each end, hiding the centre of the village of Baddeck. To starboard, on a mountain slope, stood a fantastic brick-red mansion overlooking Baddeck Bay. Beinn Bhreagh (Gaelic for "beautiful mountain"), the beloved home of Alexander Graham Bell, was built to accommodate twenty-six people plus servants. It has eleven fireplaces, ash and cherry panelling, and a dizzying assortment of towers, gables, dormers, balconies and piazzas.

Bell came to Baddeck in 1885, bound for Newfoundland with his wife, Mabel, and both their fathers. At thirty-eight, Bell was already enjoying the financial rewards of his invention of the telephone nine years earlier. The Bells were delighted with Baddeck, and the following summer they bought fifty acres at Red Head. For the rest of their lives—nearly forty years—they came to Baddeck in April or May and stayed until November. They are buried on top of Beinn Bhreagh.

Bell was a multifaceted genius, interested in everything from sheep-breeding to solar hot water heating, from sonar to the iron lung, from X-rays to jet propulsion. He is an abiding presence in Baddeck, a familiar spirit of practical curiosity, tireless work and innovation. He favoured women's rights and promoted the educational ideas of Maria Montessori, whom the Bells entertained in Washington in 1913. Traditional education, he said, "reminds me of the way they prepare *pâté de foie gras* in the living geese." The first Montessori school in America was established at the Bell home in Washington in 1912, followed by the first such school in Canada at Beinn Bhreagh that summer.

Among Bell's most attractive qualities was his youthful mind and spirit. In February 1909, a flimsy biplane called the Silver Dart, piloted by Bell's friend and colleague Douglas McCurdy, rose from the ice of Baddeck Bay to achieve the first manned flight in the British Empire. McCurdy's flight took place under the aegis of the Aerial Experiment Association, established eighteen months earlier to develop a practical flying machine. Each of the five founders undertook the design of a plane, and the group then built all five planes—all of which flew, though Bell's design flew only a few inches. When the AEA was formed, four of the five members were in their twenties; Bell was sixty.

Another member was a young engineer, Frederick "Casey" Baldwin, who came to Beinn Bhreagh in 1906 to work on Bell's aeronautical designs. Baldwin became almost a son to the Bells, and he stayed on as manager of the estate and the laboratory. His home, too, is still part of the estate.

Baldwin may have turned Bell's mind towards hydrofoils, boats which can rise clear of the water on ladders with airfoil-shaped rungs. Bell and Baldwin built and tested several cigar-shaped hydrofoil vessels at Baddeck, beginning in 1911. The first, HD-1, reached 50 miles per hour; the last, HD-4, was clocked at 70.86 miles per hour, a world marine speed record which stood for a decade. Bell dreamed of *sail-powered* hydrofoils; Baldwin, an experienced sailor, thought it impossible that any sailing vessel could ever move fast enough to get up on its foils. But Bell stands vindicated: today's fastest sailboats are foil-assisted multihulls.

In 1888, Gardiner Green Hubbard, Mabel's father, became the first president of the National Geographic Society, a sober, scholarly outfit which published a sober, scholarly journal called the *National Geographic Magazine*. When Hubbard died, Bell became president. He proposed that the society's magazine seek a wider audience. "Geographic," said Bell, meant "THE WORLD AND ALL THAT IS IN IT." He offered to underwrite the editor's salary himself for the first year—$100 a month. When the society agreed, he hired a young friend named Gilbert Grosvenor.

Grosvenor developed and guided the magazine for fifty years—and in 1900 he married Bell's daughter Elsie. As a wedding gift, Bell asked Beinn Bhreagh's boatbuilder, Walter Pinaud, to build the couple a sleek 56-foot yawl named *Elsie*. Grosvenor was eventually succeeded as editor by his son, Melville Bell Grosvenor, also an accomplished sailor. The society's president today is Gilbert Grosvenor, Melville's son— who also summers in Baddeck and sails his father's yawl *White Mist*.

Elsie remains the flagship of the Baddeck fleet. Now owned by a public trust, she is an imposing sight, with her acres of tanbark sail and her lean, racy profile. She leads the sail-past which opens the Baddeck Regatta, and she was the only Baddeck vessel in the Parade of Sail, which initiated the Tall Ships race from Sydney to England in 1984. In 1921 Casey Baldwin sailed aboard her to nearby Maskell's Harbour, with the editor of *Motor Boating*, William Washburn Nutting. During the cruise, the two discussed the possibility of a club "to promote and facilitate cruising by amateurs" and to "stimulate an interest in seamanship and the navigation and handling of small vessels." The result was the Cruising Club of America. The only vessel which flies the CCA burgee in her own right, regardless of whether or not a CCA member is aboard, is *Elsie*, and the only CCA posts outside the U.S. are in Bermuda and Baddeck.

The Bell heritage in Baddeck has become a cottage industry, spawning an Alexander Graham Bell National Historic Park, a Bell Institute at UCCB and a shower of books and dramas. Most recently, Lilias Toward's award-winning biography, *Mabel Bell: Alexander's Silent Partner*, has generated a TV mini-series, "The Sound and The Silence."

Bell seems very close at the National Historic Park, among the many volumes of "home notes" and "lab notes" in which he meticulously recorded his ideas and his experiments. The collection includes historic photographs, early telephones and the remnants of HD-4 (which, with a full-sized reproduction, occupies a large hall in the museum). The collection also includes the complete correspondence between Bell and his wife, typed and bound by Gilbert Grosvenor. Despite their Victorian stiffness, the letters in which Bell declares to the Hubbards his love for their sixteen-year-old daughter, and their responses (and her reflections) provide a touching glimpse of a great love.

Since the Bells' day — and in part because of the Bells — Baddeck has become a classic resort community: gift shops, boat tours, swimming, tennis and tea on the verandah. The harbour bristles with masts. Windsurfers and dinghies scoot back and forth like bright-coloured insects, and the ice-cream vendors on the main street do a roaring business.

We lived aboard *Silversark* in Baddeck for three summers when I was executive director of Centre Bras d'Or, an organization which intended to become the Banff Centre of the east, offering advanced training in the arts as well as a first-class summer festival. The idea drew strong support from all over Cape Breton, but the centre never found the funding to fulfil its dreams. But it did establish an outstanding Festival of the Arts, which combines top Cape Breton talent — Rita MacNeil, John Allan Cameron, Matt Minglewood — with national and international acts like Odetta, Donovan, the Elmer Iseler Singers and Liona Boyd. It also offers comedy, crafts programs, an art gallery and dramas such as the St. Ann's Bay Players' production of *Under Milk Wood* and the Mulgrave Road Co-op Theatre's play about the Bells, *Beinn Bhreagh*.

My job was strenuous but pleasant, and the festival performances were among its benefits. *Silversark* was moored in a minute cove at the Cape Breton Boatyard, near Scotty's Fish House, a little restaurant with a shady open deck. The boatyard was established by Walter Pinaud, and is now run by a gruff Yankee immigrant named Henry Fuller.

We were not well off — but, on the other hand, what would wealth be like? Suppose a person can live aboard his yacht at the boatyard, stroll over to Scotty's for chowder and a beer, and then walk up through the grounds of the Inverary Inn to the concert hall at the high school to hear Moe Koffman, The Cape Breton Symphony or the Cambridge Buskers. If one did have more money, what more could one buy?

IN THE

INDIAN OCEAN

We crept out of Baddeck on a grey after-
noon, steering for Barra Strait via Spectacle Island, locally
known as Toothbrush Island. A salutory emblem of high-rise
living, overpopulation and inadequate sewage disposal, Toothbrush was taken over by cormorants twenty years ago. Their
nests and their acid droppings killed the trees, leaving the island
looking like a toothbrush. Now even the denuded trunks are
gone, and the island lies bare.

To seaward, down the Great Bras d'Or, we saw the towering
bulk of a gypsum freighter standing high in the water, heading
for the Little Narrows quarry up St. Patrick's Channel. Gypsum
is one of Nova Scotia's main exports, quarried near tidewater
and shipped to American factories in bulk carriers like this one.

Nearly 60 per cent of the gypsum imported by the U.S. is Nova Scotian.

Gypsum, which is quarried all over Nova Scotia, actually permeates our lives. It is the only mineral which can be reduced to a powder, shaped, and then returned to its original rocklike condition. It turns up in toothpaste, crayons, blackboard chalk, cosmetics, dental fillings, white bread, papers, textiles and medical casts. Beer is often filtered through gypsum. When Hollywood builds a spectacular set and then blows it up, the set is made of plaster of Paris—so named because gypsum is common in the Seine Valley.

Above all, gypsum is a construction material. It serves as a filler in paints and caulkings and slows down the setting time of Portland cement. It is shaped into tiles, blocks and wallboard, generally called gyproc. North American plants produce 17 billion square feet of gyproc a year—enough for a pathway 10 feet wide from the earth to the moon, enough to ring the equator with a wall 100 feet high. Much of that comes from Nova Scotia. One quarry near Halifax supplies 10 per cent of the U.S. market all by itself; one quarter of North American homes have Nova Scotia gypsum on their walls.

In moments, the bulk carrier was passing astern, towering over us. They are surprisingly quick and quiet. You see one in the distance; when you next look, it is right behind you, moving at 12 or 15 knots with no fuss or disturbance.

We sailed on towards Barra Strait, looking down St. Patrick's Channel and Baddeck Bay with regret, turning our backs on enchanting crannies like the Washabuck River and the little harbour under Beinn Bhreagh where Bell once moored his floating study. Driven by a rising southwesterly wind, we beat on into Barra Strait, drawing closer to the big red church at Iona and the Highland Village on the hillside above it. Created and maintained by volunteers, the Highland Village recreates the evolution of Scottish life, from the "black houses" of Scotland to the pioneer homesteads of Cape Breton, complete with period tools and furnishings, and with Gaelic-speaking guides.

On one long tack, we passed the construction site and forged through the railway bridge. In the Lakes, the wind funnels along the channels, often intensifying and blowing harder than it would on the coast. Out in the big lake, I dropped the jib and reefed the main to ease the helm. We had a steep, tall chop rolling up behind us now; the bow wave was roaring, the wake foaming, the sails hard as sheets of metal, the flag snapping with a crack like a whip. The faces of the seas were carved and roughened by the wind, crumpled and lustrous as pewter in the sunlight.

The boisterous wind gave us a fast run down to the eight islands outside Eskasoni. Among the islands, the wind dropped off sharply. Now we were short-tacking and exploring, peering up waterways and comparing channels with the outlines on the sketch chart in *Cruise Cape Breton*. The wharf was in Crane Cove, the innermost basin of the archipelago. Mark scrambled up to the spreaders. In the dying wind of early evening we ghosted around a point of land into Crane Cove. A dozen people were swimming and diving off the wharf. As we glided closer, we could hear them talking. They were brown and young, and they were speaking Micmac. One of them dived off and swam out underwater, then surfaced and looked back at the wharf. Someone giggled and pointed. He swivelled his head and saw the black bulk of *Silversark* silently bearing down on him.

"Holy frig, sailboat!" he cried, stroking for the wharf while the others hooted with laughter.

We lowered the sails and drifted up to the wharf, a nasty-looking affair, solid concrete with long rusty steel bolts protruding from its face. The kids showed us a spot where the bolts had been broken off, and we tied *Silversark* there. Mark chatted with the kids. I checked my watch. In exactly three and a half minutes he was in the water with them, laughing.

While we stowed away, a pert young girl thrust her head through the hatch.

"Hi! I'm Mary Ann Denny, I'm a Micmac and I'm eleven years old. Who are you?"

We introduced ourselves and came on deck.

"This is Larry," said Mark, gesturing at a boy who was clutching our mast and heaving. "I'm showing him how to get up on the spreaders."

"Hi," said Larry. "Hey, this thing is *slippery*."

Two older boys stood on the edge of the crowd.

"You're from Sydney?" asked Aaron, reading from our transom.

"No, Isle Madame. The boat's just registered in Sydney."

They were just back from Maine. Many Eskasoni families spend their summers on the move, camping at Chapel Island for the mission and then moving on to Maine to pick blueberries. Young children attend a special Tribal School held at the blueberry barrens, but everyone over ten rakes berries. A family can make $10,000 to $12,000 in a month.

"Berries was good this year," said Chuckie, a scholarly looking young man. "I made $1,500."

Andrea, a young kamikaze cyclist, went below with Lulu and spotted blueberries in the galley.

"You been to Maine?" she asked.

"No," said Lulu.

"Then where'd you get the blueberries?"

The darkness came: the kids left, still laughing and teasing and chattering.

"I like this," said Mark. "This is like Europe."

An odd thing to say, ironic beyond his knowing, but it was the highest praise he could offer. A different language, a different culture, and friendly people to share it with him.

The kids came back just as we finished breakfast. We got out our shopping bags and went ashore.

"Where you going?" said a little fellow.

"To the store."

"Long way," he said gravely.

"Is it?" We really didn't know.

"Well, not such a *very* long way," he said hastily, not wanting to discourage us unduly.

"Take my bike," said a young girl. "No, I mean it. Take it, take it! Just be careful—the brakes don't work."

The store was a tiny blue shingled building almost a mile away. Our needs were small: milk, cookies, bread. Mark wanted to rejoin the kids at the wharf, so we sent him back with the bike and walked on, noting a fine church on the hillside above the road, a couple of kids with long sticks trying to retrieve a ball from a roof, a small green bungalow with a fence so elaborate it almost looked like a maze.

Just ahead was a steep, grassy roadside embankment. A black dog lay at the top, looking down at us. Then, as we watched transfixed, he rolled over the edge, spread his legs wide apart, and slid down the embankment on his back. At the bottom of the bank he rolled on his side and looked up dolefully at the two tourists who were immobilized by laughter.

We came to a street sign that said 74 Street. I chuckled.

"What's funny?" asked Lulu.

"Bright's 74 is the drunkard's wine," I said.

"They wouldn't name a road for Bright's 74, would they?"

"No, no. But I don't see a 73 Street or a 75 Street."

In fact, that madcap guess was the truth. The government insisted that all of Eskasoni's little lanes be named; the Micmacs subverted the project. Off 74 Street is a short road with heaps of kids: its legal name is Sesame Street. There's a junction called New York Corner. The road between Eskasoni and the shops of Sydney was paved only after Indians became eligible for welfare, and thus had some cash: the Micmacs still call it the Welfare Road.

The Micmac sense of humour can be a useful tool. A consultant later told me about coming to Eskasoni to make a presentation to the band council. When he arrived, all the councillors were seated around a long table. Only one chair was empty. The councillors watched stone-faced as he walked the whole length of the room to reach the empty seat: two long rows of brown, impassive faces.

He sat down—and nearly cracked his chin on the tabletop. The seat of his chair was six inches too low. The whole council roared with laughter. After that, they talked as equals.

A fancy black step-side pickup pulled up beside us, festooned with lights, chromed bumpers, overhead roll bar. The driver rolled down the window. I recognized him: a cheerful youth with a toothy grin who had been down on the wharf last evening.

"Where you headin'?"

"Lee Cremo's, if I can find him."

"Cremo's Lane, right up there." He pointed. "I think he's around."

"Thanks."

"See ya."

Lee Cremo is a little wisp of a man who drives a school bus for a living—but he is a great fiddler, selling tens of thousands of albums out of general stores and gas stations.

In 1978, Lulu's brother Pat talked with Little Joe MacNeil one summer night in Fort McMurray, two Cape Breton exiles planning a trip home. "You know, Pat," said Little Joe, "if anything happened to me, I'd want Lee Cremo to play at my funeral." They got home for the Remembrance Day weekend. On Saturday night Little Joe drove into a power pole and was electrocuted. Lee Cremo was just heading into the woods for a month when Big Joe MacNeil phoned him. The sweet and mournful melody at the funeral mass in West Arichat flowed from Lee's fiddle.

"That was a great honour for me, really," Lee told me later. "But it was a very sad thing, too. You've lost one of your greatest fans, whether you knew it or not. But I was very touched that he wanted it."

I remember that funeral: Little Joe was a popular young man, and when I got to the church people were standing in the foyer. Just in front of me was a young woman recently returned from eight years in Europe, carrying a baby in a sling around her neck. Her name was Lulu Terrio, and the baby was named Mark. She was the main thing I saw at the funeral, and Lee was the main thing I heard.

"I can transfer my own feelings to the fiddle, and the fiddle will speak it out, you know," says Lee. "If you're sad, the fiddle is the killer there, because that thing can cry, *really* cry. Same way if it makes you happy, it'll get your feet goin' automatically. It's hard to explain, really. But it happens, I can tell you that."

"Lee represents the continuing evolution of the fiddle," says Allister MacGillivray, the brilliant musician whose book *The Cape Breton Fiddler* is the first major work on the subject. "He has that vicious bowing that, properly harnessed, makes a great Cape Breton player; he has all sorts of stuff that's not documented or notated. He's like a player in the 1800s, when it was all orally transmitted, chucking in a lot of effervescence of his own that wasn't in the notes. But that's the way fiddling has survived and developed. That's how our people made it through the 1800s, when it *wasn't* written down. Interestingly enough, Lee's father was apparently pretty Scottish in his style."

Lee's father, Simon Cremo, died in 1964. He, too, was famous in rural Cape Breton. He travelled the country selling baskets and sometimes raffling them off. He'd play the fiddle for his clients. The more tickets you bought, the more tunes he'd play.

"Nobody ever lost on those tickets," Lee says with a grin. "You'd always get some fiddle tunes, anyway. We never ran into prejudice, you know. There were no hotels in those days, so we just stayed in private homes. Often the people would ask us to baby-sit while they went out for the evening. I think my father knew every child, and every dog, in Richmond County."

Lee began to play the fiddle on Good Friday, 1945. He was seven years old. When the rest of the family had left for mass, he pulled the fiddle out from under the bed and started trying to coax some notes out of it.

"In the Indian tradition, there's no music Good Friday morning," he explains. "When you go to church, they don't ring a bell; they use a little wooden block like a drum instead. And at home there's no record or radio or anything playing. I didn't know anything about the tradition, and when they got back I was goin' at the fiddle. That's the hardest tune I ever tried, too— "Pop Goes The Weasel". They had long services at the church, about two hours, and in that two hours I got that tune. But talk about sweatin' and frustrated and everything—!

"When they got back, my father explained you're not supposed to play a fiddle this day. I said 'Okay, I'll just put it away.' He said, 'You can start tomorrow, I'll even learn you'—and he did, really, next morning we got up and he started me off.

"He showed me all the fundamentals, and then he said, 'I can't place your fingers where they're supposed to go; it's your own mountain from here on, and you've got to climb it yourself. If you quit halfway, that's your business. I wouldn't force you, it's no picnic. No matter how much work you put on it, there's always somebody better.'

"I did get discouraged a few times, but he said, 'Look at it this way: all men are created equal. They got the same amount of fingers, same amount of nerves, same amount of blood—and if *he* can do it, why can't you do it?' That's the thing that kept me going, you know."

Simon Cremo also introduced his son to the woods, taking him out blindfolded and then making him find his way home alone. To this day, Lee takes a few weeks a year just to ramble the forest, not hunting, but just "studyin' nature." He gave up hunting after shooting a doe before he realized she was still suckling a fawn.

"I had to shoot the little one, too, I knew it wouldn't survive, and I felt so bad about it that I don't think I've shot a deer since." But he enjoyed fooling a fox.

The fox saw him, and froze. Lee managed to slip out of his coat and leave it hanging on a bush. Then he crept around downwind until he could approach the fox from behind.

"A fox and a bobcat will fight to the death, you know," he explains. "Well, I got about six feet behind that fox and I made a noise like a bobcat"—he lets out a mean-sounding squall—"and that fox jumped ahead so fast and so far that he banged his head on a birch tree. I was really proud of that, you know? Out there in the woods I could outfox a fox."

Lee has done plenty of touring, appearing at events like the Winnipeg Folk Festival, where one morning he won a fiddling contest. The prize was $300 and a new banjo, and when Lee stood up to receive the prize he admitted he'd never touched a banjo in his life, though he does play guitar, piano and other instruments. That same night, however, he entered the banjo contest—and won it. The MC had been at the fiddling contest that morning and remarked that "Nova Scotia Indians must be the fastest learners in the world."

Lee laughs heartily. "There's no rules that a banjo has to be tuned like a banjo," he explains, "so I tune it like a fiddle, and then I know exactly where everything is at. I knew about a pick from playing guitar, so I got John Allan Cameron and Allister MacGillivray to back me up, and we played a bunch of fiddle music. They never heard anything like it."

He later won titles in western Canada, came second in the

Canadian championships and placed fifth out of 911 fiddlers at the World Championships in Tennessee. He says he's "very competitive" by nature, and he'd love to be acknowledged the best in the country.

"But it's for my own *people*, too," he points out. "There's famous players for almost all nationalities, but nobody ever tried for Micmacs, you know? I wondered, how far would I get, for Micmacs? Well, there's a lot of places now where they know the Micmacs exist, anyhow. And they know we're not just playing with bow and arrows, either."

This time in Eskasoni, we knocked on Lee Cremo's door and left a note. But we were fated not to see him.

We walked on to a school. I wanted to see Sakej Henderson and meet his wife, Marie Battiste, a well-known Micmac educator. Marie's office was in another school further along the shore—a lovely school, centred around a high, airy library—but she wasn't there. I called Sakej, who invited us down for coffee.

The black pickup pulled up beside us.

"Where you headin' now?"

"Goin' down to see Sakej."

"See that old building, used to be a store, up there? You'll find a little lane right beside it. Runs down to the shore. That's where Sakej lives."

"Thanks."

"See ya."

We found Sakej in a bungalow on the shore, with a construction project going on at one end. A wry, rumpled, thoughtful man in his forties, Sakej doesn't look particularly Indian, but he is a Chickasaw from the southern U.S., which gives him an interestingly bifocal view of Eskasoni. Sakej straddles many realities: a Harvard-trained lawyer licensed to practice in both Canada and the U.S., he has taught at the University of California and Dalhousie. He now teaches at UCCB.

We sat in a nook looking out on the lake. The stereo was playing haunting, bell-like music written by a friend of Sakej's in New England. We had come at an interesting moment, when band members were just drifting back from Maine.

"While they're down there they haunt the Maine yard sales," Sakej said. "They buy only from Marden's in Bangor—Marden's sell goods from fire sales, liquidations and that kind of thing. Then they come home and make a year's payments on the car or the pickup, and that's it. Of course a child of ten is an adult in the berry field, and great problems arise when he goes back to school and he's suddenly treated like a child again."

Sakej likes to talk about consciousness, about the way different people see the world and their place in it. His next-door neighbour is Alex Denny, the Grand Captain—in effect, the Prime Minister of the whole Micmac nation, which stretches from Newfoundland to the Gaspé. Denny once told Sakej that the Micmacs' economic problems were based in their lack of Scottish acquisitiveness. He demonstrated by taking Sakej into a store in Iona, where he asked for a book of matches and gave the storekeeper a $100 bill. Without batting an eye, the Scot counted out $99.98 in change.

"You see?" said Denny, outside the store. "A Micmac would have said, 'Aw, take the damn things—they're yours.' "

The Micmac language, says Sakej, conditions Micmac thinking. It has very few nouns, no gender and no possessive case. You cannot say *my house, my pen, my wife*. Ownership is an alien concept; the language cannot easily express it. Micmac expresses conditions, relationships, states of being. Breakfast is "belonging to the dawn." A chair is "for being seated"—but that could also mean a rock. The language assumes constant change and flux and is well adapted to the examination of one's place in that flux, one's relation to the evolving situation. People visit and talk all winter, considering their position.

"The Micmacs are the most gregarious tribe I know," Sakej said. "They're always coming and going and visiting."

"They're Cape Bretoners," I said. "They're the *original* Cape Bretoners. Maybe the rest of us got it from them. You always notice it driving through a reserve in the middle of the night. People are on the road, walking here and there."

"Yeah, there's always a lot of movement between midnight and two A.M. It's the same thing in rain or snow or wind—people like to be outside in the storm. I love their approach to work, too. One person does the job, and three comment. It's really a form of theatre."

But things do get done. The housing at Eskasoni, for instance, is infinitely better than it was fifteen years ago, though Sakej notes that the band has a terrible debt as a result. In addition, since the band holds title to all the houses, there's a certain insecurity about tenure. When there's a divorce, for example, it's a political decision which party gets the house.

"Usually it goes to the wife and kids, and he's on the street. Often he goes and builds a little shack in 'the jungle,' in Malagawatch. Lots of divorced men over there. Twelve bands share the jurisdiction and it's really a free-for-all. The tea-drinking police kind of keep things flowing along in Eskasoni."

"The tea-drinking police?"

"The reserve police. If your kids are getting into trouble, they'll come and drink a cup of tea with you and talk it over. They'll do that three or four times before they take any corrective action on their own; you'll have plenty of warning before anything happens."

The phone rang: it was Marie. Sakej conferred quietly with her and invited us for dinner. We headed back towards the boat. Back on the main road, the black pickup appeared.

"Where you headin' now?"

"Rita Joe's."

"She's got that new gift shop over there."

"Thanks."

"See ya."

Rita Joe is the first Micmac to make a name in English-language poetry—a shy, middle-aged woman who used to come to literary events with her husband, Frank, dressed in buckskin, softly intoning her quiet, thoughtful verse:

> We are arms that are dust,
> Lips that are dead,
> Eyes that see not.
> Minds dwelling in the mist,
> Alive only in spirit.

It cannot have been easy for Rita to learn to take herself seriously as a poet, to expose her work to the cold gaze of critics, to be the only native in a room full of writers and publishers. But she always had Frank, standing quiet and dark in the shadows of the room as Rita did her reading—and Frank had died. I wanted to tell Rita how saddened I was at his going.

The gift shop was the shell of a bungalow, filled with bead-work, quill-covered boxes, baskets, leatherwork. There are no porcupines (and no skunks) in Cape Breton; quills have to be imported from the mainland. The highway bridge at Barra Strait will direct traffic through Eskasoni, and Rita will be ready. But Rita herself was away; her daughter and a friend were in charge. We bought a pair of beaded earrings, and I left a note for Rita.

"I knew a girl from Eskasoni at university," said Lulu, "Linda Googoo. She married a Swiss. I wonder what ever happened to her."

We stopped at another store. It was compact, clean and bright, and it carried everything from bananas to washing machines. We bought submarines and juice and crossed the road to sit on the school lawn. A woman came out of a nearby office building and strolled over.

"Hi," she said. "I just came to be nosy. I've seen you walking around and I wondered who you were." She worked for the school board, arranging for the placement of reserve kids in secondary and post-secondary schools elsewhere.

"I went to university with a girl named Linda Googoo," said Lulu. "Do you know what happened to her?"

"Sure, her parents live right over there, by the weeping willows. She was home last year to visit. They're living in Zurich. They've got a couple of kids in college now."

We knocked on the door, but the Googoos, too, were away. We walked on. From the top of the hill we looked down on the boat. It was aswarm with kids. Someone was on the spreaders. As we watched, he jumped. We recognized the swim trunks: Mark. When we got to the boat, we found the decks wet and sandy. Mark had spent a happy day among friends.

Marie Battiste (pronounced BAttest) teaches at UCCB, sits on the Board of Dalhousie University and plays an active role in Mic-mac affairs while also running a household, raising a family and welcoming wayfaring sailors. She and Sakej have two angelic and impish little girls, Maria Sunday Lace and Annie Winter Song, and a son, Jaime Young Medicine. Mark and Jaime disappeared together. Albert and Murdena Marshall joined us at the table. Murdena also teaches at UCCB. Albert was building the addition on the house.

"I'm not a carpenter," said Albert. "I'm a machinist, really. But there's not much difference."

"What's the difference?" I asked.

"One inch," said Albert. "If it fits within an inch, that's close enough in carpentry. You know my son, I think. Aaron."

"Oh, he's that big handsome boy we met on the wharf."

"The Micmac Adonis," said Sakej.

"Albert still thinks he's a baby," said Murdena. "He's always worrying about him."

Albert smiled. When Aaron was small, they used to supplement his education by taking him on trips during vacations and breaks—a practice, said Murdena, in keeping with "our nomadic ways."

"We'd go until the money was gone," she said. "We'd get home and see if anything was left. Yes? Good, let's go again."

After supper Albert slipped away, ostensibly to work on the addition. But when Murdena phoned later, he was home with Aaron. Despite his superficial calm, says Murdena, he has a tempestuous emotional life, which he expresses in carpentry.

"If he's depressed, he tears the house apart—doesn't matter whether he's got any funding arranged. I'll come home—oh-oh, kitchen cabinets all out in the yard. Albert's upset."

Like an artist, Albert is engaged in a relentless quest for the perfect fence. Over the years he has created and replaced any number of them. One of the first was an electric fence.

"I ran into it with an armload of wet washing," said Murdena. "BZZZZZT! What a zinger I got! I told Albert, you've got to take that thing out of there or you're going to come out and see your old mother hanging over that fence." Murdena slumped in her chair, arms hanging forward, head lolling sideways, miming the old woman dead on the fence.

Suddenly I remembered something.

"That little green bungalow near the wharf!" I said. "With the incredible fence!"

"That's our house," said Murdena. "That's Albert's latest. He had to go all the way to St. Stephen, New Brunswick, to get just the right materials for that fence."

"Alex Denny says that fence appears to be a new form of hunting," said Sakej. "He thinks it's designed to make the caribou run right into Albert's front door."

Marie and Sakej met at Harvard, where Marie did her M.Ed. They moved to Berkeley and both taught at the University of California while Marie obtained her doctorate in education at Stanford. Murdena also has a Harvard M.Ed. and a year of residence towards her doctorate. When it comes to education, it appears, Eskasoni people settle for nothing but the best.

"Why, sure," smiled Sakej. "If you're going to have a degree, why not have a really good one?"

Marie's first language is English, but she lives and works—and thinks—in Micmac. English feels increasingly unfamiliar to her. Murdena spoke no English until she went to school, and once during the evening she simply ran out of words in the middle of a story, gesticulating with her hands and unable to speak.

"I've been learning English for forty years and I still haven't mastered it," she said. "When I went to school, I was seven, and I couldn't even ask to go to the bathroom." She edged close to the teacher and listened to what the other children were saying.

"Then I said, 'Myuh luff throom?' and the teacher nodded. That was my first English sentence." She dropped her fork. "There's another thing: they've been trying to teach us to use knives and forks for three hundred years, and we still don't have it right."

Cape Breton is the capital of the Micmac nation, which stretches up through the Maritimes and into the Gaspé. Before 1750, the Grand Council met annually in Malagawatch; now it meets at Chapel Island. Two centuries of Catholicism have given a Christian spin to Micmac religion, but the old myths are not forgotten.

"As we awoke in the world naked and alone, we asked our

Creator how we should live," said Marie. "And our Creator gave us the knowledge and skills to survive—to hunt, to fish, to cure animal skins for clothing. He gave us knowledge of medicines to cure us when we were ill, medicines which come from the earth because we come from the earth and are part of the earth.

"He gave us information about the constellations and the stars, our guideposts in the darkest nights, to find our way. And our Creator gave us the knowledge of the Milky Way, which is the path to the land of the souls, and he taught us how to pray, to sleep, to dream, and what to be aware of during our dreams, where we would receive essential knowledge from the other world.

"The two worlds would be separated by a cloud that would open and fall at different intervals, and the strong and believing could pass through unscathed, but the weak and unbelieving would be crushed. To me, this describes the people whose spirit has been crushed by drugs, alcohol, boarding school, the lack of language—and the others whose spirit has not been broken, who can laugh through poverty and trouble."

74 Road, I thought. *Laughter in adversity as a mark of strength.*

"And our Creator gave us the Micmac language, to pass on all of this knowledge," said Marie, "which is why it is so important that the language should survive."

Survival: in the harsh, starless night of the global village. As we sat laughing at this hospitable table, Mohawk Warriors at Oka, Quebec, had blockaded the reserve and were besieged by the Canadian Army. One Quebec provincial policeman had died, and other lives were in danger. White crowds had stoned Mohawk women and children leaving the Oka reserve.

"All I think about these days is *blockade*," said Murdena. "I listen to the radio, I think *blockade*; I work around the house, I think *blockade*." She paused, and then laughed. "Even when I go to the bathroom I think *blockade*. That's why I take Metamucil."

To many white Nova Scotians, Oka was a distant battle in a baffling province. The Maritimes are a sort of internal colony of Canada anyway, so there is not much point in caring deeply about national events; Maritimers do not expect to influence

Ottawa any more than Puerto Ricans expect to influence Washington.

To our Micmac friends, however, Oka was immediate and urgent, far more pressing than the recent Iraqi invasion of Kuwait. People from Eskasoni had gone to Oka and come back with first-hand reports. Indeed, Micmacs were running the Mohawk communications system. There were Mohawk-speakers on the government side—but the Micmacs could convey messages for the Mohawks over open radio channels in perfect security, "just as they did for the army in World War II," said Sakej.

"The French never got anywhere until the FLQ started kidnapping," said Murdena. "Now they listen to the French. It's a pity they can't learn easier. But you know, they're so arrogant. We were supposed to have an all-day meeting a while ago in Sydney with some bureaucrats from Indian Affairs, and a lot of people put a lot of effort into preparing for it. Well, they missed their plane, and instead of arriving at nine, they arrived at one—and the very first thing they said was, 'We've got to be out of here by 2:45.' So you know they don't respect you. They just don't think you're important.

"And here's another thing: why can't we have a proper post office in Eskasoni? There's 150 people in Iona, and they've got one, and there's only 55 in Christmas Island, and they've got one—but there's 2,400 in Eskasoni, and we can't get one. We've tried, and they won't give it to us."

Good question. And why does the *Nova Scotia Tour Guide*, published by the provincial government, say that "Baddeck (pop. 965) is the largest community on the Bras d'Or Lake," while also saying elsewhere that the population of Eskasoni is 1,704? Do Micmacs not count? Or is it the government that can't count?

More darkness, closer to home. Murdena's last name is Marshall. It is a familiar and respected name in Eskasoni; one of the most prominent residents is Donald Marshall, the grand chief of the Micmac nation. The grand chief's son, Donald Marshall, Jr., was imprisoned for eleven years for a murder he did not commit. That infamous sentence, and the subsequent inquiry, graphically demonstrated the systemic racism of the judicial process. While Donald Marshall's original trial was going on, says Murdena, she avoided cashing cheques in Sydney.

"They'd see the name Marshall and the address Eskasoni, and they'd just glare at you," she says. "You really felt they hated you just for being who you were."

There are plenty of interracial friendships and marriages in Cape Breton; Lee Cremo's wife, Nellie, for instance, is an Irish Cape Bretoner from Sydney who now speaks fluent Micmac. The relationship between white *institutions* and native communities, however, is no better than it is anywhere else in Canada, as Donald Marshall's case demonstrates very clearly. Canada's treatment of aboriginal people is not just a national disgrace; it is a crime. We deserved Oka; if we fail to deal with the issues that produced it, we will deserve much worse than that.

Mark stayed overnight with Jaime — "you two can have a honeymoon night on the boat without him," Marie told us, smiling — and the next morning we awoke to a fair wind. Time to go. We walked up to the little green bungalow with the elaborate fence and phoned to see if someone could deliver Mark. No problem: one of the Marshalls' married daughters drove over and picked him up.

Although Albert had the living-room wall torn out, he seemed to be in good spirits. The problem in Cape Breton, he said, is that "you can't get materials, you can't get stock. Unless it's absolutely standard, forget it. And things are expensive. We've got infrared controls for the ceiling fan, electric eye on the outside light—that's routine in the States, cheap, $29.95, but here it's $90."

Albert knows about these prices because he has spent a lot of time working in the States. Indians don't have to go through immigration; they can move freely across the border. Sakej told me that Albert, like many other Indians, had been sent away to a church boarding school, and had been lonely, beaten and abused. But he seemed to harbour no grudge about it.

"If Joe hurt me," said Albert, "it's not a white man that hurt me, it's Joe. I can't be angry at all white men because Joe hurt me. If I did, I'd be prejudiced too. I'd be judging a whole group by what a few did to me. Here."

He tossed me a key ring with a green-dyed buckskin tassel. "You keep that, I'd like you to have it."

Lulu and Murdena had been deep in conversation. Murdena is also a spiritual leader, and one of our young friends at home was deeply troubled and had been muttering about satanism.

"I'll give you something for him," said Murdena. She picked up a sheaf of sweetgrass and began to plait it, sure fingers bending the grass swiftly in and out on itself, tying the loose ends with yellow thongs and stringing a couple of fat beads on each one. Sweetgrass is a sacred plant, gathered around the Lakes—"there used to be lots of it in Sydney, in a bog where the Woolco is now"—and traded for wild rice with tribes in Western Canada, where sweetgrass doesn't grow tall.

"You tell him to hang that on the wall in his room," said Murdena. "It attracts good spirits. They'll bring good thoughts to his mind. He'll think it's silly, but tell him to try it. And this is for you." She passed Lulu a delicate pink rose—made from wire, paper and wafer-thin flakes of maple wood.

Back at the boat, we hung the sweetgrass near the galley. Whenever I passed it, I smelled it—sweet as a memory of summer, but with a warm, comfortable aroma, like sandalwood or pipe tobacco. And, every time, the smell made me feel calm, cheerful and confident. I offer no explanation: I merely say what I noticed. It would not have been proper to steal a spiritual gift, so we did give the plaited sweetgrass to our troubled friend. But I parted from it with regret.

The Marshalls came down to the boat. Albert was all eyes and questions, wanting to know how we had built it. He was thinking of building a summer cottage, but he thought it would cost $50,000 by the time he had acquired the land and installed all the services. Now he wondered about a boat—a motor cruiser, probably. He thought he would probably buy one in Florida, where they are cheap. But he had never considered building one, and the idea appealed to him. I encouraged him. He has all the skills and knowledge, and he would make a beautiful job of it.

It was time to cast off. I rummaged in a locker, found a copy of one of my books and autographed it for them.

"Thank you," said Murdena. She smiled. "It's a Micmac custom not to let visitors leave without a small gift."

The key ring. The rose.

"Thank *you*," I said. "For all the things you've given us."

We hoisted the sails and gathered the dock lines aboard. *Silversark* fell away from the wharf, took the wind and gathered way. We looked back, calling and waving. Murdena and Albert were standing on the wharf with a cluster of kids.

The previous day, Sakej had asked me about the book I would write. It's hard to describe, I said: it's not a travel book, but I don't know what it is. It's partly a treatise on values in the guise of a seaborne tour of Cape Breton. It's partly a portrait of a community. It has elements of a book about nature. There's a lot of history in it. It's an encounter with many different people and viewpoints—

"I understand," said Sakej. "It's a book about human consciousness."

REFLECTIONS

IN

JOHNSTOWN

HARBOUR

Outside the Indian Islands a steady southwesterly wind gave us a long beat down East Bay towards St. Peter's. We sailed across the bay to Big Pond—Rita Mac-Neil's community, where Henry and Lucy Doucet's son, Father Dan, is parish priest. We tacked back to Eskasoni, then tacked again not far from Sakej and Marie's house, waving as we turned.

This was perfect Bras d'Or Lakes cruising: enough wind for good sailing, blue water and small whitecaps, green hills flanking us on both sides. It is hard to define the pleasure of such sailing; between steering, navigating, sail-trimming, getting food and drinks, one is busy enough but never too busy, and the mind is free to wander. The rhythm of the boat's motion, the sound of wind and wave, the steady unspectacular progress towards a destination—it all has a mantra-like effect, occupying enough of the mind to release its impulses to fantasy and meditation.

We passed Lochan Fad and Castle Bay, Irish Vale and Benacadie, Piper's Cove, the prominent white church at Johnstown, and the low-lying barren Red Islands. The wind eased, and eased some more.

"We're not going to make St. Peter's tonight," said Lulu.

"Let's try Johnstown," I said.

We had never been to Johnstown Harbour—which, oddly, is several miles southwest of Johnstown village. The wind had gone very light, and we bobbed slowly in towards the notch in the low-lying shore under the East Bay Hills.

Inside the bar was a cluster of micro-coves surrounded by low treed hills and *barachois* beaches. Three or four modest cottages stood on one shore; a speedboat towed a waterskier around the upper harbour. We sailed up and down the inlet for a few moments, enjoying its serenity. Picking her spot, Lulu headed into the wind. I lowered the plow anchor, and the chain went roaring out over the bow roller.

A drink in the cockpit, and then dinner and a quiet evening of card-playing and reading in the snug, warm cabin, the light of the kerosene lamps glowing back at us from varnished oak and mahogany. Late in the evening the wind came up. Lulu and Mark had fallen asleep, Mark deep in his quarter-berth, a heap of duvet and pillows and tousled hair.

I went on deck to tie off the halyard which was tapping against the mast, and to check that the anchor was holding firmly. A cool white moon hung high in the sky, bleaching out the nearby stars. The wind was north, which was not forecast. The anchor was fine. On the hills around us, the spruce trees traced a jagged graph against the pale sky.

The last night of the cruise, and the first night of typical Cape Breton cruising: at anchor in a perfect cove after a day of ideal sailing. Most summers, we stay in the Lakes and spend our nights at anchor; this summer we had spent most nights tied to village wharves. But there is always an evening when you know that the sands have run out, that the cruise will end tomorrow. An evening when you sit on deck and think of home.

My first sight of my home resulted from picking up a dusty pair of boys, perhaps ten or eleven, hitch-hiking home from a baseball game in July 1971. Home?

"D'Escousse."

"Can I get to Petit de Grat from there?"

"Oh, yeah."

I drove them along the north shore of Isle Madame. The road approached the shore and swung away, lifted and swooped over low rounded hills studded with shingled houses overlooking the island-speckled waters of Lennox Passage. Long grass rippling in the wind, lighthouses and spruce forests, brooks and bays and boats at anchor.

"Beautiful place," I offered.

" 'S all right," shrugged the boys.

I dropped them by the post office in D'Escousse, under a canopy of trembling aspens, locally known as silver oaks. Two general stores, a garage, a big new church, a brick school house, a community hall, a wharf: downtown D'Escousse. Old houses dripping gingerbread trim, clustered on the shore of a gleaming, placid harbour. *'S all right.*

I was looking for a home. I was separated, and I had dropped out of a promising academic career. I was going to be a writer, living in a village by the sea. But which village?

That September, the *Scotia Sun* advertised an "old house, on large shore lot in D'Escousse, for sale or rent." I read the ad at breakfast and by early afternoon I was looking for "the only house in D'Escousse with a For Sale sign on it." After a long search, I found what looked like the house and went next door to seek out Olive LeBlanc for the key.

"I don' know no Olive LeBlanc, me," said the brown-faced old woman next door. "But you're not in D'Escousse anyway."

"Where am I?"

"You're in Poulamon. Where the best people live."

"Can I tell them that in D'Escousse?"

"Sure, tell them that in D'Escousse. They know that already." She peered at me closely. "You're not French, you?"

"No."

"Then why would you want to live in D'Escousse? People move away from here, they don't come here to live."

"I like the looks of it."

She looked at me dubiously. Then she snapped her fingers. "You're married wit' a French girl!"

Her name is Maryann Provost, and we laughed together about it for years afterwards. I found Olive LeBlanc half a mile away. I had to wait for her son Dennis to come home from school to show me the house. Meanwhile I walked down the long, narrow field and through the woods to the shore. I was hungry, and the field was bristling with blueberries and blackberries. The shore was gorgeous: a little cove at the head of the harbour, with its own outlet to Lennox Passage behind a large, wooded island. Over the cove, gulls and terns were whirling, while gaunt herons stood meditating in the shallows.

The house was composed of two tiny ancient buildings pushed together to make one comfortable home. Parts of it are probably 175 years old, and the whole framework is pegged together just like the eighteenth-century houses of Louisbourg. It was spang on the roadside, the floor plan was awkward, and it was half-renovated in a style not much to my taste. But it *felt* right: a serene and happy little house where generations had loved and laughed and wept and died. I paid what the owner was asking: $6,000. Twenty years later, when people ask me how I like D'Escousse, I tell them I'm just surprised that it took me thirty-four years to find my way home for the first time.

D'Escousse was founded about 1718 by fishermen from St. Malo, and its name has nothing to do with Scotland, Scots or Scotch. The Public Archives of Nova Scotia volume *Place Names and Places of Nova Scotia* says it "perhaps gets its name from de Coux, a French officer who was at Louisbourg in 1747." Perhaps it does not: at that time New Englanders ruled Louisbourg, fortress historians know nothing of de Coux, and the village predates him by thirty years anyway. A more likely theory holds that since an "escousse" is a stopping-place, this harbour was a stopover en route to and from Louisbourg. Maybe so: Montreal's Hotel Meridien has a bar called "L'Escousse," and French dictionaries still list "escousse" as a period of time, among other things.

By 1752, Decoust, as it appears in the Sieur de la Roque's census, was a well-established community. One of the inhabitants, who had a farmhouse, outbuildings, a large family and some livestock, was named François Josse, apparently a Basque; anglicized, the name is Francis Joyce, the gentle old man who lived across the road from me during those earliest years.

"Ah, yes," Francis nodded. "That would be my grandfather."

Add a few "greats," and no doubt he was right. Isle Madame was named for Madame de Maintenon, the second wife of the Sun King, Louis XIV, and the names on the original land-grant maps are the names that dominate the island today: Boudreau, Landry, LeBlanc, Poirier, Samson, Martell, Marchand. When Cape Breton was French, Acadian mariners did a tidy contraband trade with mainland Canso, only six sea miles away; after Louisbourg fell, the island became the base for a wide-ranging commercial network run by French-speaking British subjects from the Channel Islands, and their names also endure: LeBrun, Mauger, Levesconte. Scots and Irish drifted in: Edmund and Edward McDonald came to D'Escousse in 1790, for instance, and their descendants are still here, speaking English with a strong French accent.

Like all of Nova Scotia, D'Escousse flourished during the last century. The first church appeared in 1815, the school in 1828, the post office in 1855. Shipbuilding prospered: the brigantine *Peter and Jane* was built here in 1823 for two Jersey traders, and big schooners regularly slid down the ways—*Mary* and *William Elizabeth*, both in 1831; *Ladysmith* in 1833; *Sea Flower* and *William* in 1835, and many others. My favourite is a little eight-ton pinky schooner launched in D'Escousse in 1852: her name was *Touch Me If You Dare*.

By 1881, D'Escousse boasted 1,492 souls, and A.F. Church's detailed map of 1886 shows half a dozen wharves and stores, a lobster factory, a forge and a hotel. There were sail lofts and sawmills, and The Skipper said that when all the fishing and trading vessels were laid up for the winter, you could walk across the harbour on their decks.

Steam, steel and Confederation demolished Nova Scotia's prosperity. By centennial year, Canada's richest founding province had become a depressed area. In 1956, the population of D'Escousse had dropped to 228. By 1971 it had rebounded to 283. By 1986 it had fallen back to 256. The gracious old homes of the last century were yielding to prefabs and house trailers when I arrived, and the grandsons of men who traded with Naples and Rio were glad of maintenance jobs in the pulp mill at Port Hawkesbury.

And so D'Escousse knows an undercurrent of sadness and loss. You can find the sons and daughters of D'Escousse in Calgary and Mississauga, in Cape Cod and San Diego. They come home in the summer, driving motorhomes and Trans Ams, and their parents are glad they are thriving. But it is hard to grow old alone in a village where enterprise has been ground down by history and profit has yielded to poverty. Of the nine homes nearest to the one I bought, two were empty, one included a general store, and the other six were supported by pensions and social assistance.

Joseph Howe told us Confederation would ruin Nova Scotia. Somewhere, he must be weeping.

Richmond County is divided roughly equally into Isle Madame and a part of mainland Cape Breton. In 1971, when I arrived, it was home to 12,734 people, all of them rural. The two largest communities were Arichat (pop. 829), the shiretown, on the island, and St. Peter's (pop 663), on the mainland. A slight majority—6,650—were of French origin, but a substantial majority—7,285—spoke English as their mother tongue. This process is called assimilation, and it has a great deal to do with the anxieties of Quebec. The census also recorded 435 people who spoke *only* French, but I have never met one.

The French population was concentrated on and near Isle Madame, and the others, chiefly Scots, were scattered from St. Peter's towards Sydney and along the Bras d'Or Lakes. Nearly 11,000 were Catholic, dwarfing the second-place United Church, with 965 adherents. Only 37 per cent of the people were between twenty and fifty-five years of age, compared with 47 per cent in Halifax.

The figures confirm what intuition tells you: this is a community where children grow up and move away, and to which they return, years later, to retire. Even those who live here often cannot work here. Isle Madame men go to Inuvik to work on oil-rig supply boats in the Beaufort Sea, to North York and Markham to erect office buildings, to the Great Lakes to sail on the bulk carriers. Some learned oil-related trades during Nova Scotia's exploration boom in the early 1980s, and they follow the rigs to Africa, Norway, Calgary.

Young friends call from Vancouver and Fort McMurray, drunk and lonely, at three in the morning. *How ya doin'? How's everybody? Well, it's all right out here, but it's not home. I'll be back in six months, a year, I've almost cleared off my bills. Listen, when I get home we'll go out in the boat, jig some mackerel. Listen, how the hell are you, anyway? How's everybody?* Phoning from a city of a million people to a village of 256: *How's everybody?*

Fine, you say, we're all looking forward to seeing you. You lie, knowing full well that most of them will be home only for weddings, funerals and vacations. It'll be good to have you back, you say, we're all looking forward to seeing you . . . .

There is the sorrow, the irony: there is no better place to live, and the children who want to live here cannot stay.

Does it matter? The Big Thinkers tell you the children are better off in Toronto anyway: high wages, dazzling opportunities, a mobile and expanding society. But why this gap in the heart, this longing for home that never really dies?

Because D'Escousse makes sense. It has its human imperfections; I would like to see it more self-confident, more prosperous, more willing to use the democratic process. I wish it were less easily gulled by political mountebanks, arid bureaucrats and cynical corporations. On election days, you can hardly hear yourself think for the baaing and braying of hereditary Grits and Tories.

But humans have lived in villages for aeons because villages are comprehensible, convenient and comfortable. A village supplies most of what people need and very little of what they do not need. Villages are big enough for some specialization of labour, small enough that people are not locked into slots. If you need people to launch a boat, form a credit union, organize a dance, put up a building, a village can provide them. Linked by ties of need, blood, habit and culture, the villagers of D'Escousse have created a warm and functional community.

Our village is too small to have any formal political structure. Along with Poulamon, Poirierville, Cape La Ronde, Rocky Bay and Martinique, we elect one councillor to the county council. The county as a whole elects one MLA to the legislature in Halifax. Along with voters in four other counties, we elect one MP to Ottawa.

But the absence of authority does not make everyone equal. Some villagers have far more influence than others, but their influence flows from their characters: their commitment, vitality, generosity, understanding, skill. Here is Alfreda Tambon, ninety years old, who retired here after a lifetime working as a department secretary at Dalhousie University in Halifax, and who took on the job of managing the North Isle Madame Credit Union, which was gasping its last. She had "no more intention of doing that than I did of going into the oil business with the Arabs." Operating out of her own kitchen, she oversaw the tenfold multiplication of its deposits. Before she retired a second time, the credit union was in its own building with two full-time staff members. For her work in the co-operative movement, Alfreda was awarded an honorary doctorate from St. Francis Xavier University.

Dr. Alfreda is always in a hurry, never as well organized as she thinks she should be, and when you see her walking to the post office and back you might think her simply a dotty old lady. She is nothing of the kind: she is a shrewd, urbane and witty woman who can skin a rabbit or a fool with equal ease. The village is proud of her—and, yes, a little amused by her, too.

But then the village is amused by virtually everyone. Its best entertainments are the stories its people tell about one another: the night a leading citizen was drinking in his power boat, fired off a batch of distress flares from sheer exuberance, and then had to reassure the Coast Guard that he had investigated the incident and seen the distressed vessel safely out of danger. The time Arthur's cow ate the mash from a neighbour's still and capered bibulously about the field before yielding very strange butter. The time Lucien's pig went down the well. The time Charlie's pig went to church. The night Frankie lost the cops in the woods, slipped home, got his truck and pulled up beside the police car to ask what the trouble was and whether he could help. "No," said the Mountie firmly. "We didn't see who the fellow was, but we'll get him eventually." The time the rudder broke on Lloyd's boat and he steered all the way home from St. Peter's by towing a bucket astern, first on one side and then on the other.

Claude Poirier is a man of influence. Claude is fifty-six, lean, brown, droll, totally bilingual. He knows all the secrets and tells none. He and his brother run the garage; Claude does the bodywork, Russell the mechanical work. Claude and Sandra raised five children in what was once a tiny house across the road from the rundown Esso station. As the family grew, the house expanded up and sideways and backward and forward. It is an interesting, welcoming, nonregulation house for a non-regulation family. It is not finished. It will never be finished. If it were finished, the taxes would go up.

Claude's income must be almost invisible, but his expenses are minuscule too. He owns the house and owes nothing on the business. He cuts his own lumber on his own land and builds onto the house himself. He and Sandra plant a substantial garden. They drive a succession of antique station wagons and light trucks, which Claude keeps alive long beyond their normal lifespan.

Claude and Russell make the garage a focus for D'Escousse's men. One goes there to hear the news, swap stories, find out what tools and skills are available for work one needs to do. Women do this at the hairdressers' — D'Escousse has two — and over coffee and at bingo games. Sometimes the men will learn about the progress of an illicit love affair at the garage, and the women through these other channels, and each group will act as though the other knows nothing about it. Then the women adjourn to watch "Edge of Night" or "Another World" just as if they weren't living in a web of passion as fascinating as anything known to Hollywood.

Children hang out at Pearl's store. Pearl and Raymond LeBlanc had five children, and the store began as a corner of the living room in which they kept pop, chips and candy. Then milk, bread, butter, eggs. The store took over half the living room. Raymond built a counter across it. Cheese, cookies, cereal. The store absorbed the living room completely. Ballpoint pens, light bulbs, frozen dinners. The living room bulged.

The new store was built right onto the side of the house. It is the size of a city convenience store, and Raymond has plans for expansion. More space out behind. Maybe a juke box and pool hall in the basement again. Arcade games. The village kids need a place to hang out and "down there everything's concrete, Lor' Jesus, and they can't hurt anything."

Raymond is a man of influence. He grew up in Arichat, on the south side of Isle Madame, and studied for two years at Université Ste.-Anne in Yarmouth County. He was municipal clerk and sheriff before becoming a paralegal aide to a prominent law firm in Port Hawkesbury. Pearl comes from Martinique, three miles from D'Escousse. When Pearl grew up, hamlets like Martinique, Poulamon and Poirierville had their own schools, post offices and government wharves, and the communities were distinct and separate. Now they are appendages of D'Escousse and Arichat, where the services have been centralized, so it is hard to realize that Pearl, even after twenty-five years, feels she is "not from here." She is from Martinique.

Raymond and Pearl are active in the D'Escousse Civic Improvement Association and the North Isle Madame Recreation Association; Raymond is returning officer for the county, a speculator in land, a former municipal councillor, an ardent Conservative, a devoted father, an occasional bigot, a regular bartender at the Saturday night dances, a phenomenal gardener, an observant student of human nature and one of my closest friends. He is volatile and generous, he can fix anything, he is cruel to animals and domineering to his wife, and he understands such mysteries as property law, probate, incorporation, and election procedures. Like a one-man H&R Block, he fills out the income tax forms for half the village.

With the support of people like Claude and Raymond, things can be made to happen in D'Escousse. Such men know who can move things and who can block them. They understand the lines of force. Their power stems from their personalities and their gifts. Claude is excellent at bringing our own people together, Raymond would be better at badgering bureaucrats.

The power of such men is rooted in our respect for their special qualities. It is a kind of power that makes sense.

For a writer, the great benefit of a village is the way you can know people. D'Escousse lacks the kaleidoscopic stimulation of the cities, but it lets me escape from the limited circle to which a writer is inevitably drawn in a city. My friends in D'Escousse include welders, fishermen, millwrights and mothers on welfare as well as teachers, potters, priests and businessmen. The longer I live there, the more I see people change and grow. An electrician becomes a politician, schoolboys become truckers and contractors, middle-aged civil servants retire and old people take their departures. Knowing them year by year, I can grasp something of the flow of their lives.

And I know them in context. I do business with Raymond, for instance, but I also dance with his wife, employ his son and his father as carpenters, buy firewood jointly with him, ask his help with my projects and chase his goat out of my yard. I have seen his kids grow up, I know how hard he is to beat at chess. I know him drunk and sober, at night and in the morning, at work and at play. I have seen him angry enough to fetch his rifle and sad enough to cry.

Raymond knows me the same way; like all villagers, we know one another as complete people, not as roles. The knowledge creates a kind of tolerance and affection which amounts to a noble set of values. I find some of Raymond's attitudes and opinions repellent, and he finds some of my ideas soft-headed and silly, but those differences do not dampen our pleasure in one another. We know too much else about each other.

Values: except in intervillage sports and elections, D'Escousse is almost noncompetitive. There is a bit of keeping-up-with-the-Landrys, and enthusiasms sweep through the village like a pack of dogs: snowmobiles, motor tricycles, vegetable gardens, trail bikes. Gardens and wood stoves were part of the traditional culture, and their revival is a steady, rooted response to a worsening economy.

D'Escousse is not puritanical, either. Parties that end before daybreak are considered rather dull, and summer is one long party. Dancing—to loud, live local music—is a favoured entertainment. In a plebiscite asking whether the community hall at

Rocky Bay should be allowed a liquor licence, the "wets" won by 382 to 12.

And love. Ah, love.

For unmarried people—including the separated or divorced—D'Escousse seems to have no prescriptions at all: celibacy, promiscuity and all intermediate practices seem to be equally acceptable. Sometimes a couple emerges from the sweaty flux and sets up housekeeping together, has three or four children and then, one afternoon, surprises everyone by getting married. In earlier times pregnancy was a common reason for marriage, and in an almost totally Catholic village, marriage meant billows of children and no divorce. So far as I can judge, a surprising number of these marriages were solid, happy unions, full of respect and companionship. It is common to see husband and wife cutting wood together, or building a house, tearing along on snowmobiles, cultivating a garden.

D'Escousse is a good place to be married. Urban life seems to draw couples apart, with its array of amusements, occupations, stimulations and associations, and the collapse of one's marriage does not really matter to anyone else. In D'Escousse it matters very much. One's closest friends are often at least distant relatives, and they can be enlisted. "See if you can talk to Louis about this," a woman asks her brother-in-law. "I can't get through to him at all." Generally he does, and often it works.

Occasionally a married person falls in love with someone else and can't confess it to the spouse. Then the whole village may engage in a conspiracy of silence. The spouse never knows, though everyone else does, and when the affair ends, the marriage lumbers on as before.

I don't mean to suggest that D'Escousse harbours no jealousy, hatred, loss, hurt, rage. But the village does show a genuine distaste for prudishness and moralizing, a recognition that humans have their frailties, that not all marriages are made in heaven and not all appetites are compatible. We shift, adapt, close our mouths and try to keep families functioning as best we can. Better an eccentric family than a broken one.

Every now and then, a love affair erupts over the village like a starburst and illuminates everyone's smiles for months. Mary Petitpas was widowed for the second time and felt lonely in her little house near the harbour. She advertised in the local weekly. Charlie Whalen, from Port Malcolm, saw the ad and came to call. Charlie was a lusty youth of about seventy-five, and in Mary he evidently saw the maiden he had dreamed of. The two fell resoundingly in love and were married; when Mary came back into the church after signing the register, she skipped and danced her way down the aisle.

They loved to walk, and for years after their marriage you would see them in the sunset of a summer evening, holding hands as they walked down one of the lanes near the shore. After Mary lost her legs to diabetes, they moved into the senior citizens' home. But they kept on walking until she died, with Charlie pushing the wheelchair. When you saw them, you could only smile and reflect that there was some justice in the world after all.

I think the village was almost as happy about Don and Lulu.

A woman without a man is like a fish without a bicycle, the feminists used to say. D'Escousse did not agree. I can say from experience that a man — *this* man, anyway — without a woman is only half of what he ought to be. When I came to D'Escousse, I was hurt, proud and independent. I wanted sex and companionship, but not a mate. I made myself into a fair cook, a passable housekeeper, a competent patcher-of-jeans.

I had no way of judging village reactions to casual amours, either. How puritanical was the priest? How powerful? Was the sexual revolution an urban phenomenon? I lived in D'Escousse like a monk and made my liaisons in distant cities. But wait: I was shaping my most intimate relationships to fit the possible opinions of people I didn't even know. The hell with that. I brought a woman home one weekend and waited for the reaction.

The village heaved an audible sigh of relief. *He's normal.*

I met Pat Terrio at the lumberyard. He was about twenty: dark, compact, rambunctious and a very devil with the women. His parents lived by the harbour in a trim house among willow trees. Arthur Terrio came of an ancient Isle Madame family. Mimi was an English nurse when they first met in wartime London. Their first two children were born in England, and the last eight in Cape Breton. The Terrios were devout Catholics, and they were not amused by Pat's style. So Pat had moved in with his brother Terry and his family.

Pat has a quiet side, and young children intrude on one's reading and music. He began frequenting my house. When I travelled, Pat took care of things. He worked at various jobs: maintenance work at the Canso Canal, bartending, construction. Eventually he became an electrician. One time, when I was away, Pat came home from a stint as a seaman to find Terry's wife had taken a job at the bank and installed a house-keeper in his room. He had the key: he stayed at my house. I found him there when I got home. In the end, he stayed four years.

Pat and I had our occasional differences—I did not always enjoy being awakened by thirty roaring revellers at two A.M. after the tavern closed—but on the whole he was a marvellous companion. I laid new floors in the house, and he rewired it. We swapped cars. We painted the house together. We took turns cooking. When one of us brought a lady home overnight, the other served the couple breakfast in bed.

Pat's brothers and sisters ranged from Lillian, then nine, to Larry, then a Port Hawkesbury businessman and father of three. I had Christmas dinner at Terry's, built a staircase with Joey, hired young Mark for odd jobs, dropped in to sample Chris's cooking at a dining room in Port Hawkesbury, and noted that Meggie evoked Unclean Thoughts. Two Terrios remained rumours: Bernie, stationed out west with the armed forces, and Lulu, who had gone to Europe the year before I arrived and who was studying biochemistry at the University of Copenhagen. In the meantime, one of my casual amours had ripened into a domestic scene that lasted six years before our ambitions diverged.

By then I had met the missing Terrios—and taken special note of Lulu, who had been home a couple of times. She had that fatal Terrio charm, and she evoked Thoughts at least as Unclean as Meggie did. By now I owned the schooner, and I had taught myself to sail her; Lulu had become an ardent sailor in Denmark. In my whole life, I had met only two women who agreed that it would be fun to cross an ocean in a small sailboat. *Hirondelle* would not do for that. I advertised her and began to build *Silversark*. Since my lover was no sailor, I expected to sail alone.

Over in Copenhagen, Lulu married a Dane. In some unadmitted corner of my mind I cursed silently and violently. Before their child was born, Lulu and her husband separated. I took note with guilty pleasure. In 1978, when Mark Patrick was four months old, Lulu moved home. I watched her at parties, felt envious of her dates and imagined sailing with her. I was not in love with her: I had no intention of being in love with her. I had seen too many Terrios break too many hearts. But a few days or weeks of sailing together would be just fine.

In 1979, alone again, I needed a crew to sail the schooner to Louisbourg. Nervous as a schoolboy, I asked Lulu. We took four eventful days, snarling our anchor line in the propeller, being stormbound for a day, then booming down the coast in a surge of sunlight and spray. Lulu was a superb, gutsy, capable sailor.

I think I fell hopelessly in love with her the first time she vomited. She had been steering, dressed in her bright orange Helly Hansen oilskins, when she quietly asked me to take the helm. I reached for the tiller, and she went to the lee railing and delivered her breakfast to the ocean. She stood up, wiped her mouth, climbed back to the afterdeck and reached for the tiller.

"Thanks," she said, resuming steering.

I had no sense of choice. *That's your mate.* Seize the moment or regret it all your life.

In Louisbourg we went dancing. I had not danced, to speak of, in 22 years. In a borrowed black dress piped in white, Lulu flashed across the floor like a little dark flame. I was forty-two, and I felt old and clumsy. But she loved to dance, so I had to learn. After all, I was going to spend the rest of my life with her. I already knew her well enough to pick my moment to tell her so.

Some weeks later, I told her: if things go on as they are, I'm going to want to marry you and adopt Mark Patrick—and sooner, rather than later. If you can't imagine doing that, please tell me and we'll quit right now. She was shocked, but not utterly opposed. Ten weeks after we had gone sailing, we were sitting in my pickup truck at Strait Motors in Port Hawkesbury. A man was filling the tank. Mark Patrick sat in his new car seat, eating Sultana cookies. Lulu's back was causing her anguish, and the doctor had just incorrectly diagnosed the problem as pleurisy. I proposed.

We were married the next May. All but one of Lulu's brothers and sisters were there. My brothers came from Vancouver and Ottawa, my mother from Vancouver, my children from Fredericton. We had guests from every province but Manitoba. The party went on for eleven days, with occasional breaks for people to sleep and work. We danced and ate lobster, drank wine and made music. Family rifts were healed and love affairs were commenced. Astounded that these two mavericks should be solemnly entering matrimony, D'Escousse threw itself into the occasion.

The service was held between two big silver oak trees in the Terrios' garden, with the harbour water chuckling behind the wedding party. It was performed by my old friend John Hennigar Shuh, once the radical minister behind the Halifax street school New Options. He was assisted by Father Dan Doucet. On John's advice, we had written the wedding ceremony ourselves. We said:

> Knowing that we are both selfish, weak and wilful,
> I give you my love without conditions.
> I will not forget that laughter heals,
>   that resentment corrodes, and selfishness divides,
>   that a child's happiness relies on our happiness together,
>   that love gives, forgives, and gives again.
> I will be neither your master nor your servant,
>   but your lover, companion and friend,
>   your partner in parenthood, your ally in conflict,
>   your comrade in adventure, your consolation in adversity,
>   your confederate in revelry, your accomplice in mischief,
>   and your associate in the search for enlightenment.
> I will be your husband/your wife, and your mate
>   and I will spare no effort
>   to be a mate worthy of the love you have given me.

In the middle of these vows, Mark Patrick, then two, tugged at my trousers and climbed up into my arms. So he was married, too.

During the service, our friend Donnie Palmer played the flute, Lillian Terrio played the piano, and later a piper led us across to the hall for the reception. Farley Mowat gave a salacious toast to the bride, and in my response, I tried to tell our friends and neighbours what this village meant to me. I told them that I had come here hurt, alone and despairing, and that they had given me their affection, their support and a share in their lives. That I had come to feel, for the first time in my life, that there was a community in the world to which I really belonged. That they had also moulded and formed a wife so perfectly suited to me that I could not even have dreamed her, lacking a sufficiently vivid imagination. That a massive wedding party and dance seemed to be a proper way to thank them for what they had done for us.

Five hundred people danced that night in the village hall, which the D'Escousse Civic Improvement Association gives free for village weddings. The band assembled by Donnie Palmer is still talked about; most of its members had played backup for John Allan Cameron's TV show. Augmented by Gordon Côté on the fiddle, they played blues, rock, jazz, jigs and reels. Tom Gallant sang a song especially composed for the occasion, "Love Is the Last Mile Home." "My theory," he said, "is that by marrying into the village, you really have been born here now." I danced with my daughter. Lulu danced with my son. We were almost the last to leave the hall.

During the reception, a young moustachioed millwright poured the wine. He was a handsome dog, and one of the guests had already lost her heart to him. He was one of the boys that I picked up hitchhiking in Louisdale, back in 1971, when I first saw D'Escousse. His name is Mark Terrio, and he is my brother. Not just in law. In truth, too.

That was ten years ago. We fenced the yard, finished the boat, bought a glorious Victorian house on the harbour, gutted it and rebuilt it. We lived and worked briefly in Banff, Charlottetown,

Baddeck, Halifax. We worked and danced and travelled and sailed.

And always our voyages ended where they began: in the salty little village by the sea which had become the final, resonant meaning of the word *home*.

Home tomorrow. I checked the anchor a final time, took a final look at the lovely serene harbour of Johnstown, and went below. Lulu rolled over in her sleep.

"Ever'thing okay?" she murmured.

"Everything's fine," I said. "Absolutely everything."

HOME

FROM

THE

SEA

We stole out of Johnstown on the lightest of breezes and spent the morning inching up towards St. Peter's Inlet. By noon we were off Cape George, with its fine old lighthouse, its freshwater ponds and its perfect uninhabited harbour. Hard to pass it by, but—

The wind freshened steadily as we tacked past Daminion's Cove, French Cove, Crawley Cove. Our anchor had tasted the mud in every one of them. Then came Sampsonville, and the gap between Beaver Island and the Sampsonville shore which we thought impassable until Doug Landry showed us the channel.

Doug's grandfather, John V. Fougère, had a big sawmill in Sampsonville. He saved the best boards for coffins, of which he maintained an inventory. One time a man traded the carcass of a deer for a bit of millwork. But it is illegal to sell or trade game, and the warden—"Crooked Neck MacLean, he was formerly from Iona"—got wind of the transaction. The Fougères dumped the deer in a coffin, and MacLean never found it. When a farmer came rowing up the inlet, towing three floating logs to be sawn, Doug's uncle Isaac set a coffin afloat and let the wind carry it down past the rowboat. When the coffin came within his view, the farmer was terrified: he dropped the logs and rowed frantically away. The Fougères had to go and retrieve both customer and logs.

It was Isaac, too, who was delivering a coffin one night when the children were sleighing on Schoolhouse Hill. The horse knew the way, so Isaac climbed into the coffin and closed it. When the riderless wagon with the coffin thundered through the glen, the children screamed, and a ghost story was born.

"Funny thing," says Doug, smiling. "Lots of ghosts when I was growing up, but they all disappeared after the streetlights came in."

We beat on through Beaver Narrows, then lowered everything but the jumbo and sailed deep into the canal. The bridge was already open; a big Hans Christian was motoring towards us, into the Lakes. Mark and I sprang ashore and towed *Silversark* through the lock and down to the Atlantic end of the canal—a miserable job, with the wind eddying around us and a big scallop dragger already moored in the berth we needed.

"I feel awful," said Lulu. "I've got a pounding headache." Her eyes were little slits, and she could hardly keep them open. "I'm going to have to lie down before we go anywhere."

She probably had a mild sunstroke from steering all day without sunglasses. Mark and I met Kert Fulmer, son-in-law of Evelina and Elio Mancini, the finest Italian cook and gardener, respectively, ever to grace Richmond County. Another time, we would have walked to the Mancinis', looking hungry and hopeful. But not with the scent of home in our nostrils.

Mark went swimming in the canal with Kert and the kids while I walked up a hill and gazed out to sea. Yellow waves with manes of foam poured westward past the end of Jerome Point. Inside the little bowl of land at the canal's seaward end, the wind baffled around, shaking the trees and raising little dust eddies behind the quay. It would take nimble sailing to get out of the canal.

Lulu woke after two hours, and we reviewed our position. It was early September: the days were getting shorter, and the wind was dropping. If we were going, we should go now—and even so, we might have trouble getting home in daylight.

"Let's go," said Lulu. "If we can sail in the fog, we can sail in the dark—and we know these waters."

We hoisted the sails. Kert held the shrouds while I cast off the last mooring lines, and the two of us gave *Silversark* a mighty shove to start her moving. While I jumped aboard, Mark hauled in the sheets. *Silversark* thrust her cheek up into the wind and sailed smoothly out of the canal, heeling over and moving quickly. A perfect departure.

We beat slowly down the bay against a failing wind. At the bell buoy the wind died altogether, leaving us aimlessly slatting in a cross sea. Then, as the light faded, the wind returned. We closed slowly with the Cape Breton shore, then tacked right across to Isle Madame. The next long tack would carry us up to the entrance to D'Escousse.

The wind was strong by now, and the little cutter was storming along. The night was dark, with black clouds chasing across a sliver of moon. Down below, Mark was reading the pale green backlit face of the Loran. The buoys in D'Escousse are unlighted: how were we to find our way in? The Skipper: *Put your stern towards Quetique Island and steer for MacLean's barn . . .* I drew that line on the chart and took off a bearing for Quetique Island. I rephrased the instructions: *When Quetique Island bears 010, tack and steer 190.*

"Dad, should I get out the spotlight?"

"Good idea! Don't shine it in anyone's eyes: we need our night vision. Only turn it on when we tell you."

I hung the hand-bearing compass around my neck. We could see all kinds of lights along the shore, and Don MacLean's barn was only one of them. I took a bearing on the red flashing light on Quetique Island light. 340, 347, 353 . . . Not yet. Don't hurry it. We rushed on through the darkness, gradually drawing abreast of the light. 358, 002, 006, 010: tack *now*.

Silversark came about with a rattle of canvas.

"Try the light, Mark."

The cold white beam sweeping over the water . . . and then a sudden flash of crimson: a buoy, exactly where it was supposed to be. Another up ahead, and a green one to port.

We sailed towards MacLean's barn until we wanted to scream, and then we tacked. The wind was blowing almost straight out of the harbour, but it was easing in the shelter of the land. We tacked and tacked again, the masthead light drawing coloured arcs in the sky, the canvas cold to the touch, the beam of the light slicing holes in the night as Mark picked up each buoy and kept it in view for us.

We eased past the beach at the tip of Bernard Island and on into the harbour. One last tack to the wharf. We could see our own blue house on the waterfront, and the boats: JJ's and Allen's and Henry's at their moorings, the masts of Bobby's and Junior's behind the wharf, Paul's and Frankie's and Tommy's, and a green boat with lights in the cockpit.

"Ronnie's boat," I said. "He finally got it in the water."

Dropping the sails, we coasted to the only free space at the wharf, behind Ronnie. He jumped on the wharf to take our lines.

"Been on a cruise, Don?" asked Ronnie.

"All summer," I said.

"Right around Cape Breton," said Mark.

"Holy Jeez, you must have seen a lot of places."

"We saw *everything*!" said Mark. "Whales and dolphins and puffins and sharks and seals—we saw *everything*!"

"We did," I said, breathing deeply and savouring the harbour of home. "But nothing more welcome than this."

SEQUELS

AND

THANKS

When we set sail, Canada was heading into a recession, and the triple whammy of high interest rates, shrinking markets and falling prices has hurt Cape Breton business badly.

At the behest of creditors, Glenora Distilleries has been reorganized, and Bruce Jardine is no longer its president. Restaurant Le Gabriel in Chéticamp has been through receivership and will open under new ownership in 1991. Good People Sea and Shore in North Sydney has finally gone bankrupt, and Dory Tuvim is back in Montreal.

In Glace Bay, Nova Aqua is in receivership, but D. Goldman and Sons is doing fine. Ross Bennett believes the assets of Nova

Aqua will form the foundation for a new company, which will succeed with the same imaginative and viable concept.

By now, it must be obvious that I have much to be grateful for—and that I owe my thanks to a multitude of people. Many of them are noted in the book and in the dedication, but I want to acknowledge a few others:

* Farley Mowat, who said over dinner, "What's the non-fiction book you'd most like to write? Well, then—!"

* The peerless Peter Livingston, agent *extraordinaire*, whose early death in March 1991 was a terrible loss both personally and professionally.

* Ron Caplan, Harry Bruce and George Butters, whose work saved me many hours of research.

* The Ontario Arts Council, who provided a small grant to help me complete the manuscript.

* Helly Hansen, Tilley Endurables and Minolta Canada, who made it possible to use equipment which would otherwise have been beyond our reach.

* Leigh Robertson of Networx, the Halifax Sony distributor, who lent us a professional-quality video camera for the voyage.

Finally, I want to thank the Cape Bretoners, named and un-named in the text, who have treated me with warmth and generosity everywhere I went—and not just during the summer of 1990, but over a period of twenty years. In "Song for the Mira", Allister MacGillivray memorably evokes their gener-osity of spirit:

> Out on the Mira the people are kind,
> They'll treat you to homebrew, and help you unwind;
> And if you come broken, they'll see that you mend,
> And I wish I was with them again.

He's right. They did. And for that, I am permanently grateful.